There is a certain amount of frustration I have with Edward Vick. As with most useful things you find later in life, either yours or theirs, the discovery becomes frustrating when you know your own development would have benefited from having them in your life earlier. With each book by Vick, my intellectual appreciation for him and his own intellect has grown. This book is no different. While it may not be for the casual reader, Vick writes to deeply motivated thinkers, who seek out the great questions, and provides a path for them to travel – to do philosophy as believers. Vick stands on the shoulders of the great philosophers of the past – and gives us something of a view of the future. He is methodical, patterned, and intentional. Each word, sentence, and passage is carefully chosen to deliver to the reader, to the novice philosopher holding the book, a careful and essential understanding of just what value philosophy holds for the believer.

Joel Watts
UnsettledChristianity.com
Author of *Mimetic Criticism and the Gospel of Mark* and
editor of *From Fear to Faith*

PHILOSOPHY FOR BELIEVERS

Every one of us has many and varied beliefs

Edward W. H. Vick

Energion Publications
Gonzalez, Florida
2013

Cover Design: Henry Neufeld

ISBN10: 1-938434-54-4
ISBN13: 978-1-938434-54-9
Library of Congress Control Number: 2013942940

Energion Publications
P. O. Box 841
Gonzalez, FL 32560

850-525-3916
energionpubs.com
pubs@energion.com

TABLE OF CONTENTS

iv

PREFACE

We are all believers. Every one of us has many and varied beliefs. We seldom think about this most interesting fact, concerned as we are with what we are, at the moment, believing. You, the reader, could very easily provide many examples. Pick up any book or newspaper. There you will have myriad opportunities to address the question, 'Can I believe that?' You will often find yourself saying, 'But that I can't believe!' When you find examples of what you can believe, you will, given a little thought, realise that you have a further belief: namely , 'I believe that what I believe is reasonable.' Or contrariwise, 'I believe that what I cannot believe is either unreasonable or not established.' So what do we believe about what we believe and about the act of believing? That is our fascinating and intricate question.

This book is intended to be an introduction to themes that concern anyone who thinks about belief, any kind of belief but in particular Christian belief. In the first instance that will be those who hold some such beliefs. But these are not the only ones who are interested in the philosophical issues which the existence of a theistic faith raises. Indeed it is often the non-believers who have the edge over the frequenters of the pew, when it comes to more consistent and prolonged thinking. This writing is for them too.

Simply let's say it is an introduction to some themes that interested persons will face and hopefully will find profitable to consider seriously. Observations that apply generally to belief will also apply to religious belief. So the writing is of general interest in elucidating those widely applicable general philosophical principles, and illustrating them in different ways. The term 'believer' has both general and specific meaning. All are believers. Some are religious believers.

The aim of the book is to state clearly some of the basic issues. If the writer achieves clarity of presentation, that does not mean that the themes will simply roll off the page into the mind of the reader. At certain points, real effort will be needed. A paragraph well understood is therefore better than a chapter skimmed and forgotten. A point well digested is progress and leads to further progress.

With each chapter, we try to provide incentives to exercise the grey cells. We do this by suggesting questions for reflection, discussion and for exercise with the pen. Write something and then hold it up for scrutiny! With some of the early chapters, we provide extensive vocabulary to suggest how the process of understanding might begin: by mastering the terms. At any rate, we shall hope that that is the way the process will also end. But we are always *in media res*. It is well to remember that and keep moving forward.

1 INTRODUCTION

Examining Beliefs
Discussing Issues
Why Be Interested in Philosophy
Understanding Faith
Argument and Proof
Where Are You?

1 INTRODUCTION:
PRELIMINARY, WHY PHILOSOPHY?

We all have many and varied beliefs. You are an individual and you think about a whole range of interesting subjects some of which are not of particular concern to other people. Your range of interest is both wider and narrower than that of other people.

As you persist you will find that much serious, productive and illuminating work has been done by philosophers in their thinking about subjects central and related to your beliefs. This is the case, even if they are not thinking specifically of particular kinds of belief, say political, religious, or moral beliefs. but of the interesting questions that arise about belief in general. You may find that you have taken for granted what such thinkers have spent great effort in reasoning about. Certainly to understand them with any seriousness, but also to attain any clarity about your beliefs, you need to know some philosophy.

Often seemingly simple questions can demand rational treatment in quest for answers. Try answering the question; 'What does that mean?' when you have made a claim. Ask that of any belief and you will begin to see that a whole multitude of issues arise demanding attention. Or just think of the terms you use. Ask, 'What does that word mean?' Or, 'What do I understand that term to mean?' You may find that you have taken for granted a great deal that you might now wish to examine further. You may then discover that you have relied upon meanings handed down to you and that you have not really made your own. It is much better to ask, 'What do I believe?' and start thinking, than to ask 'What do we believe?' and rest satisfied without any real thought with the answers you are given. Why should you get someone to give you an answer, accept it without real consideration, and thereafter take it for granted?

This book is intended as an introduction. I would like to give some guidance as you begin or continue the process of inquiry just suggested. It is intended to be as simple as makes for clarity.

1   Examining Beliefs

We said 'We believe many things'. That's not very explicit. The 'things' we believe are statements, propositions, claims. We believe many different *kinds* of belief. We might classify individual beliefs into many different classes.

Here are examples of individual beliefs:

We can trust John.
Lynne is competent for this task.
Tomorrow's weather will be fine.
Advertisements need very careful scrutiny.
That is a genuine Vermeer.
God is love.
Moses received tablets up in a mountain.

Here are some possible classifications of *kinds* of belief:

Medical diagnosis
Campaigning politician's promises
A historian's account
Claims in an ancient document
Religious teaching
Moral claims
Aesthetic claims

We can ask the questions we raise in this writing about *any* belief, however we classify it, such questions as, What motivates the belief? What reason, or lack of it, is there behind the belief? How could one argue in a rational way for the belief? What makes for the justification of a belief?

The term 'argument' has two meanings. It means

a.   a disagreement between believers. Contrary beliefs are expressed in opposed or contradictory claims. The attempt to justify them may vary. There may be no attempt to provide justification. An attempt to justify may take bizarre forms. But in this sense of the term you can have an argument simply by stating opposed beliefs.

b.   a set of statements arranged in such a way that they give support for the conclusion that is drawn from them. This is sometimes called deduction.

In discussing belief and believing we can operate on two levels. We can ask about the particular belief. Take for example the belief: 'This building is safe.' We can also ask about the fact of my holding this particular belief and then pass over to asking what makes this or any belief reasonable. Clearly there are different avenues of approach.

When you start to talk about Christian faith, even though you do not realise it you have already been engaged, I will not say 'immersed', in philosophical issues. For you already have developed certain attitudes before you fill your speech with content. You implicitly say 'I believe', whatever it is that you affirm or deny.

You then expand the statement that begins with the claim, 'I believe' with all kinds of content, with many kinds of assertion: about the future, about the past, about authority, about yourself, about the world, about the beginning of all things, about the end of all things, about life after death, etc, etc. But you believe many things, even if you do not consciously preface your convictions with the terms 'I believe'.

So a good place to start would be to ask, 'What is belief? What does it mean to believe?'

When we have spent time in thinking about those questions we might then go to some specific and important beliefs and ask the similar question, for example, What does it mean to say that you believe that God is creator? You will now see, of course, that philosophical discussion will help you to come to a better under-standing of your particular beliefs.

You ask, 'What will I achieve by engaging in such a pursuit?' You will find the best answer to that question as you immerse your-self in the activity this book invites you to engage in. There is no substitute for persistent participation. But we can give preliminary answers and say what we hope you will discover. Take just three:

Achieve clarity. Misunderstanding is often due to not being clear as to what a belief means. So we must raise and persist in an-swering the questions, 'What do the words used to state the belief mean? What does the belief mean?'

Understand what makes for reasonable support of a belief. This involves being able to see that the reasons you put forward to expound and to support your belief are rational, that the arguments you use are sound, that the evidence to support the belief is reliable.

Achieve an adequate vocabulary. A confused or inadequate understanding often results from having a limited mastery of the appropriate language. Fuller understanding results from expanding our mastery of concepts.

2   Discussing Issues

Philosophy and theology both consist in the discussion of issues. In each of our chapters we state an issue to which we then address ourselves. The point of departure in each case is with a position held by the believer. We first make a statement of that belief. We then go on to present and explain relevant philosophi-cal themes, showing what importance they have for the believer's understanding.

There is hardly any philosophical or theological position which has not been questioned and disputed. So when you hold one of alternatives it is only reasonable that you are aware of the claims, arguments and discussions that differ from your own. They may be more reasonable than the ones you are at present holding. But if you do not know what they are you cannot assess your own satisfactorily.

As you read we hope that you will learn

a. to articulate a problem, to define an issue, to recognise a significant question.

b. where appropriate, to consider different possible approaches to the issue. So we consider contrary positions and the arguments by which these are defended.

c. to assess the arguments, so as to decide which explanation is worthy, which is defensible, which appears most reasonable.

d. to reckon with the fact that our conclusion may be tentative, to be revised upon further consideration of arguments and evidence.

e. what constitutes a good argument, and what pitfalls to avoid in constructing an argument.

We discover:

that for every topic we discuss there is a philosophical literature. This includes classical statements, exploratory statements, varied and opposed points of view.

that to sample such writing seriously is an invigorating, challenging and sometimes frustrating experience — in short, a rewarding enterprise.

that there are classic treatments of particular theological issues and philosophical problems. So we do not need to start afresh when we tackle a particular issue. That means that we are learning to be sophisticated and not to think that we have made novel discoveries when we begin to have opinions about a particular topic:

that it is often only through considerable struggle that one arrives at a particular position on an issue. In that sense we make important discoveries when we come to accept or reject, attack or defend a particular position.

that such activity is fascinating, drawing us on, always with the realisation that there is more than meets the eye.

You will find that you cannot hurry understanding. Better to read a paragraph and puzzle out its meaning and significance than race through a chapter with the result that you only vaguely understand its content. Mind you, a cursory reading may be a preparation for a second or third reading as you come, again slowly, to more adequate understanding. But only as a preparation. Things take time, T. T. T. Give yourself time. Experience the satisfying joy of increased understanding as with the time you have patiently spent you come to real comprehension,

3   Why Be Interested in Philosophy?

Why should the believer be interested in philosophy? In what ways is philosophy related to theology? We can take the two questions together.

a. The language Christians use in declaring their belief and developing their doctrines has been widely influenced by philosophy. So understanding ideas and methods of philosophy illuminates and clarifies because they are directly related to the believer's usage, and often to the content of scripture passages.

b. Philosophy can illuminate particular ideas: for example *word, beginning* are creative ideas introduced in the Gospel of *John* and are also well established concepts in Greek thought as *logos, arche*. The well established meanings of these crucial terms enabled John to make significant universal claims for Jesus, whom he identifies as *logos*. They enable him to portray him as agent at the creative act. Understanding the Greek philosophical terms is essential for an adequate understanding of the claim the Gospel of *John* goes on to make, a claim no Greek would think of making: 'the word became flesh'.

You can't understand Paul's use of the Greek term *pleroma* as he battles the heretics without considering their use of the idea and others associated with it. Take the passage in *Colossians* 2:9 which reads: 'For in him dwelleth all the fullness of the Godhead bodily' (AV). Here *pleroma* is rendered simply as 'fullness' (AV). Other versions think to improve on this. RSV renders the term 'whole fullness', NEB renders the term 'complete being'. Obviously you get little enlightenment for understanding the meaning by scanning the alternative versions. Only with the original context in mind and the contemporary significance of the term can you see that the writer is making a cosmic claim for Jesus. The Gnostics had built a whole structure of the universe into the meaning of the term *pleroma*. They left no place for the uniqueness of Jesus. Paul is correcting that aberration.

We have given two instances where a depth of understanding becomes possible only with the expenditure of effort to explore how some important terms now established in the Christian vocabulary have come to be there. Think for a moment how without this understanding a reader reacts to such passages. Perhaps the sympathetic attitude would be simply to acknowledge that something important is being claimed but to leave alone such 'deep' things. Perhaps one even begins to think one's own thoughts about the terms one meets in Scripture. These may be rather vague. The constructive desire to understand may lead one to the serious discipline of inquiring further. Several passages in the New Testament reveal that the early Christian teachers were even then demanding an effort from their people to go beyond an elementary understanding, for example: 'let us leave the elementary doctrine of Christ and go on to maturity' *Hebrews* 6:1 (RSV), and Paul bemoans the immaturity of his converts at Corinth. He writes that he has 'fed you with milk not solid food; for you were not yet ready for it, and even yet you are not ready (*I Corinthians* 3:2 RSV). This plea for progress was made as the Christian leaders and their congregations faced opposition to the Christian beliefs. How can one counter error if one does not understand what one believes and also what the alternatives are?

c. It can illuminate particular contexts of exposition within which characteristic terms are used. Take the book of *Hebrews* for example with its theme of reality in the heavens, the true tabernacle, the ideal priest, beyond the shadows on earth. That reflects a central theme of Plato and the Platonists. The real is the ideal. Earthly, temporal things are shadows, lacking reality, but giving hints of the real beyond.

d. Passages of Scripture get illuminated by seeing parallels in philosophical treatments and giving them due consideration. This point differs from 2 above since here there is no direct influence between the philosophical idea and the Christian use. A case study would be the Greek concept of *akrasia* as providing similarities to Paul's definition of sin: we do not do what we see as good and we do do what we see as evil (*Romans* 7:5ff). [See chapter 9]

So in describing what happens to the original philosophical materials, we speak of adoption, adaptation, redefinition. The new context of Christian faith provides for and enables new meanings to emerge in relation to terms already rich in meaning. They become the vehicles for expressing Christian claims. Where the church finds heresy, it tackles the meanings given to the essential terms being employed, and progress in understanding is achieved in the counter play of debate and denial. So the opponent is not simply denied. Where something constructive comes out of the encounter, he is first understood.

The Christian vocabulary has owed much to philosophical discussions from its very beginning. We have only to consider some of the many terms that have been thought essential for the expression of Christian beliefs. We have already taken a few examples of some used in Scripture with direct links to philosophical discussion.

The Christian vocabulary has grown steadily from the very beginnings of Christian belief. As the church moved into different communities and encountered different languages and customs, it developed and expressed its beliefs in different ways. It was inevitable that various ways of explaining Christian doctrines would emerge. This variety of expression emerged so as to connect with the different contexts within which the Gospel was being preached. Different forms of expressing Christian faith emerged and gave rise to differing explanations. As a different context provided for different thoughts about the meaning of faith, so different theologies were created and discussions and disputes took place, even and sometimes especially within the same communities. Traditions emerged and proliferated.

So emerged the sad phenomenon that often more effort was expended in defending the tradition than in seeking further and renewed understanding. This was true not only of sophisticated traditions but also of very simple ones. Here the defence was vigorous but often without a real understanding or a willingness to understand. For that might mean revision and change.

e. We have spoken of the influence of particular philosophical ideas. We now speak of the influence of philosophy in providing vehicles for systematic expression of ranges of Christian teaching. The Greeks had developed comprehensive systems of philosophy. Here a level of mature philosophical thought emerged as in no other ancient culture.

In these systems certain guiding principles (*archai*) provided unity. So for long afterwards Christians decided: Think as Plato thought. Or, think as Aristotle thought. Then go one stage further and think how Plato might provide for Christian expression. Think Christian teaching in harmony with the Aristotelian approach. Here were resources Christian thinkers knew and employed. So in the early centuries it was the influence of Plato, characteristically exemplified in the writings of Origen and Augustine. Later in the Middle Ages Thomas Aquinas provides the outstanding example of a theologian who thought in Aristotelian terms, becoming the foundation for Catholic theology. The influence of philosophy in providing systematic vehicles for conceiving Christian themes continued to the present time. An acquaintance with such philosophical approaches provides for understanding of the Christian expressions. That is a very good reason for studying them, quite apart from their intrinsic interest.

Being aware of these considerations, we may find it enlightening to ask of a Christian teaching, 'What is the context of this particular expression of belief?' To give examples: the confession of belief in the incarnation often takes the form, 'two natures in one person'. The confession of faith in God has sometimes taken the form: 'three persons in one substance'. If you want to see the rationale for the use of these terms you have to plunge into the philosophical background where the terms 'nature', 'substance', 'person' were developed. For in fact there is a direct connection between the background context and the confessional statements. Without this background it is very easy to end up misunderstanding what the doctrine intended. So as backgrounds change, the form of expression for the Christian teaching undergoes change. 'Time makes ancient good uncouth.'

4   Understanding Faith

Our enterprise in this book is an exercise in ***Fides quaerens intellectum*** 'faith seeking understanding'. So a good place to start is with the question 'What does it mean to understand?' Then we can ask, 'What does the faith that understands do?' In clarifying what understanding means we shall be answering these questions.

We are often quite ready to use things we do not understand. We are often quite ready also to leave things we do not understand to the 'experts', the specialists. We sometimes have to. We do not know how to fix the computer because we do not understand it in sufficient detail, and moreover it is very complex. So we call in the service person who does understand.

Let's make a distinction between observing and explaining. I may see something working and be able to manipulate its workings without understanding it. Advances in science, for example in the understanding of electricity, started with seeing how things operated before attempting to explain the observations. Indeed a complex medium for explanation had to be developed before that understanding occurred. What seems an abstruse and unconnected language was required before there was a breakthrough. This is the language of advanced mathematics. Without that becoming a highly developed discipline, we would never have come to understand what electricity is, what light is. The production of the everyday things we take for granted resulted from the understanding that mathematics and accompanying theories made possible.

Then there are things we would like to understand but, because it takes a great deal of application and intelligence and often a great deal of time, we never get around to the dedication, exploration and learning that is required. Sometimes we do not achieve understanding because there is just no-one able or willing to help us with the needful explanations that would enable us to understand. So we rest content and live our practical lives with what understanding we have.

Another context for our not coming to understand as we might is that we are quite content with the understanding we have. We believe and we confess our beliefs and do not have any desire to ask any questions about them, to 'go into them' (as we say). We are often encouraged in this attitude by being members of a like-minded group with its traditions of belief and understanding. Unfortunately that sometimes breeds an attitude of rejection and even contempt for those who seek further understanding. Christian communities have ways of setting boundaries. Heresy is the name for the understandings that go beyond those boundaries, understandings that do not have the imprimatur of the group. Excommunication is the penalty for non-conformity.

You can make claims without understanding them. So, we shall make a distinction between believing and understanding what we believe, between confessing and confessing intelligently, between simply stating the doctrine and understanding the statement of the doctrine, between making a claim and being able to explain the claim, between expressing a belief and grasping the meaning of that belief.

Understanding always involves grasping concepts. Concepts are expressed in words, 'terms', and are used to construct sentences. We understand sentences only as we understand the concepts used in them. Take examples. What does it take to understand the following statements?

The earth is rotating.

The sun, our nearest star, is 93 million miles away from the earth.

Or take just the first part of this one:

> The universe 'is 45 billion light years across
> and filled with 100 billion galaxies — each
> containing hundreds of billions of stars. . . .'

Let's list some of the concepts without which we could not even begin to come to an understanding of the above statements:

> star, mile, speed, light, million, 93, near, away
> from, sun, earth, rotate universe, year, light
> year, 100, billion, across, filled with, galaxy.

Even when you understand the meaning of these concepts, it takes something more before you can really be said to understand the statements that contain them. Do you really understand what '45 billion light years' means? Can one grasp what 'hundreds of billions' means especially if you follow it with 'light years', a light year being 5,874,601,673,407.3 miles. So multiply the big figure with 45 and then add the required number of noughts! Now do you understand? But that is only the beginning!

Now make an application of this principle: Without understanding the concepts used or implied in statements, you can't begin to understand believers' claims. Then take some examples:

God brings about events in the world in answer to prayer.
Jesus ascended into heaven.
I believe in the resurrection of the dead and the life everlasting.

Consider some of the concepts in the statement of these beliefs:

Jesus, ascend, heaven, into, resurrection, life, dead, everlasting, event, bring about an event, prayer, answer, world.

5 Where Are You?

(See the chart on the following page)

The following chart may enable you to take stock of your present situation. You hold various beliefs, some of which are more important to you than others. It is your desire to be logical and rational, so that you may claim that your beliefs are reasonable. As you think about those beliefs, rather than simply assert them, you find some difficulties. The belief you are now considering poses a real difficulty. It may be because of a contradiction with other beliefs or because when you think about your belief you face a dilemma. It may be that you simply are not clear as to what your belief means. It may be because your belief does not co-ordinate with an alternative belief. You will have your own problem!

You are now faced with a choice, the first of several. Shall I simply pass on, not even articulate it to myself in any detail, but simply ignore it, even if momentarily? You had admitted that there was a problem. If you ignore it the problem remains, even if you have repressed your expression of it and it will surface again in some form.

You decide to tackle the problem and, when you do, you find that there are considerations that you had not previously made. Perhaps someone has pointed them out. Or perhaps you have heard, or read an article, come across an argument you had not previously heard. Perhaps you encounter a few new concepts that you had not known previously that set the issues in a new light and make simple repetition impossible for you.

Now you have another choice to make, a little more advanced than the previous one. Shall you go on? Since the concepts with which you have up to now been working are, in the light of the things that have been brought to your attention, inadequate, you have the choice to examine the problem in the light of the new and promising concepts. But that will take effort and possibly call for reorientation. Shall you be ready for that? If you choose at this point to go no further, the problem has not gone away. It has sim-

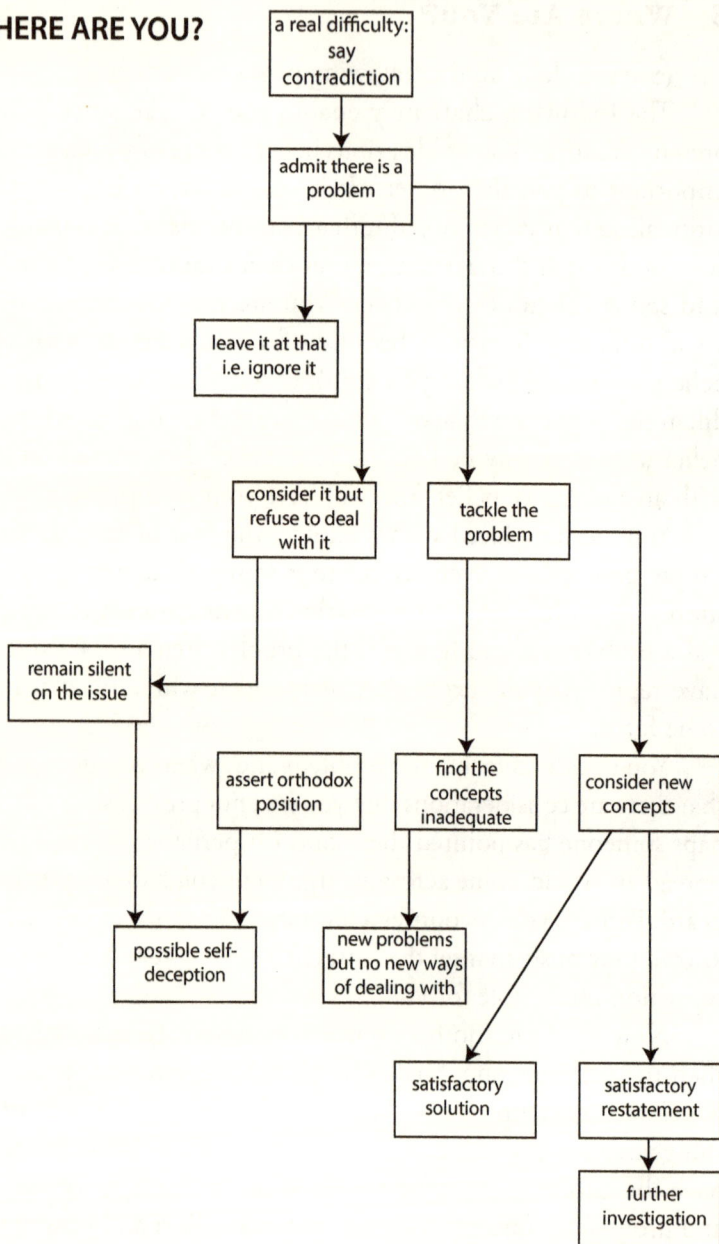

WHERE ARE YOU?

```
                    ┌──────────────────┐
                    │ a real difficulty:│
                    │       say        │
                    │   contradiction  │
                    └──────────────────┘
                             │
                             ▼
                    ┌──────────────────┐
                    │  admit there is a │───────────┐
                    │      problem      │           │
                    └──────────────────┘           │
                             │                      │
                             ▼                      │
                    ┌──────────────┐                │
                    │ leave it at that│              │
                    │  i.e. ignore it │              │
                    └──────────────┘                │
                                                     │
              ┌──────────────┐        ┌──────────────┐
              │ consider it but│      │  tackle the   │──────┐
              │ refuse to deal │      │   problem     │      │
              │    with it     │      └──────────────┘      │
              └──────────────┘               │               │
                     │                        │               │
   ┌──────────────┐  │                        │               │
   │ remain silent │◄─┘                        │               │
   │  on the issue │                           ▼               ▼
   └──────────────┘      ┌──────────┐   ┌──────────┐  ┌──────────┐
          │              │ assert   │   │ find the │  │ consider │
          │              │ orthodox │   │ concepts │  │   new    │
          │              │ position │   │inadequate│  │ concepts │
          ▼              └──────────┘   └──────────┘  └──────────┘
   ┌──────────────┐           │              │
   │possible self- │◄──────────┘              ▼
   │  deception    │              ┌──────────────────┐
   └──────────────┘              │   new problems    │
                                  │ but no new ways   │
                                  │  of dealing with  │
                                  └──────────────────┘
                                       ┌──────────┐  ┌──────────┐
                                       │satisfactory│ │satisfactory│
                                       │ solution  │  │restatement│
                                       └──────────┘  └──────────┘
                                                           │
                                                           ▼
                                                    ┌──────────┐
                                                    │ further   │
                                                    │investigation│
                                                    └──────────┘
```

ply been repressed. Maybe it will return and you will later take a different choice about what to do with the new situation.

You will then consider the new concepts and the reorientation of your thinking that employing them will require, so you find either a satisfactory solution to your problem, or you find a satisfactory restatement of that problem and that will lead you to further investigation.

Every one, I believe, will understand the moves here described. For they often occur in our everyday lives. But when it comes to our religious convictions, it is often difficult to make the choices called for at the different stages of development to maturity. Certainly some will be easy to make. Others will be difficult, so that we resist making them. For there are other than logical and rational considerations. People we know and with whom we worship will not be asking us questions about our beliefs all the time. Mostly they will take for granted that we believe what they believe, that our beliefs are similar, or even identical to theirs. That may make things harder for us when the choices are before us. For the realisation that there is not full agreement between believers often causes alienation, rather than the kind of understanding that goes by the name of tolerance. Unfortunately nothing has the power to separate believers more than the refusal to consider the reasonableness of another's beliefs when they differ from ours, and of course when ours are the widely accepted beliefs within the community in which we find ourselves. It often requires doubt for one to be tolerant.

2 BELIEF AND BELIEVING

There are different kinds of believing. Some belief is personal. Some is not. Not everything we believe is true, nor is it knowledge. So we must have grounds for assessing our beliefs. Belief is often based on testimony. So the question concerning the trustworthiness of testimony arises. It is an aspect of the more general question, 'On what grounds are we justified in believing a claim, even perhaps one that is false?' Other questions arise. Are we always conscious of the beliefs we hold? What is involved in doubting and abandoning a belief? How can we move from belief to knowledge, since we do not know everything we believe?

Scriptural writings contain testimony to historical events, persons, and communities. Many passages make allusions to what happened to individuals with names, to battles at specific times and to communities in their geographical locations. They also make reference to miracles, referring to them as on a par with natural events. Believers claim that Scripture also provides testimony to the revelation of God. Shall we apply to the claims of Scripture the same criteria of judgment we normally use in assessing historical claims?

2 BELIEF AND BELIEVING

Truth can never be told so as to be understood and not be believed.
    Does a firm persuasion that a thing is so make it so?

William Blake

1 Two Kinds of Believing

This is a book about believing, for 'the believer', and a believer is one who believes. We use the term 'belief' of both secular and religious belief. We all believe, but not all of us in the sense which the word sometimes has, when it is used of the religious believer. All believers have something in common. Our interesting exercise is to think a little about the nature of belief, about what it means to believe and make some classifications. For there are all kinds of beliefs: in people, in ideas, in reports, in products. We believe all kinds of claims to be true and others to be false.

We can thus approach this topic from two different points of view, which may turn out to be complementary. First we ask, What does the religious believer have in common with other believers? For we all believe all sorts of things all the time, often changing our minds. Second, what are the unique beliefs of religious believers that make them different from other believers?

We notice an important distinction. It is between believing *in* and believing *that*. The two meet when we trust someone. We believe *that* what they say is true and trustworthy because we believe *in* them. We take them to be trustworthy and honest because we have had experience in our relations with them. This has produced evidence that confirms the faith we place in them. When that has been established, we do not question their trustworthiness and do not always have to be assessing with questions in mind whatever they say or do.

This twofold meaning of the verb 'believe' and the noun 'belief' shows itself in the religious use. Take the two questions: Do you believe *in* God? Do you believe *that* God sustains and acts within the natural world? The first asks about relation, about commitment. The second asks about taking a theological position, asks whether you accept a particular teaching. The first is belief as trust. The second is belief in an assertion, accepting a proposition as true.

So believing is sometimes explained as equivalent to trust, sometimes as accepting a claim, making an assertion about the world and about relations within it. Take some examples of religious belief:

Belief in God
Belief that Jesus was an historical figure
Belief in Jesus as Saviour, Redeemer
Belief that some historical statements in the Bible are true
Belief that God reveals himself through Scripture
Belief that there will be post-mortem survival
Belief in life after death

It is worth noting that on occasion 'I believe in' is being used as equivalent to 'I believe that' as in these last two examples which mean the same thing.

In which senses are we to take the confessions, the creeds the Christian makes, the many and varied doctrinal claims? These are often the subject of vigorous disagreement between believers of different persuasions. For these either implicitly or explicitly are prefaced with the expression 'I believe'. It is noteworthy that such statements prefer the term 'believe' to others, for example, 'I know', 'I propose that'. It is significant that believers often prefer to preface their statement with 'I believe' rather than leave the two words out and simply say for example, 'God is the Maker of heaven and earth'. They will often say, 'I believe that . . . .' 'I believe' here expresses a personal attitude, a commitment to what the belief implies. The expression sometimes expresses a kind of hesitation, as if one did not wish to claim certainty beyond doubt. When we say, 'I believe that . . . .' rather than ' I claim that. . . .' we show that we realise that believing is not identical with making a claim to knowledge. For we do not always think that we are we making a claim when we express our belief. Often we do. But we can distinguish levels of certainty when we make a claim. 'I believe that . . . .' can express a high level of certainty. It can also preface a tentative claim.

We cannot always be assured that what we believe is true. That is what makes believing different from knowing. Belief is not identical with knowledge. Indeed we sometimes prefer to use the term 'believe' when we are not sure, even to say ' I don't know but I believe that Johnny will come today', 'I can't be sure but I believe that it was Elizabeth that I saw'. But this is not how believers characteristically use the term when speaking of many of their religious convictions. Belief is thus accompanied by different levels of conviction that 'believers' entertain. For example they would not put their belief *that* God exists (even if they would use that form of expression at all), or their belief *that* Paul was the 'author' of the book of *Romans* on the same level as their belief *in* a living God, or in their belief that they are justified by faith (an important Pauline teaching).

So we have some interesting philosophical questions to consider. We can make a preliminary list. These questions are of general interest and lead us to answers of the widest application.

What is the relation between belief and knowledge?
What distinguishes justified from unjustified belief?
How in a particular case does one justify one's belief?
Would we sometimes be justified in believing what was false?
Do we always need sufficient evidence before we believe?
Is it reasonable to believe on authority?
Can we choose to believe?

Various answers are given to the question, 'What is belief?' Let us look at some of these.

Belief is a mental occurrence, for example mere acceptance, being under the impression that a proposition is true.

Belief is reasoned assent to a proposition.

Belief is absence of dissent to a proposition.

Belief is a behavioural disposition rather than a mental occurrence.

The difference is significant. We are disposed to act in a certain way, as if what we believe were true. That means we have already entertained the proposition. A disposition is not always manifest, made public. It is nevertheless a property we possess and which, given the appropriate circumstances, we would manifest.

Belief is entertaining ideas and then preferring one or other propositions that express that idea or those ideas. We give assent to a proposition while having reasonable assurance that it is true. We have some grounds for thinking our belief is reasonable. Our route to assurance is that we have experiences that would be as they are if the proposition were true. If our proposition were true we would expect such experiences. When they happen, our beliefs are confirmed or strengthened. I believe that this recipe is a good one. So I make a casserole and it turns out that everybody likes it really well. So my belief is confirmed. I may have held it tentatively at first. Now it has grounds and is strong.

It is important to differentiate the **content** of the belief from the process of **acquiring** the belief. So we distinguish two questions: What is belief? How do I acquire belief? In view of the above observations and in view of the fact that not every belief one holds has any relation to their behaviour, that some beliefs are purely theoretical, we shall further ask, When it *is* related to behaviour *how* is belief related to behaviour?

We acquire beliefs before ever we could ask how we get them. It sometimes comes as a surprise to us when we must answer the question 'How did you come to believe that?' For, the fact for all of us is that we acquired our first beliefs before we could frame, let alone answer, that question. We believed before we knew it. We had no choice in the matter. Take (what I think has been) your former belief in Father Christmas. Then ask how you came to believe it. Was it a rational belief? You now know that it was not true. But the case raises a lot of questions.

Or draw a comparison. Contrast or compare what you believe about Napoleon or Robin Hood with what you believe about Robinson Crusoe and why. How much, in volume, have you heard of each? Who has told you? In what contexts? Why do your beliefs about these characters differ?

2 Faith

The claims of the religious person are prefaced with the words 'I believe' or some equivalent to this. The primary claim is, 'I believe in God'. These statements are, as we say, 'confessions of faith'. What does it mean to say, 'I believe'? This way of speaking is not, of course unique to the believer. Does he then believe in a special way? Since the words 'believe', 'belief', are used in different senses, a job of sorting out needs to be done to clarify what the religious use of the term is actually claiming. Such a procedure will prove illuminating.

Let us start with four sentences whose meaning we quite well understand:

a.   I believe that it's half past two.
b.   I believe in penicillin.
c.   I believe in Chelsea.
d.   I believe in you.

Note now that while there are two nouns 'belief' and 'faith', there is only one single verb corresponding to each of these. This is the verb 'to believe'. So while we talk of believing, we do not speak of 'faithing'. Because of this, the word 'to believe' may mean 'to have belief', or it may mean 'to have faith'. We must make up our minds in any particular case. We must be careful to distinguish the uses of the word, so that its various meanings do not get confused. For if they do, then the meaning of faith i. e. the appropriate meaning in the particular context is bound to be obscured. If we have alternatives in mind, we may better decide in any given context which is the appropriate meaning of the term. We shall then not simply transfer one meaning to each case, or one inadequate meaning to the particular context. For example, 'believing' might mean 'accepting as true on inadequate evidence'. Whether that is an adequate meaning will depend upon the usage to which it is put. If the context demands that usage, then the meaning it has is a proper one. But this does not mean that 'believe' will have this meaning in other contexts.

Going then to our examples: In the first instance, 'I believe' means 'I am of the opinion that', 'I am more or less certain that what I am saying is correct'. What is being affirmed is the correctness (more or less) of a fact. You could easily give other examples: I believe you can get to New York from London in five hours; I believe that Mary is Jane's cousin; I believe that Sara Jones is a pen-name for Susan Jenkins, etc.

In the case of b and c the term 'I believe in' expresses the confidence appropriate to what is believed in. 'I believe in penicillin' means that you would recommend its use, you would use it yourself, because you anticipate it would produce benefit when used. 'I believe in Chelsea', a football team, means that you think that they are likely to have success rather than failure. In both of these cases the confidence expressed is tested by future performance. If penicillin produced such dreadful side effects that outweighed its future usefulness you would not talk this way about it. If Chelsea never won a game for the whole of the season you would soon lose that confidence. 'I believe in' in the sense 'I have confidence in' is a statement which you can alter if you find that things don't turn out so as to support your confidence. You have to wait and see!

We may not be aware of the total range of our confidence. We assume beliefs, which we only make explicit when there is some demand upon us or when they are called into question, or when perhaps, for methodological purposes, we feel that examination is called for to make them explicit. The physical scientist has a confidence of this kind. He assumes, that is to say he believes in, the reliability of nature, accepting the principle of uniformity as the foundation for all his work. Such an assumption is irrational in the sense that he is never able to give decisive and finally convincing reasons that this is so. But his whole activity is based upon this belief being a worthy one. That belief is a non-scientific assumption which, when made, he finds makes his scientific work possible. He too has faith. That his methods 'work' is sufficient to sustain that faith.

In the case of d, we have an example of an expression of personal trust. 'I believe in you', spoken by a father to his son, by a voter to his representative, by a friend to his friend, means 'I trust you'. The term is now being used on a personal level. Of course, it might turn out that such trust is wrongly placed. If you have confidence in a friend and speak to him about private matters and find that the secret is kept, your confidence is maintained. But can you be absolutely sure? What if the next time you share a confidence you find that someone later knows about it? Or what if one day you find a knife in your back? But people do trust one another. They do act as if there is not going to be this let-down. They are willing to venture on the assumption that the future will bear out their trust. But they also know that there are quite specific ways in which such trust could be shown to be misplaced. But they do not expect that it will. In this fourth sense, then, 'I believe' means I have trust of a personal kind.

3   Belief, Testimony and Knowledge

> 'I'll do the impossible. What you believe in, I'll believe in.'
>
> John Steinbeck, *East of Eden*

'I can't believe that !' said Alice.

'Can't you? The Queen said in a pitying tone. 'Try again: draw a long breath and shut your eyes.'

Alice laughed. 'There's no use trying,' she said: 'one can't believe impossible things.'

I daresay you haven't had much practice,' said the Queen.
'When I was your age I always did it for half an hour a day.
Why, sometimes I've believed as many as six impossible things
before breakfast.'

———

The Christian religion demands and offers belief. Some people
find it impossible to believe, to accept the demand to have faith.
For others it is because it is impossible that they confess to the occurrence of a miracle to bring about such belief. It is not only the
sceptic who talks that way when he explains that he cannot believe.
The believer sometimes says the same, in a reverse, positive way: 'It
required a miracle to bring about my faith.' Take the words of the
non-believer classically expressed by David Hume, *On Miracles*:

> The Christian religion not only was at first attended
> with miracles, but even at this day cannot be believed by any
> reasonable person without one. Mere reason is insufficient to
> convince us of its veracity: and whoever is moved by faith to
> assent to it is conscious of a continued miracle in his own
> person, which subverts all the principle of his understanding,
> and gives him a determination to believe what is most contrary
> to custom and experience.

We can discuss the issues on different levels, by asking the
following questions:

What does it mean to believe?
What can you believe and what can you not believe?
Can you choose to accept a particular belief?
Can you choose between beliefs?

Basic and fundamental questions for the Christian believer are
what it means to believe in God, to believe that what the sacred
writings present to us is true.[1] That second question is one which

———

1   Does faith in God justify belief in the authority of Scripture? What
does belief in the authority of Scripture entail? Questions arise that
demand definition of the understanding of God, of the meaning of
faith and of the coming into existence of the many writings of scripture,

the non-believer can also ask. Both believer and non-believer will ask, 'Are we to take as both authentic and as true the claims that the various writings of scripture make?' Both will also ask, 'Why does the believer take these writings to be authoritative in a way the non-believer does not?' 'Is it possible to establish common ground over the difference of approaches?'

We have distinguished two meanings. The term 'believe' sometimes means 'to have faith'. It also means 'to have a belief.' The distinction can be illustrated by considering two sentences.

I believe in God.
I believe that Jesus spoke of the Kingdom of God and of the Son of Man.

The term 'believer' has two meanings: a person who has faith. It also means one who assents to particular beliefs, who accepts purported claims to be true. Those who share faith (belief in one sense i.e. 'belief in') do not always share beliefs (i.e. 'belief that'). For example, both may share belief in having faith in a loving God, and yet disagree about what they believe (assent to) about the problem of evil and suffering, or about scripture and its interpretation.

Christians, like other theistic believers, have writings they consider to be not only authentic but also authoritative. For the Christian believer is interested in both the present and in the past. The writings, called 'Scripture' make frequent reference to events that happened, to people and peoples who lived in the past, to places which now no longer exist. So historical questions are often of importance. It is relevant to ask why, if so.

These documents are sources and provide testimony. They witness to persons, events, beliefs. Sometimes the writing is the only witness to the events it purports to report and interpret. Such

---

historical as well as theological issues are inevitably involved. Give a truncated answer to these questions and the result will be an inadequate understanding. For a careful treatment of these issues see Edward W. H. Vick, *From Inspiration to Understanding*.

testimony is thus available for the kind of scrutiny the historian directs to historical sources.

The believer and the unbeliever share something in common. They both make claims about historical events based on evidence available generally, in particular from written documents. What each claims about a particular report will depend on the background beliefs they hold. They may both agree that *Mark* was the source of a miracle story, but then disagree about whether the miracle actually took place. The dispute may be on a theoretical level. One believes in the universality of natural law. The other believes God has ways of intervening into the system of nature. Those are the more fundamental beliefs. One believes that allowance must be made for the truth of reports in a sacred book that would not be made in other cases. The other believes that reports in a sacred book are to be evaluated according to principles of historical evaluation that are universal.

The unique testimony of Christians also has a present aspect in that the believer is now making a claim not simply about the past but also about the present. He or she is testifying (1) to something that has happened to them, something that is claimed to validate belief, and (2) claiming that, fulfilling the same conditions upon hearing testimony, it can also happen to the hearer.

How is this testimony validated? Some such testimony is validated by a two stage process. The hearer believes the proposition. What the testator claims to have experienced, or claims other people have experienced, the hearer also experiences.

What then results, it is believed, is that the testator's claim is justified. That is a common experience. The sufferer says that when she took Pillpal her pain ceased. You believe her and take Pillpal and your pain ceases. The effect confirms your belief in her testimony. It was true testimony.

Reference to other peoples' experience is not direct testimony as is testimony to one's own experience. But it may well be evidence, and in a secondary sense it is thus also testimony. 'John has become sober and honest after coming to believe' is a different kind of evidence from 'I have become sober and honest after coming to believe'.

One dictionary defines belief as 'mental assent to or acceptance on the ground of authority or evidence; the mental condition involved in this assent of a proposition, statement, or fact as true' (*Shorter Oxford Dictionary*).

When would we, indeed when do we, accept what someone says as true? When do we give assent to their claim on the basis of their testimony? Put the question in terms of the definition above and it becomes: 'When does someone's testimony have such authority that we believe, i.e. give our assent to, what they say?' Or alternatively, 'Why do we hesitate or entertain doubt or suspicion about it?'

The question we are asking is 'When is belief justified?' We might also consider whether there are circumstances where I could justifiably believe something that was not true. We could not 'remember' something that is false. If we thought we had remembered something false, it would not be remembrance but delusion or deception. But in contrast to remembering could we *believe* something false? So we need to ask, 'How is evidence, independent of the person's testimony, related to my giving or withholding assent to their report?' Maria testifies that she saw Phyllis at the concert yesterday evening. I met Phyllis this morning and, full of enthusiasm she described the performance she heard yesterday. So I am confirmed in believing Maria's testimony.

Now for a few examples. Apply the questions suggested above to the following examples:

The witness says that she saw the car swerve and hit the lamp post.

The witness says that he saw a man walk through a closed door.

The witness says she saw a ghost in the library.

The witness said that he saw water flowing upwards.

The reporter claimed that the Frenchman ate three hundred and twenty four snails.

David Hume considered that when the Indian prince or the inhabitant of Sumatra refused to believe that water froze, that belief was a reasonable one. So he thought that it is reasonable sometimes to believe something that is false. There is no reason to disagree with that. We are now ready to discuss what makes for reasonable belief, what justifies belief.

To express a belief you do not always have to preface the remark with the words 'I believe that'. Normally when you make a statement you intend your hearer to understand that it is to be taken to be a true statement. When you say, 'Mary is coming tomorrow', it is clear to anyone who takes spoken sentences as we normally take them that you believe it. A false statement or a lie is under normal circumstances, i.e. unless we have grounds for doubt, taken to be true. When we believe a false statement we take it to be true. That is why people lie.

A proposition is a statement, i.e. a sentence that expresses either a truth or a falsehood. It is a claim and it is either true or false, but not both! It is a sentence that makes an assertion. The following two sentences make claims. 'Today is the twenty-ninth day in February.' 'Leila's maternal grandfather is six years younger than she is.' Note that the first is true now, the 'now' being as I write in the second month, but it will not be true tomorrow but only again four years from now. The second will not be true tomorrow either, but for a different reason. It is a logical impossibility. Define the terms correctly and there is a contradiction. The passage of time has nothing to do with its truth or falsity. We do not look for evidence for its falsity because we cannot. When we understand the meaning of the terms we know that the claim is false. Sentences that make claims are called propositions. They can be either true or false. We may or we may not believe them. As we have just seen, they make claims in their different ways.

In contrast, 'Get up!', 'What a beautiful morning!', 'Let us move forward.' are complete sentences but they do not make claims. They are not propositions. They are not statements. One is a command. One is an exclamation. One is an exhortation. None of these can be true. Nor can they be false. Such a sentence that may be true or false is a proposition. We respond appropriately to each of these different kinds of sentences in different ways. But we cannot believe these three kinds. Take an exclamation for example. Jane says, 'What a lovely day!' and wants you to take this as an exclamation rather than as a claim. Jenny says, pointing to the facts, 'It's pouring with rain and the river is overflowing. So it's not appropriate to say, What a beautiful morning.' 'Oh! But it is!' says Jane, 'I have just heard that I have passed my exam!' Reacting thus appropriately is not the same as believing, asserting, claiming. An exclamation expresses an attitude. It does not make a claim. But the attitude may or may not be appropriate. What makes the attitude expressed in an exclamation appropriate will, of course, be some state of affairs about which a proposition may truly be made. Hence Jenny points to some dismal facts which seem to make Jane's happy exclamation inappropriate, only to be countered with Jane's stating a different fact which makes her expression of delight appropriate for her.

Sometimes sentences that have the form of propositions and so appear to make a claim may function differently. They may express an attitude. For example, 'That dog is a terror' (which has the form of a statement) may mean effectively that I am expressing an aversion to the beast! Something like 'Ugh!' Or I am sounding a warning: 'Keep well clear of him!' When Jane says, 'I've passed! I've passed!' (which has the form of a statement) she is expressing her exultation and means effectively, 'Wow! Whoopee!' as well as giving you the information that the examiners have passed her. It has the form of a statement but in effect it is not only a statement, but also an exclamation. It is to be taken rather as an expression of delight than a statement of fact. It does have these two functions of course. But one is predominant! Some religious sentences are like that. It is a matter of recognising both the function and the status of the particular sentence. Take and consider for example 'God loves us as a father loves his child'. It may be intended as an exclamation of contentment, or as a claim, sometimes both!

Some things we believe are justified and others are not. I may or not be justified in my belief about a perception, an event, or an abstract proposition.

To answer how you would justifiably affirm or deny a claim, you must ask the general question about the grounds on which one makes claims. There are two basic answers to this question: First, 'It stands to reason!' where 'reason' means logical consistency. The statement has to be true given the meaning of the terms and the relation asserted between them: e.g. 2+2 = 4. The statement is logically necessary.

The second sort of ground is that there is sufficient evidence to verify the claim. The evidence may be direct. It is given to me by some experience I am having or have had. I have seen, heard etc. Or, the evidence comes to me from reliable witnesses. Mary told me she saw, heard etc.

Having asked the general question and given your answer you then can go to the specific case and apply it there. Try the examples that follow:

The sound I am now hearing is a car exhaust. (To hear is to perceive.)

The flower I am looking at is yellow. (To see is to perceive.)

What I smell is lavender. (To smell is to perceive.)

People never have illusions.

There are pink elephants.

The earth is flat.

Not all claims are concrete. Some are abstract. You may or may not be justified in your belief about an abstract claim. First of all, of course, you have to understand it. You may then believe it. You may then not believe it. Your belief depends upon your understanding. If you do not understand Pythagoras' theorem, you cannot believe its conclusion. You may pretend to assert it. But without comprehension you neither believe nor can you make a genuine assertion. Your stating it may give the appearance of an understanding you do not have.

Consider the following:

20 litres is larger than 10 gallons.
The end justifies the means.
Knowing involves believing.
A necessary condition for believing is understanding.
The interior angles of a triangle amount to two right angles.
A large dog is a better house dog than a small dog.
Boojams are inflabulated.

An interesting issue arises. When one affirms a belief one does not understand the conformity that results may be artificial and/or hypocritical. You may appear to agree with the majority when you have not reached an understanding of what it is you appear to assert. So you give the impression that you believe. Such artificial agreement is often welcomed by the authority or the company! At least you are off the hook.

Sometimes a belief is justified and sometimes it is not. Even if what I believe is true, I may not be justified in believing it. On the other hand, I might be justified in believing something false. So we need to address the question of how a belief is justified. From what we have said, it is clear that a justified belief is not the same as a true belief, not the same as knowledge. So, now we shall ask, What is knowledge? Is it a special kind of belief?

Note that in logic we define an argument as a process of reasoning. Statements follow one another and are connected in such a way that we draw a conclusion and say that we are justified in doing so. If the argument is a sound one, the conclusion will follow from the preceding sentences, which are called premises. In such a case if those premises are true the conclusion will be true. Look at the following argument.

You can justifiably believe a false statement.
Knowledge involves believing a true statement.
Knowledge involves justifiably believing a true statement
Therefore, you cannot know a false statement.

Nor can you know a true statement unless you can justifiably believe it.

Does it also follow from:

> You cannot know a true statement if your belief
> is not justified:

that

> Justifiably believing a true statement constitutes
> knowledge?

If testimony is to be credited and provide justified belief, (1) the attester must be honest. This is the sincerity dimension, and (2) she must also have sufficient knowledge or experience to form a true belief. This is the competence dimension. For example, If Pamela testifies on the basis of a lucky guess that Samantha was in Nottingham yesterday, she cannot transmit justification or knowledge to Peter, the person to whom she speaks. What she testifies to is true, but it is a fluke that she believes that it is true. It is even more of an accident that the one to whom she testifies believes the true statement.

So their belief is not justified and an unjustified belief is not knowledge. I may believe that what she says is true. Her belief was not justified. But what about Peter's. Is his belief justified? If you say that it is, will you also have to add that he does not know what he believes? I can believe what I do not know. I can believe what I am not justified in believing. Also it is quite possible that I might justifiably believe something that is false. Think of circumstances in which this might be the case. The one above is an example.

Questions to think about:

Are there other reasons why my belief might not be justified?

Since a justified belief may be a false belief, what more must there be for a justified belief to constitute knowledge?

On what basis would you consider a belief to be justified by someone's testimony? This might be either someone's verbal account, a report in a newspaper, or what a textbook says.

But you may be justified through my testimony even if I who testify am not justified in my belief. Whether you are justified in your belief will depend on (1) The way I attest to Samantha being in Nottingham yesterday, and (2) your background information about me and about the circumstances. Can you work out this example? Then make up one of your own of (1) justified belief, (2) unjustified belief based on testimony.

Statement of principles:

A belief based on testimony is justified provided the believer has adequate grounds for taking the attester to be credible regarding the proposition in question. Belief constitutes knowledge only provided the one testifying knows the proposition and provided the one hearing, the one who comes to believe, has no reason to doubt either the proposition or the attester's credibility about it.

So if I have reason to think the attester is trustworthy and has no motive for deceiving me and has a good ground for believing what she says and perhaps also is in a position of authority, or has access to special knowledge, then my belief is reasonable and so is justified.

Questions:

Was it reasonable for many thousands of people for long periods of time to believe that the earth is flat, i.e. were they justified in so believing a falsehood? So is one justified in believing something at one time but not at another time?

Think of examples of justified but false belief.

4 A Summary of Some Issues

a. Our question is: How does testimony produce belief?
b. Distinguish inferential and non-inferential beliefs. Ask, Are all beliefs which are derived from testimony inferential, as in the following case?
Premises: The witness seems reliable.
Evidence: The statement the witness makes fits in with what I know about the case.

Conclusion: Therefore, it is reasonable that I believe that statement.

c. Perception is necessary for the formation of beliefs grounded in testimony. I must hear the testimony. A basic belief is one not based on other beliefs. The beliefs evoked by testimony need not be based on premises at all, i.e. they can be non-inferential.

d. The epistemological question is: 'How does testimony yield justified belief and knowledge?' Certain conditions must be fulfilled if testimony is to provide knowledge to its hearer. If I who am testifying do not know that p [p stands for 'any statement'], you who hear my testimony can't come to know that p on the basis of my attesting to it. If I do not know but only pretend that I do, you cannot know what I testify to. For example, if I do not know, but only surmise, that I am getting a good return on my investment, and testify to you that I am, you, the hearer, cannot know. You may believe but the belief may turn out to be false. Whether you are justified in believing me depends on other considerations.

However, even if I am not justified in believing it, my testifying to it can provide you with justification for believing it, by providing the main materials for your becoming justified in believing it. The way I attest to the proposition, together with your background justification regarding me and the circumstances, may give you justification, independent of whether I have such justification.

e. If testimony is to be credited and provide justified belief, (1) the attester must be honest, and so fulfil the sincerity dimension, and also (2) must have sufficient knowledge or experience to form a true belief, the competence dimension. For example, say that Pete testifies on the basis of a lucky guess that Bob made a deal with Mary yesterday.

What he believes is true, what he testifies to is true, but it is a lucky accident that his testimony is true. But he does not know that it is. Suppose I believe his testimony. I may or may not be justified in my belief. Whether I am must be determined by considerations about my previous contacts with Pete, and my present grounds for taking his testimony to be true, e.g. my experience of his previous reliability as a giver of testimony. There is irony in such an example. His belief is a true belief, but for him it is not justified since it is a fluke that he got it right. So since his testimony is true, and will turn out to be known as true, he may, because of that, be taken as a reliable witness, not only in this case, but in other instances. The question is whether my belief is justified as the grounds for his reliability in other cases than this one.

f. You may be justified through my testimony even if I, in testifying, am not justified in my belief. Whether you are justified in your belief in my testimony will depend on first, the way I attest to say, Samantha being in London yesterday, and second, your background information about me and third, independent of your considerations about me, your awareness of the circumstances to which I am testifying

g. Statement of principles: A belief based on testimony is justified provided the believer has justification for taking the attester to be credible regarding the proposition in question.

Belief constitutes knowledge (1) provided the proposition is true, (2) provided the one testifying knows the proposition and (3) provided the one hearing and coming to believe, has good reason to believe or has no reason to doubt either the proposition or the attester's credibility about it.[2]

---

2 Cf. Robert Audi, *Epistemology*, pp. 136-138.

5   **Validating Testimony**

Christians, like other believers, have writings they consider to be not only authentic but also authoritative. The Christian believer is interested both in the present and in the past. The writings, called 'scripture' have frequent references to events that happened, to people and peoples who lived in the past, what they did, what they said, what happened to them, the writings that survived them. Historical questions are often of primary importance. But their importance is to be distinguished from other kinds of importance.

We rely for our knowledge of the past on the testimony of those who lived and left evidence of their living. Such sources provide testimony to persons, events, beliefs. Sometimes the evidence is in the form of writing about the events it purports to report and interpret. Such testimony is thus available for the kind of careful scrutiny the historian directs to historical sources. Such scrutiny reveals the importance of that past to the present. How is this testimony validated?

The testimony of Christians has a present aspect in that the believer is now making claims about what is present. Christians testify (1) to something that has happened in the past, something that they claim is essential for their belief, (2) and claim that, fulfilling the same conditions, can also happen in the present to the hearer. Some such testimony is effective and is validated through a two stage process: The hearer believes the proposition about the experience of others. What the testator claims to have experienced, or claims other people as well have experienced, the hearer also experiences. What results, it is believed, is that the testator's claim is justified.

Reference to other peoples' experience is indirect testimony. I can testify that since he became a believer Sam has become a better person. Statement of what has happened to the speaker is direct testimony. But it may well be evidence, and in the secondary sense of testimony it is thus also testimony. 'John has become sober and honest after coming to believe' is a different kind of evidence from

'I have become sober and honest after coming to believe.' If there were no other way of knowing either about Sam or about me, such testimony, the conditions being right. would be sufficient to provide justification for my belief.

6   Different Kinds Of Beliefs: The Book Of *Acts*

The book of *Acts* in the New Testament provides us with examples of many kinds of beliefs. We may not be aware as we read scriptural writings that understanding them demands several kinds of belief. Some of these are more easily achieved than others and some are not achievable at all by some readers. A typical Christian 'believer' will hold the following beliefs and so could preface each of the following propositions with the statement 'I believe. . . .' Those marked with an asterisk are amenable to historical assessment. As such they can be verified or falsified empiricially. The others are not amenable to such assessment. That is to say they are beyond historical confirmation.

Luke wrote the book of *Acts.**

Acts was not the first writing Luke composed.*

Luke used various sources in writing the book.*

Luke's account is in detail literally true and so trustworthy as a report of actual events. For example, Luke gives a trustworthy account of the day of Pentecost in chapter 2.

Peter healed the lame man who came to the Temple by being carried, and left leaping about in his joy.

Luke records amazement of the crowds at the healing of the man lame from birth.*

The healing was a miracle.

The crowds were amazed.

Luke knew by report about the conversion of Saul on the way to Damascus.*

Luke's report of this conversion is authentic.*

Saul was converted on the way to Damascus.*

Luke was a companion of Paul and accompanied him on some journeys.*

Paul lived two years in his own house in Rome.*

Luke could have written about the last months and the death of Paul, but (as far as we know) he did not.*

What is most interesting about these beliefs is that they are not all of the same kind. So, since our task is to analyse what it means to believe, we will distinguish the kinds of belief we have instanced in this list.

These beliefs fall into different classes:

Belief about historical fact e.g.: about the book
Belief about what the book says took place
Belief about the trustworthiness of the evidence of testimony
Belief in miracle i.e. that the unusual event reported took place
Belief in the possibility of an event which either did not happen or of which we are ignorant.

Some of these overlap. For someone who believes that the supernatural can and does intervene in the natural course of events there will be a different assessment of reports about extraordinary events from the one who does not so believe. One will be sceptical about purported testimony to such events. The other will simply accept that testimony. An interesting case is that of the believer who readily accepts reports of miracles within his own religion but is sceptical about those from another religion, even if they are similar. This raises the question about the demands of consistency in the process of evaluation of reports and testimony.

The non-believer and the believer would agree about several of the beliefs listed. The 'non-believer' would have reservations about several. The beliefs both might agree about are the ones starred on the above list. We may go further and ask whether there could be disagreement about any of the above between believers calling themselves Christian. The one principle all would agree about is that a physical event not considered possible today, for good reasons that can readily be given, could not have happened at any previous time. So people of a different religion have difficulty with reports of miracles claimed within a religious context different from their own. Sometimes this causes them to question the possibility of miracles claimed within their own religious context. If a physical miracle cannot happen now and we can give good reasons for that claim, then it cannot have happened at any time. We know that a lame man is not instantly healed by the mere words of another, that atrophied limbs are not at once made operative, we do not say restored, because, in the case we took as an example, the man was lame from birth. So the believer either does not give the matter thought and takes the account as literally true or, after reflecting on the passage, finds an explanation he can accept but others cannot.

7   Consciousness and Belief

How many of your beliefs are you conscious of at this moment? Why none at all! Of course, now that the question has been asked you can start recalling one after another till you have an exhaustive list. You can then say, 'These are my conscious beliefs now.' But does it seem strange to talk about an unconscious belief?

We are interested in the concept of consciousness for two reasons. So we can pursue our discussion

in relation to belief: whether to hold a belief I have to be conscious of having it. Must it be explicit to my consciousness? There are related problems, to explain what it means to lack the awareness of a belief/to be aware of a belief.

in relation to the possibility of holding contradictory beliefs: lacking awareness of one, or of both, or having awareness of both.

in relation to the idea of personal identity. Is identity of consciousness the criterion for identity of the person?

What does having the consciousness of a belief, being conscious of a belief, mean? Are either of the following correct?

You don't have to be conscious to have a belief.

You don't have to be conscious of it, to have a belief.

We are not conscious of most of the beliefs we have at any given moment, even when we are conscious. To produce such a sentence, we use the word 'conscious' in two different ways. There are other ways as well.

a.   I am conscious if I am not unconscious, i.e. not under anaesthetic, not suffering the effect of a wallop on the head, not in a dreamless sleep. For example, I have been in a coma. But I have now 'come round'. So I am conscious. This is the intransitive use of the term.

b.   Contrast to this the transitive use of 'conscious'. This may take various forms, variations of a basic mode, namely 'I am conscious that . . . .' I say, 'I believe that I once lived in Nashville.' 'I am conscious that p ('I once lived in Nashville'). In this case the belief in the proposition is explicit since the content of the proposition is held before my mind and I assent to it. But I can be said to have the belief even when I am not at the moment aware of its specific content, even if I am not now holding it in my consciousness.

What does it mean to believe, say, that Mary was espoused to Joseph? Must the belief be explicit in their consciousness for anyone to say that they believe the proposition? Do I still believe it when I am not thinking about it, when a lot of other things are in my mind, when my concerns of the present have pushed it and many other beliefs out of my conscious thought. Am I a believer when I am asleep?

Take for example, 'I believe Elizabeth is in the library'. My first level of awareness is of the belief. The belief is explicit in my mind. I am now assenting to the proposition 'E is in L'. There is also a second level of belief. That occurs when I am aware that I am entertaining this belief. I step back, so to speak, and think of myself thinking my belief. If I express this I will say, 'I am now aware that I believe that Elizabeth is in the library'. The second level of awareness occurs when e.g. I am aware of my belief that. . . . or when I am aware of my awareness. So, 'I believe Elizabeth is in the library', is a first level belief. So, I go looking for her. I walk here and there in the library. Then I reflect on my state of mind and become aware of my belief that Elizabeth is in the library. This is a second level awareness. I am aware that I believe that Elizabeth is in the library. If later I reflect on an act I did not notice at the time, that I walked to the opposite end of the room on the strength of my belief, I am now aware that I may not have been explicitly aware of it then when I was taking significant action at the moment of taking it. Yet I must have been in some sense conscious of taking it, to enable me to have taken it. It was my act, after all. My action is like that of the motorist who avoids an obstacle in the road but at the time is not consciously aware that he is doing so. Such sub-conscious acts sometimes reveal our beliefs, even if while performing those acts the belief that stimulates the act is not then conscious nor the act consciously connected with it. If someone had met me and asked what I was doing rather than say, 'I am walking in the library', I would have said, 'I am looking for Elisabeth'. If he asked, Why? I could then have said, 'Because I believe she is here, somewhere', thus appealing to my belief as a reason for my action. I may of course have wanted it to be the case that she is in the building. This might lead to the consequence that, holding fast to my belief, I do not consider the evidence that she is not in the library. It is then that self-deception might take place. I do not permit myself to examine the evidence for what I believe, since I do not want to have to abandon it. There may be at some level a refusal to be aware of my belief. Does that happen? Why would I refuse to believe something that I do not know is false?

An interesting footnote can be added to these remarks. Some propositions are not compatible with explicit awareness, and turn out to be in some cases rather amusing. For example, if I said, 'I believe that I have forgotten that once I lived in Nashville' you would probably laugh. That 'claim' involves a contradiction, as the following one does not; 'I believe that I have forgotten where I put my purse'. You will easily discern the difference between the two!

8   Accepting, Doubting And Abandoning A Belief

a.   Sometimes we consider a proposition but do not yet believe or disbelieve it. When does entertaining and examining a proposition become believing it? Is there such a thing as half-belief? Consider the following as possible stages:

Being aware that there is a proposition to consider
Entertaining the proposition
Giving myself reasons for thinking it may be reasonable to believe it
Being disposed to assent to it
Giving my assent to it i.e. believing it.

A note needs to be added. For the fact is that we sometimes find ourselves believing and are not aware that any process has taken place. The child can hardly help believing in Santa Claus. She just does. Sometimes we do not have to 'make up our minds'. They have already been made up for us. Once we are aware that we have not really done so before, we can as thinking beings reflect and consider those unexamined beliefs responsibly.

b.   b [= a in reverse] We can readily find examples of the processes of coming to accept a belief, and also of coming to abandon a belief. When does questioning and doubting a belief become abandoning it? The process is something like the following:

Ask what the belief means
Work out its implications
Consider the evidence for and against it
Ask further about its rationality, e.g. Is it consistent, illuminating?

    Compare it with alternatives
    Give myself reasons for calling it into question
    Doubt it
    Revise it
    Abandon it
    Replace it

c.   If I do not understand, at least to some extent, what I say I believe, my profession of belief may well be an empty one, a kind of front with little or nothing behind it, something akin to a child holding up a banner, not understanding what is written on it. If, for example, I assert that Scripture is inerrant, I may never have asked some of the questions involved in the preceding paragraph. But I consider some of the implications of the belief as I ask, Can I really believe the Hebrew text when it says that an ass can speak because impeded by an angel, that the word of a prophet can cause an axe to float, that a captain can win a battle after he has given the sun a command to stand still?

To examine other scriptural, Christian claims you will have to ask yourself rather sophisticated questions, and find reasonable answers to them. Some of us write books to help you in the process!

d.   You realise there is a distinction between believing and knowing. You have always been certain about your beliefs. But you may realise that believing and being certain is not the same as knowing. You may nevertheless hold firm to your beliefs But then you must admit you cannot be arrogant about them, cannot treat them as if there were no questions to be asked about them. Self-assurance and certainty about belief does not mean knowledge. A certain humility is always appropriate in holding and expressing one's beliefs.

e.   About doubt. At this stage, the people who think they know every answer, or worse still, every question, are the ones who may be able to help us the least. People who have gone through an experience similar to ours a long time ago, and who have now found working answers to their questions, may have forgotten how hard-won their conclusions and attitudes were. It's easy once you've found a working answer to forget the process of struggle that led up to it. It is easy then to be unsympathetic.

Those who have not gone through what we go through in this period simply live in a different world from us, and speak to us in a language which does not connect. We hear the words and see the concern. We know their affection and appreciate it. Yet sometimes the very finality and placidity with which we are told disarms us. It may even — if we are deeply troubled by such dogmatism — lead us to reject not only the unsatisfactory answer but also the very quest in which we are participating. This is a gesture of despair, but quite an understandable one.

FOR FURTHER READING

D. J. O'Connor and Brian Carr, *Introduction to the Theory of Knowledge*, Brighton: The Harvester Press, 1982.

Phillips Griffiths (editor), *Knowledge and Belief*, London: Oxford University Press, 1967.

Elizabeth Maclaren, *The Nature of Belief*, London: Sheldon Press, 1976.

BELIEF AND BELIEVING: WORK SHEET

1. There have been several questions inserted into the text of this chapter. Go back and give your answers to them.

2. Is there a basic meaning for the term 'belief'? Write a paragraph explaining what you take 'belief' to mean. Give examples.

3. 'I wish I could believe that!' Is there any possibility that you might come to believe what you wish to believe?

4. Think of something you wish your friend would believe. State it explicitly. What might you do to help her believe it?

5. How does one establish the reliability of testimony? Think of a witness in a law court, and also of how to assess historical witness, for example the trustworthiness of written materials.

6. Must decision always precede belief? If not, what then? What would make you change your belief? Find a worthy example, say — the last time you made such a change.

7. What makes the difference between a justified and an unjustified belief? Give an example of each.

8. How does it happen that you change your belief?

9. There are many different ideas about God. Perhaps you do not believe in the God I do not believe in. Since there are many ideas of God, does the idea you have of God make the difference to whether you believe or not?

10. Should we distinguish between superficial and radical doubt?

3 EPISTEMOLOGY AND RELIGIOUS BELIEF

We all profess many and varied beliefs. For the most part we consider our beliefs justified. To go beyond justified belief to assert knowledge is to make a stronger claim. It is a step to a new dimension. We discuss the distinction between belief and knowledge, and the possible relation between them. What is it that provides a justification for what we believe? For sometimes we believe what is not true. One can justifiably believe what is false. One can also believe what is true without being justified in believing it, a condition to be avoided. We discuss the relation between Justification, Knowledge and Truth.

3 EPISTEMOLOGY AND RELIGIOUS BELIEF

1   Terms and Problems for Consideration

Episteme is the Greek word for 'knowledge.' *Epistemology* as 'theory of knowledge' addresses itself to the questions: 1. What is knowledge? How much knowledge do we have? 2. What are the sources of our knowledge? This question is answered by speaking of belief, perception, memory, consciousness, introspection, reason, testimony. 3. What is the relation between belief and knowledge? How are our beliefs justified? What are commendable features of belief? 4. If truth is desirable, what features distinguish true from false beliefs? If we wish to commend a belief we might say that it is rational, or that there is good evidence for it, or that it is well grounded, or that it is justified.

Consider these terms: justification, memory, remembering, recalling, recollection, testimony, evidence, knowledge.

Here are some questions about these terms. Can I be said to remember something that I do not now recall, something tucked away, as we say, 'in the back of my mind'? Is it alright to say I remember an experience, something that I have not myself experienced, as in the following example? A friend tells me what happened last night. There was a performance of *Hamlet*. Tomorrow I remember what she told me. But what is it that I am remembering? Am I remembering the event? Or a report of the event? Would my memory provide evidence for what happened last night?

I read in a history book what happened in 1066. What am I remembering when I say that I remember 1066? Does my memory connect me with the event? I read about the feeding of the five thousand. I remember what I have read. What is it that I am remembering? In one case I can check up and find out whether there was a performance of *Hamlet*. In the 1066 case I can relate the accounts of William the Conqueror's assault with other reports of later and contemporary events and work out a consistent account. If it hangs together well and does not make unwarranted demands upon my credibility I then accept the initial report as highly probable, if not true. That is until a better explanation may possibly be given. We deal with the interesting topic of 'best explanation' later.

So far we have talked about believing. What justifies me in going beyond saying 'I believe' to saying 'I know' something? In the case above, my remembering what my friend said as evidence for what happened last night, can I say that I remember what happened last night on the grounds of what she told me? Or rather should I say that I believe it?

Could I be justified in saying that I remember having done something I had forgotten doing, but which someone told me I had done? They say to me, 'Don't you remember meeting Jeremy at the seaside last October?' If I accepted their report but did not remember I would then be believing that the event happened. If I then recollected the event I would be remembering, rather than believing on the basis of testimony, and so have direct and not indirect connection with the event. We sometimes speak of 'jogging the memory'. But I may not have been able to recall the event in which they said I had participated. I could hardly then be said to be remembering it. I would simply be believing that I had done it on the basis of their testimony. A person suffering from serious amnesia would be in this situation many times over. So what is it about another person's testimony that would lead me to believe it? When would I not believe such testimony? One reason would be that I do not want to recall unpleasant things, unfavourable things. So I could resist recalling them and may unreasonably deny the veracity of their testimony to those events.

Some distinctions: **Memory** – the general capacity for re-membering and recalling: like a storehouse. Because we have this capacity we can remember and recall what we have so remembered. **Remembering** – the actual repository of events, things, proposi-tions. They are available for recall. There are things we remember i.e. store in the memory which we may never recall unaided. But given certain stimuli they could be recalled. **Recalling** these items.

We often claim to know events in the past, and propositions about such events, on the basis of our remembering them. If some-one else remembered what we had forgotten we have a certain access to past events. We are thus dependent upon their memory of the events. This is often available to us in their writing. Often memories conflict as do the reports based on those differing mem-ories. So we have to have some means of assessing those reports. So we may well ask whether such claims to true belief or to knowledge are justified by the appeal to memory?

To claim that memory is a source of knowledge is to claim that beliefs are grounded in memory. So to clarify what we mean by a memorial belief we need to consider whether there are direct causal connections between what we remember and our memory of it, that is to say whether the event is the actual cause of the memory directly or indirectly. So we distinguish between direct and indirect remembering.

I recall yesterday's birthday dinner because I participated in it. The event itself is the cause of my remembering, since there is a direct chain connecting the event with my recollection. That is direct memory. I remember yesterday's dinner even if I was not there, since my colleague, whose testimony I take as reliable, tells me about it. I have present testimony to a past event that immedi-ately becomes past testimony to a past event. The past event is now lodged, along with many other events, in my memory storehouse. I may recall it at some future time. This is clearly a different kind of remembering because its basis is different. It is indirect memory. So I can truly believe the proposition about yesterday's dinner in the latter as in the former case. In both cases the dinner is the cause of the belief which I have about it. The cause is either immediate or mediated by testimony.

Distinguish between a memorial belief caused by a past event and one which is not so caused. The latter belief is one in which my memory has no role in supporting the content of my belief. Suppose I take a non-poisonous drug unknowingly and later I become strangely ill. My feeling ill causes me to believe I have been poisoned. I then remember taking the drug and make a connection. So indirectly my taking of the drug causes me to believe I have been poisoned, but indirectly causes the belief. So it is not a memorial belief (cf. Audi, p. 57). A belief about the past is a memorial belief only if it has some causal connection to a past event, even if that connection is hard to specify. When such causal connection is established we take it that memory provides genuine knowledge.

Take the case of written documentation of events. The author of such writing may or may not have had direct experience of the events he reports. So there are questions to be asked before we simply accept what he has reported. We assess rather than simply accept.

The believer should also follow this procedure in assessing reports in written documents. No reports should be exempt. The problem arises in particular under two circumstances: first, when there are conflicting reports and secondly, when events of quite extraordinary character are reported. We are never in a position of having directly experienced events that the testimony reports which took place before we were born. On the basis of their reports we believe them or we do not. We have no experience nor initially any memory of them. So we assess first whether the events reported are possible, i.e. not beyond the bounds of what we consider possible, and that within that restriction, whether there is reliable evidence that the event happened. It is not always the case that purported evidence is decisive.

What do we mean by evidence? What are the standards by which we normally decide whether to accept, reject or reserve judgment about what purports to be evidence? For our purposes, consider just the evidence of testimony. I accept one person's testimony and I question another's.

2   Belief, Justification, Knowledge and Truth

Justification has something to do with truth. When we engage in the process of justifying a belief we are looking for grounds for considering the belief to be true. We do this particularly when the belief is called into question.

Knowledge is a kind of belief that satisfies further conditions than are required for justified belief. Justification of a belief is a necessary condition for knowledge. But having a true, justified belief is not sufficient for knowledge.

A self-evident proposition is so called because it is true with no need of supporting evidence. For example: The man who is taller than the boy who is taller than the girl is taller than the girl. This proposition is self-evident taken by itself. It needs no further explanation or support, to make it evident. Our resultant belief exhibits epistemic immediacy. It is a truth of reason, i.e. a truth knowable through the use of reason only, as opposed to one known through sense experience. If I pay attention to the proposition I can, in doing so, see the truth of it and thus in believing it, know the proposition. If I understand a self-evident proposition I am justified in believing it. If I believe it on the basis of adequate understanding, I know it.

Justification of empirical beliefs is also related to truth. An empirical belief is one that is based on observation, experience or experiment. I believe that there is a wall before me. That means that I can take it as true that there is a wall before me. In doing so, I can appeal to a clear visual impression. I can see the wall. This impression is confirmed by other impressions. I can touch it. When a belief is justified, it has a property which we take to count toward the truth of the belief, and so toward knowledge. My reason alone tells me that, like 2+2=4, the statement is true.

But justified true belief may in certain unusual cases not be knowledge. Knowledge need not be justified true belief. I can believe and claim truthfully 'My pencil is on the desk' and not know that it is. How this is possible is very interesting.

I see a pencil on the desk. My pencil is a unique one. I assert, 'My pencil is on the desk'. In fact the thing I see on the desk is a pencil exactly similar to mine. So I do not see my pencil. But I am not claiming that I do. I take for granted that what I see is my pencil, making the assumption that a thing that is exactly similar to another thing is that thing. What I do not see behind the computer on the desk is actually my pencil. So while the statement I made is true, I am justified in making it on the basis of my seeing *a* pencil. What is not true would be for me to say, 'I see my pencil on the desk'. But I cannot be said to know that my pencil is on the desk. I draw an inference from

> I see a pencil on the desk.
to
> I see my pencil on the desk.
Then I draw another inference to
> My pencil is on the desk

My conclusion depends on my assumption, my theory if you like, that what is exactly resembling is the same, that if A is qualitatively identical to B, A is B. That is a false assumption and a false assumption in an argument leads to an invalid argument, and probably to a false conclusion, certainly to an unwarranted conclusion.

If I were asked to pick up *my* pencil, I would not do so. I would pick up *a* pencil, the pencil I see on the desk. If my pencil were then produced I would after some examination and consideration come to see my error.

This illustration makes clear one very important point. I can be in error when I most reasonably believe, when I cannot give reasons not to believe, when I can give good reasons for believing. So the somewhat disturbing question arises. Should I examine the grounds I give myself or simply assume them for my reasonable belief since

I now know that a justified belief may be false. In speaking about 'belief', we are talking about the many, many beliefs we hold, not only in a religious context but in general. But in the religious context we must consider not only the very basic belief in God, but also many particular beliefs. For the Christian professes beliefs over the whole range of Christian topics.

To summarise:

> You may be able to justify your belief.
> You should still examine it.
> After examination it may be that you should revise it.
> Why? It might be false, or inadequate, or held on the wrong basis.

The relation of truth to justification is more complex than its relation to knowledge. While justification has some relation to truth, it is not an easy matter to specify what it is. Justification in some way counts toward truth. Justification is in some way truth-conducive. This assumes that the basic role of justification is as a means to truth.

3   Perception as a Source of Beliefs

Perception is the apprehending of something in the world by means of the senses. I see a pencil on the desk. I smell the onions. I hear the dog bark. I see and hear a jet plane. Questions then arise. How do we obtain information about our environment by using our senses? Since our senses often deceive us and things are often not as they seem, when is this information accurate, in view of mistakes and illusions?

Perception gives rise to beliefs, perceptual beliefs. These are beliefs we acquire as part of perceiving. If we describe our perceptions in propositional terms, we then say 'I saw a fox.' or 'There is a fox.' We believe that the propositions that express those beliefs are true. But such beliefs may be false. I may confuse the thing I see and identify it as a fox, whereas it is actually a dog. In that case my belief will be false. But a true belief may be based on the same perception. My companion will truly identify it as a dog. There are ways of deciding which identification is the correct one, and of settling between different claims. We both see the same thing. I see it as a fox. He sees it as a dog. In such a case it is relatively easy to decide which is the correct claim. At other times it is difficult. Sometimes it is impossible. When conflicts arise it is helpful to understand if they can be resolved and then go on to ask how? How does one resolve debate between alternatives that are difficult to assess? Scientists are doing this all the time. So is there any sense in which we can claim that our beliefs about the world are justified or true?

The problem is that we only have access to the world in the context of our theoretical beliefs about the world. All our observations of the world rest on our assumptions, upon our beliefs about the world. Does that mean that we have no direct access to the external world?

The following is a list of assumptions and categorizations we impose on what we are observing so as to arrive at our beliefs about the world and what is in it.[1] Take for example the belief, 'There is a green field in front of me.'

> My senses are normal.
> The conditions under which I am observing are normal.
> What is before me behaves in certain ways.
> I am entitled to use a scheme of classification in which fields, green things, figure.
> What I am now experiencing is similar to what I have experienced in the past.
> My memory is reliable.
> (Possibly) there is an external world in which there is regularity.
> I am a subject of experience, continuously existing and with a reliable memory of such things as I am now experiencing.

---

1   Cf. Anthony O'Hear, *What Philosophy Is*, p. 87.

4 Critical Question: Relevance for Religious Claims

Because we do not have direct experiential access to the world, and because our theoretical beliefs about the world are not directly and conclusively supported by our observational levels of judgment, in what sense(s), if any, can we think of our beliefs about the world to be justified?

If statements about God make assumptions or imply statements about the world and if our knowledge of the world is questionable, statements about God are also questionable. Is there some special way of grounding such religious claims?

For the believer there are two sorts of question, one of which all of us make whether religious or not. What do we believe about the world? The other sort is peculiar to the believer: How does what we believe about the world relate to our claims that God acts in various ways within our world?

Of course the non-believer asks the former kind of question too. Having assumptions that differ from those of the believer he may come to quite different conclusions about what happens in the world. Both of us live in the same world. So the debate will be about the assumptions that give rise to lines of argument that produce differing conclusions.

As a necessary condition for making religious claims, e.g. that God is love, that God superintends the affairs in the world, that God guides human history, that God will judge the world, we have to consider what we think about the world. We have to think about what we can reasonably believe about the universe. This is an exercise in thinking about what we think. We may not be aware of making the following assumptions that guide our thinking. We take them for granted even if we have to be reminded that we do:

> The world is orderly.
> Its order can be understood.
> We can frame laws about its operations.
> The laws we frame lead us to remarkable discoveries.

We also claim to know a multitude of established facts about the world, and about the forces that are active within the world, from the minutest to the most extensive, from the inner structure of the atom to the remotest galaxies and the forces that maintain them and so maintain our existence.

What we may say about God and God's relation to the world means that we must think of him in relation to the world, a physical entity, and to ourselves as human beings in a physical world. Our talk about God will be governed by what we know about the world and so how we think about what we know.

5   Holding Religious Beliefs

Two questions are basic to religious epistemology:

> How do we come to hold beliefs? H.
> How do we come to present, defend, and argue for the beliefs we have come to hold? D.

Within conservative Christianity these two questions have received interesting but often questionable answers. These answers have given rise to ambiguous terms such as these: **fideism, evidentialism, presuppositionalism.**

A constant incentive has been the desire to find a safe area to secure one's faith. When we were children playing tag, one of the rules was that there was a safe haven. If you got there you could not be tagged. Anywhere else you could. For some believers the desire to put the quest for certainty beyond any doubt, to provide unquestionable grounds for belief provides the motivation for claiming a 'safe haven'. Once achieved that would put one's belief beyond question, beyond the kind of question that leads to ambiguity, to doubt or to uncertainty.

(1) Presuppositionalism

Let's start with **presuppositionalism.** The answer to both questions H and D is by appeal to a presupposition or to a set of presuppositions. A **presupposition** is a supposition antecedent to knowledge. It is an idea assumed as a basis for further conviction, for argument, for activity. It is a preliminary assumption on which to base an argument or even to raise a system of thought. To provide the grounds for such, it is assumed to be true. So it is not 'just a supposition'. It is the true supposition.

Taken as such, its status, meaning and function is different from suppositions taken in other spheres. There you ask, Suppose that this may be true, what follows? Or simply, just suppose for the sake of argument and exploration that p, where p stands for the proposition you are presupposing. That is the regularly employed method of the detective and the scientist as they seek to solve a problem or come to a conclusion. In the context of our discussion of religious epistemology, the term is being given a particular connotation. It stands for a claim that is not to be questioned rather than functioning as a heuristic device.[2] For if the supposition taken as a heuristic device is not fruitful, i.e. if it does not produce results, it is abandoned. The presuppositionalist's presupposition is never abandoned, and indeed never defended. That would be the posture of the so-called 'evidentialism', if we assume that the evidentialist's presupposition is open to disconfirmation by examination of evidence.

That leads to the question, Why take your presupposition as true, rather than as a heuristic device for the exploration of

---

2 A **heuristic device** is an idea or set of ideas provided expressly for the purpose of investigating, researching, arriving at a conclusion, solving a problem. When entertained it makes possible research, ideas, conclusions otherwise not attainable. It is constructive if it leads to the result of solving a problem, advancing knowledge. So the detective says, 'Let's assume that Jones was in the Smith's house at 4.30. The scientist said, 'Let's assume that waves pass through the medium of ether'. In each case the aim is to arrive at acceptable conclusions. In each case they might add, 'and see where we get'. You make the assumption and argue from it, look for evidence for it, to let you see what you might discover. If you find you have to reject it, you have made some progress. There is one less option. If it is fruitful in leading to a new truth it has served its purpose.

knowledge? Why not retain it only in consideration of the results it produces, as enabling the best possible explanation or alternatively reject it if it does not. For even if you take the presupposition to be beyond question, you have to test the results it leads to. The alternative is to take them as themselves already beyond question. But the whole point is that you have assumed, and not concluded, that the presupposition is beyond question. But when one attempts to explicate that presupposition it becomes obvious that it is both ambiguous, questionable and in fact misleading.

Does not the serious question also arise, How do I come to assume my presuppositions? Where did they come from? For, once I did not have them. I surely did not start by simply asserting a belief as bedrock, i.e. unquestioned, but held the belief as one among other beliefs. And there is a preliminary presupposition namely, I believe my presupposition will render truth for me, or guarantee beliefs I already hold. It's a presupposition about the presupposition, and leads to a regress.[3] It quite destroys the claim of an unquestionable starting point

Moreover, there is much more that is being taken for granted as true or valid. These are the general presuppositions we all take for granted, the general conditions for rationality. The presuppositionalist's presupposition and its function are simply assumed to be rational. Both the assertion itself and the function it is held to perform must be held up for examination. The presupposition asserts:

> the Bible is to be taken as true and its world view is be taken
> as the context and basis for all assertions we make.

---

3   The presupposition about the original presupposition is that it is true. So we have a regress. We have regressed to a presupposition about that original presupposition i.e. that the presupposition about the presupposition is true and that leads on and on and on to an endless series of presuppositions about presuppositions. The result is that the 'solid foundation' disappears. Even if the original presupposition was false in the first instance, the subject who believes it is still involved in an infinite regress.

The problem is that to say 'the Bible is true' is a gross oversimplification. As soon as you begin to expatiate the idea it becomes extremely ambiguous and questionable. What actually is it one is asserting to be true?

The issue is over the status of the Bible and its interpretation. That interpretation renders the doctrines of fundamentalist Christianity. While it is a phenomenon within fundamentalism and so is of restricted interest it raises some important epistemological questions.

(2) Evidentialism

The assertion that the Bible is true without further question entails also an assertion that a particular method of interpreting the Bible is the correct one. and produces a system of doctrine that is also beyond question. In pursuance of this question of the status of the Bible what has come to be called **evidentialism** takes a different line. Both alternative views agree in their belief that the Bible is true. There is no need for proof or discussion of that assumption. Whatever further beliefs are held are grounded on that presupposition. So evidentialism is itself a form of 'presuppositionalism'. But that term has already been pre-empted. What follows is that appeal to the Bible, and so the quotation of statements selected from any writing in the Bible is sufficient basis for doctrinal assertions concerning God, freedom etc.

For evidentialism, you examine available evidence to support the belief that the Bible is true. Belief in biblical claims, reports, and stories is substantiated by evidence, for which you engage in searching, assuming that you will discover it even for biblical testimony to most unlikely phenomena and their causes.

The supporting presupposition in the case of the evidentialist is that the claims made in the very varied 'books' of the Bible can be shown to be true. Therefore one goes in search of 'evidence' for that truth. One interprets the claims the Bible makes as being open to confirmation by available evidence. One then produces an apologetic that presents that purported confirmation, be it of historical, geographical, astronomical and other phenomena. The further hidden presupposition is that faith is in some way dependent upon possessing and understanding evidence.

Readers who wish to pursue in some detail the questions of the status and function of the Bible, and the complexities involved in its interpretation, might consult my writing, *From Inspiration to Understanding: Reading the Bible Seriously and Faithfully.* Here you will find detailed consideration of issues which the views we are discussing here raise.

The quite serious question for both of these approaches is whether it is appropriate to think of the Bible as a storehouse of truths that can be assented to, in particular historical facts and religious convictions. Also whether it is not a distortion of belief, a misunderstanding of faith and a misrepresentation of the Christian's response to the revelation of God, to engage in searching the writings of the Scriptures for confirmation of facts, so as to provide a demonstration of faith.

We often find a very seriously held belief that the confirmation of claims by evidence in some way makes the fact of Christian faith reasonable. How could the truth of the various assertions about purported historical events make reasonable my act of faith in Jesus Christ. I even heard that if Noah's ark could be found and documented that would show that not only the biblical account was a true one, but that one then might on those grounds (and on basis of the authority of the scripture that contained the account) reasonably be persuaded to accept Christian faith. How could such 'evidence' have any relation to my faith in God? How could confirmations of biblical claims, say the most worthy results of biblical archaeology, show that a commitment in faith is reasonable (we shall not even talk of 'proof') and so provide basis and material for a theistic apologetic? The demand to recognise confirmation of historical claims is of a quite different order than the call for faith.

(3) Fideism

We turn now to the third of our terms, **fideism.** The term is unfortunate because it is both problematic and has become pejorative. It stands for the view that it is through faith and not via reason that we arrive at the distinctive truth of Christianity. Stated simply: *We come to truth via faith, not reason.*

August Sabatier wrote,[4]

> Faith, which, in the Bible was an act of confidence and consecration to God, becomes an intellectual adherence to an historical testimony or a doctrinal formula. A mortal dualism starts up in religion . . . . If, by a subtle theology, you succeed in rationalising dogma, do you not see that you destroy it in its very essence.

Sabatier is protesting that faith has been forgotten in the mistaken quest to ensure true belief, important as true belief is. The definition of faith has become distorted. Faith has now become doctrine, dogma. Obviously it is important to see what is meant by 'faith' and what by 'reason'. Sabatier saw faith being turned into rational dogma, 'rational' because either identified with or made dependent upon the results of reasoning or being amenable to demonstration.

Fideism attacks the idea that we arrive at truth by a process of reasoning, by examining the evidence and then pronouncing that, satisfied by the result of reasoning, we can then affirm the truth of Christian faith. But since faith is not arrived at by reasoning, and also cannot be demonstrated, it does not follow that, either with reference to faith or to the Bible, there is no constructive place for evidence or reasoning. If that were so, faith would become irrational. There is a difference in saying beliefs are rational only if supported by faith and that beliefs are beyond reason.

The targets of fideism are the positions of evidentialism, that beliefs are rational only if supported by evidence. Support by evidence must be carefully defined. It might signify that evidence

---

4 *Outlines of a Philosophy of Religion,* pp. 46, 47.

supports a proposition to a certain degree of probability and that you are warranted in believing the proposition if the evidence reaches a certain degree, say 75 per cent, but not if it is only 25 percent. Such talk, however, is quite irrelevant to faith. I do not bet that faith is certain and its beliefs are true on the basis of an assessment of what I take to be relevant as 'evidence' for belief. It is one thing to believe that faith is reasonable, and can be shown to be intelligible. It is quite another to claim and to believe that either faith is demonstrable or the product of a probability game.

That does not mean that there is no place for reason in thinking about faith. We constantly ask, 'What is rationally acceptable?' as we live our lives in many dimensions and as we try to avoid error and believe what is acceptable. It is quite proper to ask whether there is a place for Christian faith within the sphere of the rationally acceptable. As we give an affirmative answer to the question, we may take a further step and inquire: What is the justification for faith? Here fideism answers, in opposition to evidentialism, that we can hold beliefs not supported by evidence. Fideism also registers opposition to the presupposionalist assumptions that to hold beliefs without further support is rational.

Two Concluding Observations

We must beware of oversimplification. This might lead to the belief that the three approaches we have considered are alternatives, each one stating an adequate position worthy of belief if only one of them is chosen. You can find an article telling how one believer found that presuppositionalism was unacceptable, and so moved to the second and embraced evidentialism. Discontent with one made it necessary to accept the other as a replacement. One package is rejected. The other package provides an accepted alternative. One accepts that others are 'going' concerns, acceptable alternatives. But you can't just move from one to the other. The important and much more demanding way is to consider issues, one by one, rather than to accept a package of already defined answers to issues.

The various packaged positions get associated with theologies inherited from the Reformation. The Calvinistic and the Arminian set a range of alternatives in consideration of the Catholic theology of Thomas, with his emphasis on showing faith to be reasonable, notably in his *Five ways (Quinque Viae)*, the so-called 'proofs' for the existence of God.

But there has been most extensive and fruitful discussion in the last two centuries that provides essential material for consideration, but is overlooked in the context we have been discussing, often on principle! Is the basis of this neglect in a further presupposition, 'Recent theology is in error' or is that position simply a required corollary of the presuppositionalist's programmatic assumption?

FOR FURTHER READING

Audi, Robert. *Epistemology.*

O'Hear, Anthony. *What Philosophy Is.*

Morton, Adam. *A Guide Through the Theory Of Knowledge.*

EPISTEMOLOGY AND RELIGIOUS BELIEF: WORK SHEET

1. Concepts: give definitions.

faith, theistic belief, religious beliefs, reason, rationality, knowledge, justification, direct justification, reason without justification, degree of justification, requirements for reason, rational belief, positive justification, acceptance, presumption, cognitive attitude, non-cognitive propositions, inferential beliefs, non-inferential beliefs, a priori, empirical, a posteriori, evidentialism, experientialism, ontological argument, argument from motion, teleological argument, perceptual analogy to theistic belief.

2. Distinguish cognitive and non-cognitive sentences.

3. Distinguish between inferential and non-inferential beliefs. Give examples.

4. Relate the concept of knowledge to the concept of belief.

5. Give reasons for taking religious statements non-cognitively rather than as making claims. Draw a parallel to moral statements.

6. Is religious knowledge possible? A priori? On the basis of experience?

7. What is the difference in approach between the ontological and the teleological arguments?

8. Distinguish rationality about belief and justification of belief. Which is the stronger term? Why?

9. Is belief on the basis of testimony inferential?

10. Can one have a concept of something without knowing that it exists, e.g. a diamond weighing seven kilograms. Could one recognize something without having a concept of it?

11. How does one arrive at a concept of God? Does the concept you form of God have influence on whether you believe in God?

12. Give examples of inferential and non-inferential beliefs? Is belief on the basis of testimony inferential? What of the following?

You see a cassowary. You see a print in the soil. Gill says. 'I saw a cassowary.' In each case you say, 'A cassowary was here.'

13. 'God speaks to me.' Is such a statement to be taken literally. If so why, if not why not? How could one know that it is God speaking (revelation) or listening (to someone praying). Can there be different kinds of appeal to evidence?

14. To the atheist who asserted that God does not exist, Billy Graham said, 'That's strange! I spoke to him this morning.' Discuss the implications.

15. What is the status of a concept of something that does not exist, held by a person without knowing that it does not exist, e.g. a diamond weighing seven kilograms.

16. Could one recognize something without having a concept of it? What of a concept of something with contradictory features: a human body that survives without protection in space.

17. Does the perceptual analogy (I hear Eileen speaking) help us to understand a theistic claim, e.g. that God speaks?

18. Give reasons for construing religious statements non-cognitively rather than as metaphysical claims? Draw a parallel to moral statements.

19. Fred believes that he can prove the existence of God. He believes that to believe in God you have to be able to prove that God exists. Frederica believes neither of these. What is the issue between them?

4 MEANING AND TRUTH

We often assume that what we say is clear, simple and straightforward. But if we are faced with the questions, 'What do you mean?' 'What does that mean?' we are often puzzled to know how we should answer. We must take this puzzlement seriously. For we may be affirming what we do not understand. How is that possible? Why would anyone do that? Indeed, some dogmatically oriented Christians, i.e. those with a set of doctrines traditionally accepted and well entrenched, may emphatically claim, 'We have the truth' where 'the truth' means 'our system of doctrine'.

Behind every statement about Christian belief is the assumption that the belief is true, that claims, for example, about God, about history, about resurrection, about freedom are true. But to see that they are true, they must first be seen to be reasonable. They must first be understood.

4 MEANING AND TRUTH

1 Sentences and Statements

A sentence is an arrangement of words that make an intelligible utterance or expression. Some such arrangements have a truth value. They express what is either true or false. We can classify such sentences as first: either true or false. These are cognitive. We call these sentences 'statements', 'claims', sometimes 'propositions'. 'My bed is warm' is an example. Others are neither true nor false. These are non-cognitive, such as commands, exhortations, for example, 'Get up!', 'Out of your bed!'

2 Word and Sentence

Words are used to construct sentences. As used in different sentences the same word can have different meanings. Indeed it may be ambiguous in a given sentence. If the word being used ambiguously can bear different meanings its significance in a particular sentence may not be immediately clear. Puns sometimes make good jokes! So I am told that Ivor has gone to the bank. If you want him you will find him there. I want him. So I set off. But where do I go? He works at the high street bank. But he is also a fisherman. Today is his day off. So I make my way to the river to find him. I have put the word 'bank' in a context and given it a meaning appropriate to that context. I have read the sense of the term 'bank' as meaning 'river bank' rather than 'financial bank'. That is the sense of the term I believe to be at this moment appropriate. I make for the river bank because I believe that the term refers now to that location and no other. The term 'bank' has both senses, and so different references. To understand the term 'bank' I must first discern the sense it bears in the particular context. Then I may be able to figure out its reference. The context in the sentence determines the sense.

Sentences are either		
Cognitive	or	**Non-cognitive**
Inform		Advise
State fact		Warn
Assert		Exhort
Make claim		Admonish Command Question
Can be true or false		Cannot be true or false
Examples		
Jesus is coming again		Jesus is coming again soon (unspecifiable)
Jesus is coming again before 2050		We can't know when
Jesus is coming again within 20 years		No limit can be set

3   Sense and Reference

Different terms can have the **same reference** but **different senses**.

For example take the following terms:

The resident of 10 Downing Street
The prime minister
The leader of the Conservative party
The C-in-C of British forces.

Each of these terms refers to the same person. That constitutes their identity of reference. The fact that descriptions of the subject differ constitutes their variety of sense. If someone is not aware that the terms have a single reference he may think that different people are being designated by the different terms.

Each of the three subjects of the following sentences has the same references as does each of the three predicates.

> The prime minister of the UK met the president of the US in 1941.
> The resident of 10 Downing Street met the resident of the White House.
> The C-in-C of the British forces met the C-in-C of the American forces.

This may lead to an interesting situation when two people are in conversation and are using different terms for the same object. One describes a person in one way, the other describes him in another way. They think there are two objects. They do not realise that they are talking about the same object. So they draw the conclusion that here are reports of three different meetings.

4 Truth Value

There are two truth values. A statement is a sentence which is either true or false. Truth value is the status of a statement being either **true** or **false**. The truth value of a sentence is its being true or false.

'The earth is the centre of the universe' has the truth value false.

'The same 92 (and more) basic elements are found throughout the universe' has the truth value true.

5 Belief

If we preface a false statement with the expression 'Peter believes', we determine the truth value of the whole sentence with its subordinate clause in a different way from that which we employ to determine the truth value of the subordinate clause which follows it. We have to determine whether or not Peter in fact believes the statement. If he believes it then the statement is true. For example, 'Tycho Brahe believed that the earth is the centre of the universe' is a true statement while the sentence in the subordinate clause, 'the earth is the centre of the universe' is false. If you preface a false statement with '*X* believes that' the resulting compound sentence may be true. The criteria for assessing the truth value of the different sentences is different. The same observation may be made about sentences with other prefatory phrases: 'John claims', 'Elizabeth reports', 'The Daily Waffle informs', 'The Bible says'. The preface may be more complex e.g. 'John claims the Bible says. . . .'

6   Kinds of Judgments Contrasted

We make judgments about **what happens** within the world as with the judgments: The clock is out of order. Jonathan will not repay the loan. Mother's cake is the best.

We make judgments about the **reliability of testimony** and the status of historical evidence. [See the chapter 'Belief and Testimony'.] We sometimes make a **grand judgment** about the world, about life as a whole, about the meaning of history. Such a judgment about the totality is called a *Weltanschauung,* **a world view**: e.g. The cosmos is God's creation. Human history is meaningless. Time is running out for mankind.

(1) Kinds of statement and kind of confirmation

Different kinds of statement are subject to different kinds of confirmation.

The egg is frying in the pan is an empirical judgment, confirmed by appeal to sense experience: look, listen, smell.

Churchill met Roosevelt is historically confirmed. Look up the evidence in the appropriate records; interview people present at the meeting.

The universe is expanding is a scientific judgment. Confirmed by observation and inference within a theory.

God loves us like a father loves his child is a religious conviction, confirmed by appeal to interpreted experience, or to the claim in a sacred text.

So we may define 'meaning' in terms of sense and reference. In cognitive sentences a reference can be specified. The statement is either true or false.

A sentence may look like a statement, i.e. one which is making a claim. But when it is examined carefully you find that it does not do so. It seems to state a claim, but when closely scrutinised you find that it is not functioning in that way. It is not asserting a specific fact, as it seems to be doing. It seems to be meaningful as a claim but on careful examination it is qualified in such ways that the term turns out to be meaningless as a claim. It has a different function. The following has become a classic example.

7   The Gardener: A Modern Parable[1]

Once upon a time two explorers came upon a clearing in the jungle. In the jungle were growing many flowers and many weeds. One explorer says, 'Some gardener must tend this plot'. The other disagrees, 'there is no gardener'. So they pitch their tents and set a watch. No gardener is ever seen. 'But perhaps he is an invisible gardener.' So they set up a barbed wire fence. They electrify it. They patrol it with bloodhounds. (For they remember how H. G. Wells' *The Invisible Man* could be both smelt and touched though he could not be seen.) But no shrieks ever suggest that some intruder has received a shock. No movements of the wire ever betray an invisible climber. The bloodhounds never give cry. 'But there is a gardener, invisible, intangible, insensible to electric shocks, a gardener who comes

---

1   Antony Flew, *New Essays in Philosophical Theology*, p. 96-7.

secretly to look after the garden which he loves.' At last the
Sceptic despairs, 'But what remains of your original assertion?
Just how does what you call an invisible, intangible, eternally
elusive gardener differ from an imaginary gardener or even
from no gardener at all?'

The point is that if you qualify a sturdy looking statement long
enough, it becomes meaningless and can no longer function as a
claim, but must be taken in another sense. The case of the invisible
gardener applies this point to the theistic claim that God is love
and loves us as a Father loves his children. The original confident
claim gets qualified over and over again until it 'dies the death of
a thousand qualifications'. An earthly father is frantic in his efforts
to help his child dying of cancer, but the Heavenly Father 'reveals
no obvious sign of concern'. The original bold assertion is modified
so that it becomes empty. God's love, we are told, is not like our
love. God's love is inscrutable. We may be reassured, but then begin
to wonder what such assurance is assurance against. If we cannot
understand God's love, what do the qualifications assure against?
Finally the apparently emphatic claim is rendered meaningless. It
dies the 'death of a thousand qualifications'. It ceases to function as
an assertion. The sentence cannot be taken as a statement.

Another example is the claim that the end of the world is
nigh, i.e. is imminent, expressed sometimes in the claim that Jesus
is coming soon. We all know how to use the word 'soon', and to
use it meaningfully in different contexts. But it can be so qualified
that it ceases to have any cognitive meaning and so cannot be either
true of false. The claim has been made for two thousand years, and
since the arousals and hopes of the nineteenth century we have
heard it constantly and insistently to the present time. Neither the
term 'soon' nor its synonyms have any content if no limit is set
for the length of time it has reference to. But this refusal to state a
limit becomes the principle: we cannot specify a particular length
of time as the limit within which the event will occur. To qualify
the original meaning by saying that the term 'soon' has no limit
is to render it meaningless and so incapable of being true or false.

It then amounts to saying, 'The end is near, but we have no idea when'! In short, 'We don't know what *soon* means'.

TUTORIAL T<small>RUTH</small>

There are several theories of truth.

Correspondence Theory

'To say of what it is that it is, and of what is not that it is not, is to speak truly.'

Aristotle's dictum.

Ask almost anyone whether a statement is true and you will under normal circumstances get a ready answer. Ask the same persons how they can say that the statement is true and you will also get a ready answer. To the question 'What makes the sentence a true sentence?' the answer you will most likely get is that there is some state of affairs in the real world to which the sentence refers and it is this that the words in the sentence as well as the sentence as a whole refers to. In short there is a correspondence between the sentence and what is there.

The quotation above expresses this idea. There is something that is. When I say of what is that it is, I am speaking truly.

This is the commonly accepted explanation of truth. A claim is true if it reflects what is real, what actually exists or has existed. The following would be examples.

The egg is in the frying pan	a common sense judgment
Churchill met Truman	historically confirmed
The universe is expanding	scientific judgment
God loves us like a father loves his child	religious conviction

We know what an egg is. We know what frying pans are. We know, what the condition of 'being in' something is. So we know what the first of the above sentences means. We decide whether the sentence is true by finding out whether there actually exists a state of affairs to which the sentence refers, whether, that is to say, the sentence represents a state of affairs, whether to the sentence there corresponds some reality or other, whether there actually is an egg in the pan.

Let's make the distinctions we are taking for granted here. The important one is between **word** and **sentence**. We must be quite clear as to the meaning of the individual constituents in these sentences, and of the relation that is being claimed between them before we can make a judgment (on some basis or other) about the sentence as a whole, whether the claim is true or false.

We can state the principle involved in the correspondence theory of truth as follows:

A statement is true if there is a correspondence between

> (1) the thing that is true: a set of words constituting the statement and
> (2) the thing that makes it true: the existing state of affairs, what obtains in reality.

(1) Sentences, statements, propositions, beliefs and thoughts constitute what is *said* by a sentence, *believed* by a believer, *stated* by a statement. For example I say, 'The pie is in the oven'. That is a statement which reflects the entity it expresses, namely 'there is a state of affairs in the real world to which the sentence 'corresponds'.

(2)There is the thing to which the proposition corresponds. What is it? It goes by various designations **Reality, a fact, a state of affairs, a situation.**

This amounts to saying: The proposition p, (where p stands for any statement whatever) is true if and only if it corresponds to the fact that p. This is the point of Aristotle's dictum quoted at the beginning of this tutorial.

A proposition is a linguistic entity. For the sake of economy we use the term p for a proposition, any proposition. We are using the term 'proposition' here as a synonym for 'statement'. It also has a more abstract use: for the abstract entity a statement expresses truly.

A fact is a **thing in the world.** Even if we did not frame the true proposition p, the *fact* would exist that p. Whether or not we frame the true assertion 'The pie is in the oven', the pie is in the oven. When we compare our propositions with the facts, we are talking about something other than ourselves. Put in economical form that reads

P (any proposition whatever) corresponds to the **fact that *p*** (the situation that exists).

Notice that there are three features of truth as defined by the correspondence theory;

(1) the structure of the sentence making the claim

(2) the referential relations between the parts of the sentence and reality

(3) the nature of the reality referred to, as independent of the mind.

To put it in a nutshell:

Let *a* stand for an object. Let *F* apply to a range of objects
So *a* is *F* is true if there is an object to which *a* refers
That object is among the objects *F* applies to.
Take our sentence 'There is a pie in the oven'.

The terms 'pie' and 'oven' relate to parts of reality, to some form of objective reality, '**in** the oven' refers to a **relation** to an object. If that relation exists between the real objects of the statement then the sentence makes a claim, and so the sentence is a **statement**, (the term for a sentence that makes a claim and so may be true or false) and the claim is true.

The realities are **objective** and **mind-independent**. There are such things as pies and ovens. There are such relations as **being in**.

The sentence is true if there is a correspondence between the sentence and the facts. The correspondence theory of truth assumes **realism**, the view that realities exist apart from minds.

Note that the theory does not tell us which sentences are true or false. Nor does it entail any doctrine of truth. It tells us what it is for a sentence to be true or false. It does not tell us which specific entities exist. Which entities exist is established according to the appropriate methods of inquiry, often empirical ones. We see the pie, we see the oven, we see that the pie is in the oven.

We gave other examples of statements: historical, scientific and religious claims. So a few further simple comments seem in order. Reference to past events such as those established by the historian are established by the appropriate methods the historian employs. His entities are realities that have existed in the past. The statement, 'Churchill met Truman' is confirmed as a true statement by the employment of such methods.

Something similar is to be said concerning scientific statements. The appropriate evidence is established within theoretical contexts proposed by the scientist. These are shown to be appropriate if they bring results, in increased understanding and discoveries.

The religious case is similar to the ones already cited only where the religious statements are historical, have reference to what exists or happens, or to what has existed or has happened in the world. But the theological statement given above is of a different kind. The question to be asked here is whether there is any way of making intelligible reference to the entities and relations in the claim. The methods that we appropriate in the other cases we instanced seem beyond reach in the case of statements about God. The employment of analogy (between the love of God and the love of a father) complicates matters.

Coherence Theory

The basic premise of the coherence theory of truth is that a true proposition coheres with a set of true propositions. If in doubt you ask, 'Does this proposition cohere with the set of true beliefs?' Coherence theory denies that we can move beyond our system of beliefs to get to a mind-independent world.

You can't get outside thought to an independent world of facts. You can only get to another thought or proposition. Having then amassed a whole series of such propositions you can put them together to make up a consistent set. Truth is then defined as a coherent relation between those propositions. It is then proposed as a true view which over its extent hangs together. There is no need for reference to extra-mental entities.

What does it mean to say that we define truth thus? Does it mean simply that the idea of coherence is that of consistency, that a belief is true if it is consistent with a set of beliefs taken to be true?

While this approach may explain science and theory construction, there is a basic problem, namely the difficulty of defining the relation of coherence. Shall we define coherence in terms of consistency by saying that there is harmony between all the propositions under consideration, that there is no contradiction between the statements proposed within the theory?

Take examples: The scientist provides a theory, say the general theory of relativity, and accepts it as his guide, provided only that there is no major inconsistency between the propositions asserted within it.

The theologian may propose an explanation of the basic Christian belief of the Resurrection of Jesus in terms of a coherence theory. Not able to provide the historical evidence for his belief, and in consideration of the problem of the status of such a claimed unrepeatable and miraculous event, he may rest content with a coherence theory, and claim that resurrection provides the **best possible explanation,** by coordinating all the available evidence in a thorough-going consistent manner. Each proposition provides 'support' for the others, or makes the others more probable, or is connected to the others through chains of evidential support.

Consistency is a necessary but not a sufficient condition for truth. A thoroughly consistent system might be irrational. Moreover, there could be rival but internally consistent systems of explanation. One of these may well be taken as the **paradigm**, and widely accepted. See below [13.8] for Kuhn's treatment of scientific revolutions. But there could be several conflicting systems. So shall we appeal to the best evidence? If we now appeal to the relation of **entailment** by arguing that the best evidence for q is the case where p **entails** q, we are defining coherence in terms of truth.

Or is there a more specific relation between coherent propositions making up the set? For example, a mutual capacity for one to explain the others, and the others to be explanatory of the one? What is at the heart of the theory is that a set of propositions is believed to be true.

But how extensive is this cohesive set of propositions to be? For us it will always be restricted. For our human resources are limited and we come at some point to the extreme limit of our knowledge. At any one point in our history our knowledge and beliefs are limited, the present included of course. On any account of coherence, at any stage of history, to the very latest moment, the 'now' in which we live, our knowledge is limited. The range of our beliefs is always restricted. So will anything less than a fully comprehensive set of beliefs suffice for such a theory? That would entail an omniscient being whose knowledge of truth extended to the most comprehensive. That being would know every truth that could be known. But that involves that he knows truths of which we are unaware.

But the theory of coherence cannot admit that a proposition may be true even if it cannot be known to be true. God could and does know truths which in our limited condition we cannot know. So the truths we cannot know but an omniscient being can, cannot be included in the set of beliefs which constitute the range of our knowledge of truth.

Redundancy Theory

The sentence 'p is true' says no more than the sentence 'p'.

For example to add 'is true' to the sentence 'It is now noon here' says no more than the original sentence. To say 'It is true that it is now noon here' says no more than 'It is now noon here'. So are we to conclude that the addition is redundant and can be dispensed with?

The two propositions are **logically equivalent.** So it follows that we do not need the concept of truth. We are not describing the sentence p by these predicates. Note that the sentence p is the subject of the sentence 'p is true'. The function of the predicate 'is true' is not the same as that of 'is red', 'is late', as in the sentence 'Dinner is late'.

It functions like an emphatic adverb like 'really', or 'certainly'. There is no separate problem of truth. The two sentences 'p is true' and 'p' must have the same **truth values** whatever proposition we substitute for p.

One problem for the theory is that it does not follow from (A) that (B):

(A) The truth value of any proposition p is identical with the truth value of the proposition 'p is true.'

(B) p and 'p is true' are identical in meaning.

It is often the case that identity of truth value is a sign of identity of meaning, as in the case, 'John is a bachelor', and 'John is an unmarried man'. But not always. The concept of **sameness of meaning** or **synonymy**, is debatable. If two propositions are identical in meaning they must be logically equivalent. But from this we may *not* infer that if two propositions are logically equivalent they must be identical in meaning. For example:

(C) This figure is a circle

(D) This figure is the locus of all points equidistant from a given point.

The two statements (C) and (D) are logically equivalent but are not identical in meaning.

Find your own examples of sentences which are identical in meaning but not logically equivalent.

FOR FURTHER READING

O'Connor D. J. and Carr, Brian, *Introduction to the Theory of Knowledge.* Brighton: Harvester Press, 1982. pp. 164-185.

Scruton, Roger, *Modern Philosophy.* London: Sinclair-Stephenson, 1994. pp. 97-111.

MEANING AND TRUTH: WORK SHEET

1. Cognitive sentences can be true. Non-cognitive sentences cannot. Explain with examples.

2. Distinguish sense and reference. How can two different terms have the same reference?

3. How does one resolve ambiguity of reference, for example in the sentence: That performance was only a *dress rehearsal.*

4. What is a 'world-view'? Do you have a world-view? Is there a common modern world-view about the cosmos?

5. The parable of the gardener illustrates the narrowing function of sentences when repeatedly qualified. Explain. Can a proposed apparently wide-ranging statement really end up by being empty, i.e. saying nothing?

5 EXPLANATION

Explanations often conflict. Then further explanations are provided for the conflicting beliefs. It is a question of finding reasonable grounds. When we make explanations we often cite causes. We often of necessity associate ideas with other ideas, producing an argument, as we put together a series of ideas and then draw conclusions. There are good and bad ways of doing these things, of making inferences by deduction or induction. Explanations demand theories. So, we discuss levels of explanation, explanation as deduction, causes as explanations, common sense explanation, historical explanation. Sometimes we must rest content with finding the best explanation. Our aim in all this is to provide rational belief.

5 EXPLANATION

1 Levels of Explanation

There are levels of explanation. What satisfies one person will be only the beginning for another. 'That's too complex for me!' says one. 'That's too simple and rudimentary for me!' says another.

There are limits to explanation. These are sometimes set for us in spite of ourselves, by the limited interests, capacities and knowledge of those who have instructed us thus far, and by the range of opportunities we have had, by our intelligence, by our interests, by our choices.

In some contexts and for some minds explanation may be unwelcome even if they had the capacity to understand. One just sees no need for making explanations. Why not just accept the position? Go on! Just accept it! What good does explaining do? For some an explanation would be intolerable if complex. For some it would be intolerable if simple. For others it would be welcome only if simple.

There are different theoretical backgrounds to contrasting explanations. Your theoretical outlook will influence your argument and your conclusion.

So, why should I listen to your explanation? Is it because I think you are wrong that I do not want to listen to your explanations? Is that a good enough reason? You want an explanation either when you do not already have one or when you are not satisfied with the ones available. You don't want an explanation when you think you could give a better or a more adequate one yourself, when you are satisfied already, when you do not want to change your mind or have your position challenged, your outlook disturbed.

Religious questioning, like any other questioning, demands explanations. So it will be either one you have already given yourself, or one you do not yet have or one to replace another found unsatisfactory. Questioning with serious intent indicates either that the inquirer is not satisfied with the explanations he already knows, that he is looking for an explanation he does not yet have, to be assessed as to its plausibility.

An interesting situation may arise. The inquirer considers several explanations. He thinks in the context of a theory or two and then puts various explanations side by side for comparison. The detective, the scientist, the believer all think in this way. The aim of each is to come up with the best possible explanation that they can give. Sometimes the preferred explanation results from various tests the inquirer has devised. Sometimes the explanation cannot be tested. Such explanation may provide different contexts for their thinking. Such explanations we call theories.

2   Explanations Demand Theories

Inquirers create theories in their attempt to explain the data, the evidence, the phenomena, the elements of the problem. If there are several possible explanations the problem can then be considered, first in one context, then in another, first in the light of one theory, then in the light of another. If there is a team of inquirers, the different members of the team may have different theories in relation to the subject matter they are thinking about, the propositions, the data, the phenomena. They then make comparisons, conduct arguments in the endeavour to show which of the explanations is best. Sometimes there is fact, evidence, testimony, confession to confirm one in preference to the others. Sometimes there is not. Sometimes, with several explanations available, they may draw the conclusion that no one explanation settles the question. But the hope is that one explanation may, for given reasons, be favoured as the best explanation. When this happens there is sufficient warrant to accept it as worthy of belief provided certain criteria are met, and, failing another better explanation. By inferring to the best explanation one may justifiably think one has reasonable grounds for believing that explanation. The problem is that the preferred explanation may not be true, even if it is the best one can find. So the problem of uncertainty and the invitation to agnosticism even then present themselves.

To justify your belief you have to defend your theory in the context of which you conducted your inquiry and made your explanation. Let us see how this works. One believer insists that there is no problem with the view that miracles happen and so can assert categorically that he has no difficulty in believing the reports of miracles. No doubt he will make reservations at some point! Another accepts that while extraordinary and unrepeatable events in nature occur — they are always occurring in history — we have to recognise as a reasonable explanation that the order of nature requires us to draw a line between the possible and the impossible and judge that some kinds of event are not possible and so do not happen and have not happened.

Imagine a criminal investigation that leads to two theories and two different conclusions on the part of two detectives. Think then of a religious dispute that produces (at least) two different beliefs, in the context of two sets of background convictions (theories). This provides us with a model for conflict between believers.

But there is a basic difference between the believer's and the detective's explanations. The detective can expect that some evidence will turn up that will settle the case. The scientist likewise, in framing his theory and making judgments within its context, will hope that the predictions he makes on the basis of his belief will lead to results that will at least indicate that the line is worth pursuing. He will as a result continue to employ his theory. If the proposed explanation is falsified that will not be the end of the matter, even for the continuing employment of the theory. He will go on thinking and testing, perhaps at some point revising, the theoretical background with which he was working. That makes for progress in understanding.

Since the believer is dealing with the transcendent, he will sometimes admit that the knowledge he desires is beyond him. Sometimes the believer's conviction is neither verifiable nor falsifiable. So he may choose to leave the question open. Or he may sometimes dogmatise!

3   Explaining An Unexpected Healing

Take for example a difference in explaining a healing. The believer may be ready to claim that God healed the patient without being either ready or willing to explain how the healing took place. The medical professional will give a detailed analysis of what has taken place with reference only to any natural, physical agencies. He will expect the believer to accept his medical, scientific explanation, one which includes no reference to an act of God. It is as such an atheistic or agnostic one. But the believer himself may ask whether there would be any point in confessing God's action in the healing if the medical explanation is sufficient. He might reflect, 'Is it not superfluous to introduce extra explanatory entities when you already have been given a convincing explanation?' He may remember Ockham's razor, *entia non multiplicanda*: '(explanatory) entities should not be multiplied.' The *entia* i.e. 'explanatory entities' are concepts, hypotheses, theories. Perhaps he might conclude that since no further explanation is being given by the religious claim, that claim is not to be taken cognitively as elucidating a state of affairs. Rather than an explanation it is to be taken as an expression of an attitude on the part of the believer, an attitude of gratitude, a feeling of dependence. He may recall that a word for miracle in scripture is *semeion*, 'sign'. Miracles are signs of the inexplicable presence and activity of the divine and occasions for humility and thankfulness. They are best seen as occasions for feeling rather than incentives for explanation! Best to exhibit gratitude than cleverness!

The medic may himself be a believer and, while giving his physical explanation may also be ready to allow divine agency without professing to be able to understand it. He can only confess it. He cannot explain it. He does not face conflicting explanations of rival situations. The scientific, medical explanation cannot be faulted or denied. These claims do not conflict with the believer's assertions since they are not on the same logical level. The problem for the believer is that some similar or identical medical situations result in different consequences, sometimes recovery, sometimes death, without the medic being able to explain why there was a difference.

4   Conflicting Christian Explanations

As another example take the conflict between the creationists and their opponents. We can clearly see in this case that the theoretical backgrounds of these two positions are opposed. We need not detail all the elements of those backgrounds to make the point. Just take two.

On the one hand, *Genesis*, for whatever reasons, is to be interpreted literally. We then give an alternative scientific account for the coming into being of the universe and of human life within our solar system from that given by the scientists, be they physicist or biologist. Conflict is inevitable.

On the other hand, *Genesis* was never intended as an account of the physical origin of the universe but rather as a worshipful confession of the majesty, transcendence and universality of God. The Hebrew account is a 'didactic and polemical argument for the cosmic and divine origin of Sabbath rest'.[1] We can produce a rational account of the origin of the universe without such reference to the transcendent. Taken as a confession of the transcendence of God it is of a quite different order and as far as rivaling that secular account, *Genesis* is irrelevant. Since that is the case, the two accounts cannot conflict.

Given opposed theoretical assumptions, it is clear that approaches and conclusions made within the context of conflicting

---

1   Cf. Herold Weiss, *Creation in Scripture*, p. 41..

theories will differ. The resulting conclusions are in opposition and provide the background for further exposition. When the creationist claims to be making an alternative scientific account of the origin of the universe, conflict with the secular physical explanation is inevitable.

Take another example. Why do Christians differ in explaining the significance of the Lord's Supper, the Eucharist? The names given already suggest difference. One says, The ceremony is memorial. The other says, The ceremony is re-enactment. Without going into detail, it is clear that in the background there are quite different assumptions, quite different 'approaches' to enable the parties to come to their opposed conclusions. These differences in theory concern ministry and priesthood, remission of sins and the function of ceremony in the mediation of that remission.

A further example is provided by the conflict between Protestant and Catholic over the explanation of how sins are remitted and the place of the individual in the process of salvation. The differing theoretical backgrounds provide the context and occasion for the development of differing and opposed doctrinal explanations of the ritual and also have led to the differences between the rituals themselves.

5 Explaining Explanation

Definitions: What is an explanation
Here are two definitions:

'that which produces understanding how or why something is as it is'

Oxford Companion to Philosophy.

'that which makes clear or accounts for'

Shorter Oxford Dictionary.

What is involved in making an explanation, e.g. of the following quotation? Here we read that the ideal kind of explanation is one which is closest to the type of explanation the scientist gives.

This is sometimes called the **analytic argument**. Toulmin² contrasts it with the **substantial argument.**

> The idealisation of analytic arguments … lies at the bottom of much epistemological theory, as it has developed from Descartes to the present day …. The respects in which substantial arguments differ … from analytic ones have been interpreted as deficiencies to be remedied, gulfs to be bridged. As a result the central question of epistemology has become, not "What are the highest relevant standards to which our substantially backed claims to knowledge can aspire? But, can we screw substantial arguments up to the level of analytic ones?"

6   Explanation as Deduction

To explain this quotation involves making clear the meaning of the concepts used. It also involves saying what the reference to Descartes means, i.e. clarifying an historical connection. It then demands expounding the issues involved in the claims that are being made. We shall content ourselves with making a single point. For Descartes, mathematics provided the model of explanation. One moves by logical steps from one proposition to another and then draws a conclusion. The conclusion is proved by the rational process. He coupled this conviction with the further conviction of the fallibility of the senses. So the deductive, geometric model became for him the norm for proper reasoning. It provided the standard for adequate explanation. Other thinkers could not be content with such a model and discussion is continuing.

Such **scientific explanation** is sometimes taken to be the model for *any* reasonable explanation. That is the concern of the quotation above. So we ask: What is a scientific explanation? What distinguishes a scientific from a common-sense or ad hoc explanation? Why has scientific explanation of a particular sort sometimes been taken as the model for any reasonable explanation?

---

2   Cf. Stephen Toulmin, *The Uses of Argument,* pp. 125ff.

Hempel's **deductive-nomological explanation**. There are two basic requirements which any scientific explanation must meet. The first is that of **explanatory relevance**. Our explanation of a particular phenomenon, say the appearance of a rainbow, will provide good grounds for the appearance which we now witness, and so will provide some grounds for expectation of a similar occurrence in the future. If it is adequate it will serve as a ground for making predictions. It does so by specifying necessary conditions. The second requirement is that of **empirical testability**. If I should attempt to explain the eclipse we have witnessed by referring to dragons, or the occurrence of a cure of a disease or the occurrence of a pregnancy by reference to the activity of angels, I should not be able to conduct a test. Such references would not constitute reasonable explanations.

Scientific explanations are arguments. They involve a sustained process of reasoning. This has to do with general laws and particular facts. X is the **explanandum**, what is to be explained. We fit the phenomenon X into a pattern of uniformities, by specifying laws, and then detail the **particular circumstances** relevant to the particular phenomenon, X. One theory, the Cartesian, is that the reasoning process is a deductive one, i.e. it moves step by logically acceptable step towards a necessary conclusion. It is like the logic of a geometrical theorem, where we prove the conclusion. So we call such accounts 'explanations by deductive subsumption under general laws'. *Nomos* is the Greek word for 'law'. Hence the term '**deductive-nomological** explanations'. This is a familiar theoretical explanation of scientific explanation. It is not the only one.

7   Causes As Explanatory

Beside the scientific there are several other kinds of explanation. We explain facts, when we say why events happened, why something is as it is or what it is. We explain regularities when we say why, when we give an account of the same thing happening over and over again, such things as the changing of the seasons, the melting of ice, the ebb and flow of the tides. Often we pick out a particular fact and specify that this is the cause, and so provide a kind of explanation of an event or fact. Such common sense explanations usually satisfy us when we ask, for example, Why did the car skid? Why did the cake burn? Why does the telephone not ring? Why is Mary crying? Why does Andrew have a fever? In each of such cases we search for one or more crucial causes, a cause being something without which the effect would not have happened, and so is a necessary condition for it to happen.

The question is, What sort of account constitutes an adequate explanation for the particular phenomenon or general phenomena in which we are interested?

When we ask other 'Why?' questions we follow a similar procedure. Why does the pope oppose contraception? Why did Paisley believe that the Pope is antichrist?

8 Common Sense Explanation

In making explanations we instance causes. So in answer to the question, What is the cause of *x*, this particular phenomenon, i.e. in response to a demand for explanation, we often cite one particular cause. Why did the slate fall off the roof? Because the builder did not fix it securely enough. Why did the first World War start? Because of a shooting in Sarajevo. In doing so we satisfy ourselves by pointing to a relevant, particular cause. A common sense explanation of this kind often satisfies us, even if it is very truncated. The one cause to which we then refer may not be a sufficient condition, even if it is a necessary one. Often it is the immediate cause, the one that sets the effect in motion, so to speak. Usually it is one which is immediately accessible.

9 Historical Explanation

What of the historian? Are the processes of reasoning an historian employs to be identified with those of the scientist, when scientific method is defined in terms of the deductive-nomological explanation? For the historian speaks of causes, in addressing the question, 'Why . . . . ?' He attempts to give a satisfactory account of an event, a series of events, a period, a personality, a movement. In the effort he addresses such problems as: Explain why the French Revolution occurred. Explain why Churchill was unsuccessful in the immediate post-war period. But there are serious objections to the theory that historical explanation follows the above model. When the historian employs the idea of cause, it is in a different sense from the above. Moreover the historian is not interested in constructing laws based on repeated uniformities to explain unique historical events. Such cannot be subsumed under general laws. An extension of 'the regularity interpretation of explanation' to the work of the historian is not possible. When the subject matter is an historical event there can be no question of going over the same ground again and varying one or more factors to see what difference it would make, as is the procedure so often applied in the quest for scientific knowledge. Nor can there be the framing of laws based on regularities and then attempting to see the event under scrutiny as an example of a universal law. By definition the historians' subject matter is unique and unrepeatable. To account for the unique historical event involves isolating the unique causes for that particular, not by attempting to subsume it under a general law.

10 Standards

'The claim implicit in an assertion is like a claim to a right or to a title' (Toulmin, p. 11). Knowledge consists in putting forward claims. These require confirmation. Claims presuppose standards. To ground them entails both construction of argument and production of evidence for those claims. What are the grounds upon which we are entitled to credit one account of past events in preference to others? Here philosophers divide. Some answer: to the degree they approximate the scientific explanation which subsumes statements under a law (Popper and Hempel). Others assert that historical explanations are unique (Collingwood and Dray). Frederick Gardiner examines in what senses the historian employs a causal interpretation (Cf. bibliography for references).

11 Finding the Best Explanation

We want to avoid false beliefs. We want to acquire true beliefs. How do we go about achieving these ends? Would you take any of the following maxims seriously? Which would you take seriously if modified? How modified?

> Believe whatever you read in the papers.
> Believe everything your teacher says.
> Believe what the majority in your group believe.
> Believe whatever is written in a particular book.
> Believe only what you consider reasonable.

We like to think that our beliefs are reasonable. So we sometimes try to justify them. To accomplish this we give an explanation, and whether we consider other explanations or not, we implicitly think that the one we give is the best possible explanation. Hence the idea of 'inference to the best possible explanation'. Justifying our beliefs, is what Inference to the Best Explanation is about.

Consider three kinds of believing:

Believing irrationally. We believe irrationally when we have no possible justification for our belief. e.g. that a curse will always cause harm, and when we give bad 'reasons' for our belief.

Believing justifiably. We believe justifiably when we give a reasonable explanation for our belief. What is of interest here is that we may believe justifiably even if the explanatory reasons we give for our belief are false. It is sometimes reasonable to believe what is false, for example it was quite reasonable in pre-Copernican days to believe that the earth was flat, as it is quite reasonable for young children to believe that Santa Claus favours them and brings gifts, both being lies deliberately told them and that surround them on all sides for extended periods of their lives.

We believe what is true, e.g. some drugs such as penicillin, produce effective cures.

What then is a satisfactory explanation? What makes one explanation better than another? Why is it that some people prefer explanations which others reject? When you consider alternative explanations how is it possible to make a judgment as to which is the **best explanation**?

Here is a body of data that needs explanation. Here are beliefs about it.

Here are proposals to justify the belief.

Here are alternative explanations of the data.

One method of obtaining beliefs about the data is by following these simple rules:

Consider the body of data in the context of alternative explanations.

Select the most acceptable explanations. The following are the criteria for making a judgment between alternatives:

> simplicity,
> expansibility,
> explanatory power
> consistency with our other beliefs
> consistency with the evidence
> fruitfulness.

A belief is justified, where 'best explanation' is understood in terms of these pragmatic virtues. So, we conclude, that theory gives a better explanation than any other by most adequately meeting these criteria So it is the one we should believe.

There is an important question. Does believing the explanation on the grounds that it is the most to be preferred to inferior alternatives mean that we accept it as true? Or do we not rather accept it as probably irrational not to believe it? If we accept it as true how are we defining 'truth'? Are we or are we not justified in assuming correspondence to reality, realism? To give an answer to this question we start the process all over again.

Such a strategy can be employed on different levels to different subject matters. You can try it out by attempting to explain for example:

> Why people do things they do e.g. buy a ticket
> How the physical world is made up
> The construction of an atom
> Whether there is life after death
> How a scriptural book came to be written
> Why dogmatic people refuse to consider an alternative

In ordinary life we most often explain our experiences by making reference to the 'observable entities of common-sense realism'. We hear an unusual noise and we say, 'That sounds like a tree crashing.' Then we coordinate it with the gale force wind that we hear is blowing, look out of our window and that satisfies us. In such a case we know that a real cause produces an observable effect. We then affirm with confidence, 'The old oak has finally succumbed!' That is to state a fact. We then explain it by observing; 'It was rotten inside and the gale was too strong.' That is a satisfactory common sense explanation. A scientist might give a much more complicated account.

In science, physicists refer frequently to unobserved and unobservable entities. We do not observe electrons. But we employ the concept of electrons (and several others) in explaining the construction of the atom. We then are satisfied that we have an acceptable explanation in the context of an acceptable theory.

Many claims made in the name of faith differ from claims made by a process of inference from historical and scientific evidence. How, if at all, are such claims to be justified? What is 'best explanation' in such cases? Some claims made in the name of faith are historical claims, e.g. that certain events took place in the past. Let's here confine discussion to such claims.

Sometimes we attempt to explain the unrepeatable and unexpected counter instance to what we have regularly experienced. Not every unrepeatable counter instance is a miracle. But we often encounter tales of such in religious literature presented as if historical, for example the immediate restoration of normal sight to the blind, the instantaneous restoration of atrophied limbs, the unexpected defeat of an overwhelmingly superior army, resurrection.

So we must ask questions about such accounts. How did the report get to the page? What do we make of the claim that the writing is making? The writing gives its presentation in terms of the supernatural. What is the best explanation of the report that we are getting at least second hand and behind that what are we to make of the event?

Take the case of the exorcist who casts out the demons that caused the disease and so restored health to the sufferer. Consider some explanations. On the one hand: The testimony in the written report comes from people who believed that demons caused physical deformity and who also believed that some people had the gift of casting out the demons and thereby produced the healing in the moment of the casting out.

> They believed their testimony to be trustworthy.
> The writer reported their testimony.
> The writer also believed that testimony.

Then there is an alternative explanation. Demons do not cause disease. Demons are (to say the least) problematic and cannot feature in a reasonable medical explanation of a physical restoration, or deterioration. So the literal interpretation of the story is to be rejected. This means rejecting the occurrence of the event as reported.

Then we find an explanation of the significance of the story, and give an account of why the story was told and preserved. Reference to such miracles focuses our attention upon the person of the healer, and sets that one apart from ordinary mortals, giving him a special significance for the believer. His teachings and his demands therefore are to be taken with the utmost seriousness, in particular should he be believed to have raised the dead.

You may think of other explanations. Give them all to yourself, assess them according to the criteria suggested above and then decide which of them is the 'best'. Having made the decision in this rational way, you may assure yourself that you are then justified in your eventual belief.

We can distinguish the inferences we are drawing in this process. We will be saying to ourselves with conviction some if not all of the following:

> These are the most likely causes.
> This scientific law is true.
> This is a reasonable historical reconstruction.
> This is what is most likely to have happened.
> This is an unacceptable explanation.

The best explanation we can give at present may not be the best explanation in a few years time. The qualification 'best' indicates there are other explanations. We can compare ours with these alternatives and by so doing put the adequacy of ours to the test.

To make the judgment that a particular explanation is the best we can give assumes that there are inferior alternatives that are set aside. We consider that our best explanation is at present preferable to any alternative. We then accept it. We accept it for what it is. Minimally, that means it would be irrational not to believe it or maximally that it is justified and rational. Does that mean we have sufficient warrant for certainty, for assertion? Does that mean we accept it as true? If so we have at least an implicit understanding of the concept of truth we are ready to accept.

But in some cases of historical investigation there is no possibility for testing the historical hypothesis. Sometimes there is no possibility of providing an hypothesis that can be tested. The reason is simply that the material for such historical reconstruction simply does not exist. In particular cases we will assume our inference is reasonable but cannot and do not wait for evidence because there won't be any, given the limitations under which we think. We then conclude that historical investigation in some such instances is not appropriate. One can speculate beyond the evidence. To do so may provide interesting fictional or quasi-fictional accounts. The framing of theory in history is of a different order and function from the construction of theory in science.

12 Two Examples of Believers' Claims

(1) **A Traditional Christian doctrine**: The Resurrection of Jesus as physical resuscitation.

How could you check the claim that Jesus rose from the dead or Luther's claim that Jesus took our human body into the heavens at the ascension?

The resurrection of Jesus has been interpreted in different ways:

(1) The dead body of Jesus became alive. Jesus lived again after his death.

(2) Faith in the resuscitated person of Jesus emerged shortly after his death. He was then confessed as Lord (*kurios*).

(3) and so the Christian community came into being.

What are the necessary conditions for (3)? Are both (1) and (2) required? Is (1) a necessary condition for (2)? Are (1) and (2) two separate events or are they to be taken as one? Is it the case that the Resurrection as a physical event is significant for the Christian only if the resurrected person becomes the object of faith and as such the foundation of the Christian church? Is it only in the context of Christian faith that the Resurrection has meaning? If that is the case, is Resurrection, conceived as a physical event, a necessary condition for the emergence of Christian faith? Is the Resurrection of the physical body of Jesus the necessary prelude to the communal confession of faith in him, and so the foundation for the coming into being of the Christian community? We remember that the only testimony and reports of the beginnings of Christian faith and of the Resurrection are by those who became believers in Jesus as the Christ, themselves passing on testimony which they had in their turn received. There is no other original context for the Resurrection than the emergent faith of the Christian community, the event of the 'upper room' and later of the witnessing to their resurrection experience.

(2) William Miller's exegetical speculation

Miller read passages in the book of *Daniel* and then speculated about the 'cleansing of the sanctuary' (8:14). He taught that the earth was the sanctuary and that it would be cleansed with the coming of Christ at the Second Advent. This 'cleansing' meant both destruction and deliverance. He made complex calculations, coordinated biblical passages with historical events and references to periods of time found in scripture. On that basis according to biblical prophecy he predicted the end of the world at a particular time, October 22, 1844. It did not take place. Then, it became a matter of waiting to see whether the event would occur at a newly fixed date.

Now emerged several different proposals. These provide materials for discussion of 'best explanation'. Our question is, 'What is the best explanation of the failure of the Second Advent at the predicted time(s)?'

When the expected event did not take place, some explained the non-event by claiming that they had got the date wrong. So what was needed was a new calculation of an alternative date when the expected event would occur. But again it did not. So after the revised date had passed, that alternative was shown to be false and could no longer feature as an explanation. With the failure to materialise, it became obvious that providing alternative dates was proving to be a failure of explanation. The procedure had to be abandoned.

Immediately after the 'Great Disappointment' of October 22, 1844, as it came to be called, Hiram Edson provided an alternative explanation based on the same ideas as Miller advocated, that there was a sanctuary and that it was to be cleansed (taking, as did Miller, an interpretation of *Daniel* 8:14 as starting point). This was an alternative to the explanation that had been universally accepted by those who expected the end of the world in October 1844 under the persuasive preaching of William Miller. Edson's idea was to relocate the sanctuary. The sanctuary is transworldly. It is in the heavens. He proposed that the earth was not the sanctuary, as

Miller had proposed, to be cleansed by destruction at the coming of the Christ, but rather that the sanctuary was in the heavens and provided a 'place' for the Christ to engage in special activity before the final judgment. So time would continue. The time of the end is not yet and indeed is not known.

Great sighs of relief resulted. The disappointed and disillusioned followers of Miller could, if they wanted to, revive and reconstruct. They could now engage in further speculation and, by a process of complicated inference, guided by different assumptions, develop an elaborate theory of the divine activity in the heavens before the final denouement. Of course there was and is no possibility of present verification as there had been in the case of Miller's date setting. With no occasion for any kind of testing, here and now in the present world, if there were to be any verification or falsification it would have to be eschatological. The only possible evidence for the Advent would be to experience it! The important belief would be confirmed only at the end. If it did not happen and so not confirmed then, no one who thus believed would ever know they had been wrong. Believers in the Advent would have to wait for that confirmation as the followers of William Miller waited for confirmation of his prediction. He predicted a date. Failure at that date meant that the theory was false, and entailed its rejection.

Could anything possibly be retained? Some of his spiritual descendants content themselves with speaking about an undefined and indefinable, and so irrational, 'soon' for the Second Advent, thus removing totally the element of time from the explanation.

But there is another explanation related to the original sanctuary predictions. It is to say, 'Since we were wrong in our interpretation, we must start again by framing a totally new approach to apocalyptic writing. We have to consider why the hoped for confirmation of the speculations about the Second Coming, the *parousia*, has not taken place.' The explanation is required because such speculations were in principle misguided from the outset. The hermeneutical procedures employed in interpreting Scripture by arbitrarily co-ordinating selected but unrelated passages, here a little and there a little, produced a system that raised hopes and then produced bewilderment and distress. The modified explanation cannot be acceptable. What is demanded is a rejection of that hermeneutic.

It is clear from this illustration that the choice between explanations should not be hard to make.

13 A Question About Rational Belief

Rational belief does not, by virtue of being rational, constitute knowledge. Justified belief may well be false. But if we maintain a justified belief, whether we know or do not know whether the belief is true or false, at least we know that we are not irrational. Does that suffice? Or should we only be satisfied with a belief we know to be true? We may, of course, think that our belief is true, when it is justified! We must also be concerned about the question of truth, a topic discussed in chapter 4, above.

So a **historical belief** is justifiable provided that an explanation is given and that the subject accepts the explanation as the best available. Take the case of a historical belief that depends upon the evaluation of written texts. Often the only materials for such evaluation are a limited number of such extant texts. These will be taken as possible testimony to the event. The essential and important proviso is that criteria relating to testimony as evidence are respected. We must thus consider the issues involved relating to acceptable testimony. [See chapter 2]

In the case suggested, two areas of investigation must be respected as represented by the following questions:

(1) What constitutes a satisfactory explanation of the context and origin of the texts?

(2) What general assumptions related to the contents of the text are to be respected? Respect means they are relevant in this investigation.

The kind of explanations we accept in our everyday affairs will apply in our consideration of written texts that we examine. For example, if we do not accept the possibility of physical miracles in our ordinary affairs, what possible reason could we give for allowing them in assessing ancient texts when we are considering them as possible evidence for what took place in the past. We cannot simply refer them to the transcendent acting within the physical universe, for that in itself requires a most serious assessment. What we can accept them for is evidence for what people once believed and also employed as appropriate vehicles for expressing their convictions and beliefs. But that is quite a different matter.

We feel that, when we are able to give what we consider a good reason for our belief, we are justified in being certain about it. We may be, shall we say, hopefully certain! But this may be irrelevant to our discussion, since certainty has little relation to the truth of a proposition, or to its justifiability. Certainty is a psychological state and can accompany all ranges of belief. So it is still a belief, our belief, even if we are only relatively certain about it. We remind ourselves that false beliefs can sometimes give the best explanation possible. But we had better be careful in the status we give to our claims to certainty. Knowledge is something other. For centuries, no one (except a very few) questioned the belief that the planets moved in cyclical orbits. Then, Ptolemy's epicyclical explanation of the movements of the planets was the best available. Also. for multitudes and for centuries the geocentricity of the universe was taken for granted.

The theory of 'inference to the best explanation' contrasts with a purely **empirical theory**, which claims that all our knowledge is derived from experience. Not all the concepts we employ are defined in terms of experience. The advantage of inference to the best explanation is that it utilises concepts not derived from experience and so achieves a richer level of explanation. While we do not experience them, we take **unobservables** into our explanation. We include them in our consideration, e.g. sub-atomic particles, in the context of quantum theory. They have explanatory value in providing us with explanations we could not otherwise obtain.

When a theory explains all the data and does so better than other theories, we may conclude that the theory is true. **One infers** from h^{be} to h, from the fact that a certain hypothesis would explain the evidence better than any other hypothesis that the hypothesis is true. It is at any rate then the subject of justified **belief**. But to move from justified belief to **truth** is to make a **grand inference**.

There is a risk that we shall be wrong. The theory may be false, even if the predictions it enables us to make may be true. But a false theory, at a given time, may provide the best explanation possible, or whenever explanatory value takes precedent over truth value or when no definitive confirmation is possible. Moreover in due course further consideration of a false theory may give rise to a more adequate theory. So inference to the best explanation may have pragmatic value. It is sometimes not irrational to believe a false theory.

14 A Historical Note

In ancient Greek thought a distinction gradually emerged between explanatory theories and theories about the nature of explanation. Thales, Empedocles, Anaxagoras, and others proposed explanations of natural phenomena. Plato's theory of Forms offered at the same time both a systematic explanation of things and also an epistemology of explanation. He was explaining explanation as well as explaining reality.

Aristotle, however, seems to have been the first thinker to differentiate explicitly between investigating what causes what and investigating the nature of causation itself. For him there were four different kinds of cause that an explanation of physical phenomena could cite. The formal cause is that in virtue of which a thing is the type of thing that it is. The material cause is the stuff, whatever it may be, that is shaped by the formal cause. The efficient cause is what produces a thing; and the final cause is the purpose for which something is produced.

To illustrate:

This item is a pot.

Its material cause is a quantity of steel

Its formal cause is the shape it exemplifies.

Its efficient cause is the source of the pot, the workman with his tools that produced it.

Its final cause, its *telos,* is the cooking it was made to enable, the purpose for which it is or will be used.

Today we recognise only Aristotle's 'efficient cause'. But of any object we can ask various different questions. Aristotle's other three 'answers' direct us to different explanations.

The Greek word for 'purpose', 'goal', 'end' is *telos*. We get our English word *teleology* from it. The idea for which it is used theologically is that the cosmos can be understood in terms of design, another key translation of *telos*.

Medieval philosophy echoed Aristotle's ideas about explanation. Indeed his concept of 'final' causes supplied a convenient foundation for religiously orientated teleology. Teleological explanation appeals to a kind of design in nature. Natural events and processes achieve aims. There is a relation between means and ends such that in the natural process means are adjusted so as to achieve ends. In Thomas Aquinas this issued in the arguments for the existence of God, the *Quinque Viae*, the 'Five Ways'. These argue from effect to cause. He argued characteristically from design we can discern in nature, as effect, to a Designer, which he identified with God as Cause. This has come to be known as the teleological argument.

Francis Bacon (1531-1626) took the decisive step of segregating teleological explanation from scientific explanation. At the same time he correlated an observable characteristic with a form. He generalised from particular instances to the law. The particular occurred in accordance with a general characterisation. There was a hierarchy of these laws. Some were more comprehensive than others. He supposed that the more comprehensive the explanation that a law achieves, the more certainty it has. There was no place for theological explanation. The road to science opened up new themes for philosophy.

David Hume (1711-1776) held that such causal laws state the constancy with which one particular type of observable phenomenon succeeds another. He attacked the view that such regularity in nature as expressed in natural law was necessary. He argued that the feeling that this succession occurs necessarily is to be explained as being merely the outcome of a regular association between the idea of the earlier phenomenon and the idea of the later one. It is because we easily move from the idea of universal regularity to that of necessity. Whether or not Hume is right about this, the dominant model for explanation in the natural sciences seems to require the citation of one or more laws which, when conjoined with the statement of relevant facts, entail occurrences of the phenomenon or of the uniformity that is to be explained. For example the movement of the tides is explained by relating the observed phenomenon to the law of gravitation.

Bertrand Russell (1872-1970) argued that such laws should specify not a causal process but the correlation of one natural variable with one or more others. But, when we want to derive a technology from scientific knowledge, we shall need to know what causes a desired effect. So we need to distinguish between different levels of explanation, in that while, for example, the disappearance of a patient's infection may be causally explained by his antibiotic injection, the operation of that causal process is in its turn to be explained by co-relational laws of biochemistry. And for discovering this kind of deeper and more comprehensive explanation it will often be necessary to devise appropriate new terminology. Moreover, it should also be noted that some scientific explanations cite statistical probabilities rather than determinate laws.

Further questions arise, especially in the social sciences, about the explanation of specifically human behaviour. For example, Hempel held controversially that in historical inquiry the pattern of explanation to be sought accords with the same covering law model that applies in the natural sciences. Collingwood argued, again controversially, that the historian achieves understanding of other people's actions by the re-enactment of their thoughts in his own experience. And in any case we cannot overlook the fact that people's rational acts often need to be explained teleologically — that is, in terms of what their aims are and what they regard as appropriate means to achieve those aims. It is the present thought not the future satisfaction of our aims that helps explain what we are doing to achieve them. One should not think of teleological explanation as a kind of influence exerted on the present by the future.

BIBLIOGRAPHY

P. Achinstein, *The Nature of Explanation*. Oxford, 1983.

R. G. Collingwood, *The Idea of History*. London: Oxford University Press, 1966.

William H. Dray, *Philosophy of History*. New Jersey: Prentice-Hall, 1964.

Patrick Gardiner, *The Nature of Historical Explanation*. London: Oxford University Press, 1961. Cf. Part three for discussion of the historians' understanding of cause.

Carl G Hempel, *Aspects of Scientific Explanation and Other Essays in the Philosophy of Science*. New York, 1965.

Philosophy of Natural Science. Englewood Cliffs: Prentice-Hall, N.J., 1966.

W. C. Salmon, *Statistical Explanation and Statistical Relevance*. London, 1971.

Stephen Toulmin, *The Uses of Argument*. Cambridge: University Press, 1964.

Edward W. H. Vick, *History and Christian Faith*. Nottingham: Evening Publications, 2003.

EXPLANATION: WORK SHEET

1. Explain the term 'explanation.' Analyse what you have done in giving your explanation

2. Give an explanation of the following:

I am here tonight

I expect the store will shut at ten tonight

The pie burnt

In 1939 England declared war

There will be a full moon tonight

Mary believes Napoleon is her uncle

Pythagoras' theorem

Why there was a rail crash

Why there is a precipitate in the test tube

Why Mary is crying

The fact that there is a rainbow in the sky

The meaning of the word 'necessary'

The fact that the slate fell off the roof

3. Now try to say what in each case it was that you explained. What does 'because' mean?

4. Comment on these explanations:

Galileo saw moons of Jupiter because there was a fault with his telescope.

God causes storms.

Demons cause disease.

Tony likes noodles because he is Italian.

Subatomic particles are unpredictable. The human brain is composed of such particles. Therefore, nothing is determined, i.e. determinism is false.

5. Explain the following terms:

entailment, justification, conclusion, warrant, relevant cause, standing conditions, necessary condition, sufficient condition.

6. Should we distinguish between different kinds of explanation, for example: common sense explanation, ad hoc explanation, scientific explanation, historical explanation? Do these or some of them have anything in common? Do different subject matters require different kinds of explanation?

7. Religious explanations are of very different kinds, dealing with different kinds of subject matter. Specify and differentiate. Do you find common features with other kinds of explanation?

6 EXPERIENCE AND GOD

The basic claim of the Christian theist is that religious experience is the source of all knowledge. How shall we define 'experience'? Is there such a reality as religious experience? If so, does religious experience provide grounds for making claims about God, for example that he is a God of love? Distinguish between the meaning of the two terms 'experience' and 'experiences'. Is it possible to test experience for authenticity? We give reasons why the philosopher is interested in experience.

6 EXPERIENCE AND GOD

I

1 Experience: Different Kinds Of Question

We can talk about experience in many different ways on different levels. That is also obviously true in the religious context. We shall ask various questions concerning experience, and concerning religious experience, specifically whether there is such a thing.

We shall address three such questions.

a. What experiences do religious people have? What kinds of such experience are there?

We have no difficulty in finding examples, in describing such experiences and classifying them.

b. Are there convincing arguments from religious experience to the religious object?

There are many ways of experiencing the world. One that has impressed many people is perception of order in nature. Can we move logically from the order discerned in the world to the religious object, God? We shall assume that discernment of order in the natural world is not a religious experience.

c. Is there a way of defining the distinctive religious experience so as to distinguish it from all other kinds of experience? Is there a characteristic *kind* of experience we may recognise and identify as *religious* experience and on its basis speak of the religious object (God)? If so how?

Is there such a thing as distinct and universal religious experience? Is there a 'religious dimension' in human experience, comparable to the moral or the aesthetic dimension? If so how shall we characterise it? If so will it be distinct from all dimensions of experience we may recognise?

For the theist the question of God is involved when the question of the purpose of existence is raised. At such point in our lives we may be faced with the question of the meaning of the whole, when 'openings into the depths of life' lead us to ask about the ground and goal of our existence.

2   Recognising Experience

Within the Christian faith there are many groups. Some religious groups recognise and value certain experiences. Other groups recognise and value different experiences. What is thus valued is taken as normal and can be expected, even demanded. If your faith is good, the condition will show up in your experience, defined in a specific way. These expectations are frequently expressed by specifying discernible, even psychical and physical, exhibitions.

We have now moved to another meaning of 'experience', by distinguishing experiences valued by those particular Christian communities from the basic religious experience. We thus distinguish 'religious experience' from 'experiences'. [See the next section, 3]

Christian churches have defined the coming of the Holy Spirit in many different ways. Some speak of it very vaguely, professing the need for the Spirit and from time to time claiming community revival. So members make efforts to discern the Spirit, strive to manifest the signs that the Spirit has come, and make predictions of what the individual and the community will experience with the coming of the Spirit. In making these specifications each community is guided by its particular doctrine, by its own theology. What is evidence of piety and what are manifestations of faith and holiness reflect the doctrine of the particular Christian community, and over the broader spectrum the particular religious community. A genuine 'believer' will have particular experiences.

In giving recognition to its leaders, and requiring that they be instruments of the Holy Spirit, the Christian community will often demand that they have particular experiences, such as visions or audible revelations. They favour the leader who claims that his special experience or experiences, whatever their nature, are a direct revelation from God. The community recognises the experience and acknowledges or endorses its source as divine and with it the claim to leadership. Each community has its own criteria for giving such recognition. But not every claim to experience is an authentic one, and the standards the community employs may not be appropriate. For example, that a person can perform an unusual physical feat is no guarantee of a divine endorsement nor does it provide confirmation of a qualification for leadership. A community may have been surprised at the person's performances and claims. Its reaction may be to wonder at the performance, may be to endorse the claims. But they may be mistaken. They must explain how a physical or psychological performance could possibly authenticate dogmatic pronouncements, demands, or claims to authority. There may be justifiable scepticism.

We recognise that the fundamental question we can ask is whether there is some feature that distinguishes the religious experience from any other kind of experience, and specifically for the Christian believer whether there is a kind of experience that can be identified and distinguished from other kinds of experience as distinctive Christian experience. That is what a philosophical approach demands.

Within the totality of my experiences there are experiences of many sorts, so we can then classify the various particular experiences into kinds of experience, making more and more general classifications. For example we see, hear, touch. So there are sensory experiences. We feel sadness, exultation, grief. These are non-sensory experiences.

3 'Experience' and 'Experiences'

For there is an important difference when we speak of religious 'experience' and religious 'experiences', Christian 'experiences', and 'Christian experience'. For within an identifiable type of basic experience, many kinds of experience, 'experiences', take place. For the Christian there are many different experiences that can be identified within the overall designation of 'Christian experience', for example the experience of guilt, the experience of relief with the forgiveness of sins, of being guided, of deep peace, of being called to a vocation.

To take a further example: Let us say that the basic religious experience is defined as a feeling of dependence. It will find expression in the varied experiences the believer has within the religion. When it provides the definition of the Christian's religious experience, the basic 'feeling of dependence' will then be further defined by reference to the saving grace of Jesus Christ, and manifested in the many particular experiences of the Christian, such as penitence, gratitude, confession, forgiveness. To point to the fact of the experience of dependence is to single out a kind of experience that may plausibly be claimed to be distinctive of the religious experience. The idea may be qualified by speaking of a feeling of *absolute* dependence, as for example by Friedrich Schleiermacher (1768-1834), whose purpose in framing such definition is to identify the distinctive common feature of a distinctively religious awareness. Other examples that make this attempt are those of Rudolph Otto who singled out 'awe' and Paul Tillich, who defined religious experience as 'ultimate concern'. [See Tutorial at the end of this chapter.]

To make a general definition of the phenomenon of religion we must address two questions:

Q1: Is there a general framework for interpreting the many historical religions? Is there a common definite structure to these religions?

Q2: Is there a 'religious dimension' to human existence?

John Smith claims that

'It is possible to show that there is a religious dimension to human existence and also that the historical religions do have a common structure without also claiming that either the dimension or the structure exists by itself.'[1]

The suggestion is that we approach the Religious Object through the medium of the religious dimension of experience. How that dimension is to be defined is answered in particular cases by suggestions as to how it shows itself. 'Feeling of dependence', 'awe', 'ultimate concern' are such attempts to articulate it.

4 Different Sorts Of Experience

There are different **kinds** of experience. One way of classifying these kinds is to observe that some relate to the world beyond the subject. Others do not. There is a distinction between those that in some way are related to realities beyond the one who is experiencing and those which do not. To make this distinction we shall speak of (1) the **structure** of the experience.

By 'structure' we mean how the experience is related to the world. Take two instances. I feel dizzy [D]. I see a tree [T]. The structure of these different experiences is in contrast. In the case of D, there is nothing external, independent of the subject. If I feel dizzy there is nothing that I am dizzy about. In the case of T there is. The subject senses or seems to sense a particular object, a tree. We call these respectively and tentatively **subject/content struc-ture** and **subject/object structure**, simply to differentiate between them. For the subject is of course conscious in both. In the case of T, the consciousness is such that I can ask questions about an object of consciousness, e.g. What is the relation between my sensing an object and the object sensed? In the case of D I cannot. I may ask what caused the dizziness. But that is a different question.

Then we take note of differences in (2) the **content** of the experience.

---

1 John E. Smith. *Experience and God*, p.98.

Is it pleasurable, painful or neutral with respect to pleasure or pain? Different experiences have different hedonic content. D is usually judged as 'not pleasant'. So you can ask, What is it like to be dizzy? For strictly sensible experiences it is not difficult to provide a description. But when it comes to non-sensory experience, i.e. ones with no sensory content, it is not so easy. What is it like to be sad, to experience joy? Often there are physical accompaniments to the experience but these are not of the essence of the experience. They do not define it. Joy is not identifiable with the expressions of satisfaction the subject makes. Sadness does not consist in the wails and tears that express it. But each has its own distinct quality, whatever the expressions may be.

There are different sensory modalities: smelling differs from hearing and both from seeing. As-experienced, i.e. phenomenologically, colour content is different from auditory content. What it is like to hear is different from what it is like to see.

So, let us begin with the idea of the structure of religious experience. Is it something about which we ask, Does this experience relate to an object beyond the experiencing subject? In addressing this question we first try to answer, 'What is the distinctive content of the religious experience?' The two questions are related.

As we have seen, it is important to distinguish what we are calling 'religious experience', singular, from the many experiences the believer has in the context of his faith. Some of these will be essentially related to faith, such as relief at the remission of guilt, sense of being called to a particular vocation or task. Some will be ordinary experiences of everyday life interpreted in the light of faith and so experienced as having religious significance, such as a feeling of well-being, having food to eat, having a good night's sleep (I was puzzled as a child when my father in his morning prayer thanked God 'for the rest of the past night'), and coincidences of different kinds.

When we apply this distinction to religious experience we can receive both sorts of answer. That can be confusing. For there are many types of religious experience, even within a particular tradition.

Believers make claims on the basis of religious experiences. One of these is quite basic. It is that experience reveals the reality of God. This claim is fundamental to Christian theism, since all other claims and confession relate to this belief in God. So it is essential that the experience appealed to be carefully elucidated. What is at the very heart of theism is said to have been revealed and manifest in the experience. There is a pattern to be discerned.

For the theist, the reality of God is revealed in experience as the solution to human ills, however the problem of the human is defined. Such revelatory experiences have made a significant difference to the diagnosis and solution of the fundamental problem of the human condition. The particular traditions define this problem in their particular way, for example, as disobedience to divine law, as lack of love. So the relevant experiences are taken to be 'soteriologically central.' We discern through them what is wrong in the human condition, what puts it right and where we stand in the scheme as individuals seeking salvation, enlightenment. The solution put here in the most general terms is called by different names in different traditions. In various ways, 'salvation' comes to the believer.

5   Experience and God[2]

The crucial question about religious experience is how it connects with the reality of God. Claims about arriving at the reality of God may take two forms.

---

2   As is obvious from footnote 1, this is the title of a book by Professor John E. Smith. He contends that to make a general definition of the phenomenon of religion we must address two questions:

Q1: Is there a general framework which can be produced for interpreting the many historical religions? Is there a common definite structure to these religions?

Q2: Is there a 'religious dimension' to human existence? The suggestion is that we approach the Religious Object through the medium

These may be placed on a spectrum. At one end is the claim to immediate experience of the divine reality. God is disclosed without a medium. The subject is in immediate relation with the divine reality. There is nothing in between the experiencing subject and the religious object experienced. Mysticism provides an example of such unmediated immediacy. At the other end of the spectrum is the claim that by a process of inference from well chosen premises we can attain to the reality of God. So that reality does not need to be experienced. We end with a concept of God, nothing more. A third approach insists that experience is always mediated through a process of interpretation. Experience and interpretation are interwoven. To speak of the disclosure of the divine, the reality of God, involves experience as the medium of encounter. It is experience as mediated and interpreted. Such disclosure is neither immediate experience of God, nor is it inferred knowledge of God produced by a process of argument.

To speak of the disclosure of the divine, the reality of God, involves experience as the medium of encounter. It is experience as mediated and interpreted. Such disclosure is neither immediate experience of God, nor is it inferred knowledge of God produced by a process of argument. These are unacceptable.

II

6   Why the Philosopher Is Interested in Religious Experience

We have indicated two approaches to our topic. (1) The first is to examine the assertion that the basic religious experience substantiates the claim of God's reality. This is what we have attempted in the first part of this chapter. (2) The second is to explore whether

of the religious dimension of experience. How that dimension is to be defined is answered in particular cases by suggestions as to how it shows itself. 'Feeling of dependence', 'awe', 'ultimate concern' are such attempts to articulate it.

there is an analogy between experiences claimed by believers as religious experiences and ordinary experiences, where we take for granted what has been called **the principle of credulity**. Before we consider Swinburne's statement of the principle of credulity, some explanation is needed.

Philosophers sometimes appear to talk in obscure ways. They do so because they take into consideration what people often overlook. If a poet (Longfellow) can say, 'things are not what they seem', the philosopher will give reasons why. The fact is that we do not always make a correct judgment about what we sense. Perception may mislead. So, taking this into account, the philosopher says, 'I seem to see a red pencil.' By using the expression 'I seem to' he suggests that what he sees may not be what it seems to him to be.

In spite of this allowance for doubt, it is usually the case that what seems to us to be so in our ordinary experience is probably so. So we quite reasonably judge that the way things seem is the way they are. So in our ordinary course of life we do not say, 'I seem to see a pigeon', 'I seem to hear a loud noise', 'I seem to be touching a tennis ball'. We only use the term 'seem' when we have some doubt about what we are perceiving.

The question is whether there is an analogy from such ordinary experience to religious experience. In our ordinary experience we often move easily from the content of our experience to the object of the experience. The analogy proposed is quite simple. Mary says, 'I see a thrush.' We readily take this statement as evidence that there is a thrush to be seen. We confirm this by seeing a thrush ourselves or alternatively getting reliable testimony from other sources to the same effect. Those sources will claim, 'We see a thrush', 'We have seen a thrush'.

Call this procedure an application of the principle of credulity and apply it to the religious case. Joan says, 'God spoke to me in a vision.' Peter says, 'God directed me by giving me a sign.' Both believe that they are making a report. Both are claiming, 'We have experienced God (in action).' Does the principle of credulity apply in both cases? Should the statement be prefaced with the phrase, 'It seems to me that . . . .'

a. The difference between them is that in our ordinary cases we have access to many confirming cases. Here we can show that when someone seems to perceive something, in most cases the something actually exists. So it is most probable that in the particular instance, say, the next case I perceive something, that will also be the case. We know of many instances when someone has said, 'I see a thrush' and where we and other people would say the same. Moreover we could take a photograph of the object.

b. The argument from analogy produces a probable result. But such a result will not suffice in the case of religious experience. Here an argument to a probable result is unsatisfactory. Christian faith demands an absolute. A probable God, i.e. a God shown probably to be a reality according to an argument from analogy is not the God of Christian faith.

We shall now quote and consider Swinburne's statement

> It is a principle of rationality that (in the absence of special considerations) if it seems (epistemically) to a subject that *x* is present, then probably *x* is present; what one seems to perceive is probably so. How things seem to be is good grounds for a belief about how things are. From this it would follow that, in the absence of special considerations, all religious experiences ought to be taken by their subjects as genuine, and hence as substantial grounds for belief in the existence of their apparent object. It seems . . . intuitively right in most ordinary cases . . . to take the way things seem to be as the way they are.[3]

When I say, 'I see a thrush' I take it as evidence that there is a thrush out there. I don't question it. But if my colleague in a moment of stimulated repose or inebriation says, 'I see a pink elephant,' or more moderately 'I seem to see a pink elephant' I do not think that he means that there is a pink elephant out there. The following similarly phrased assertions are statements about experiences.

---

3   Richard Swinburne, *The Existence of God*, p. 254.

I seem to see a thrush.

I seem to see a pink elephant.

These are statements about our experiences. The structure of the two sentences is the same. The implications are different. We take them differently.

The believer claims to have an experience that God speaks to her, even that God appears to her, that an angel directs her, claiming that the angel is a messenger from God. She then takes the experience to confirm her belief that God exists and is active in specific ways.

7 Analogy Between Religious Experience and Sense-Perception

The question: Since we often readily allow experience, sense perception, as a source of knowledge shall we allow such religious experiences also as a source of knowledge? Should we grant religious experiences a similar status to sense-perception as a source of knowledge of an experienced object? We must raise the question of the criteria for allowing experience as a source of knowledge.

Differences between sense-experience and religious experience:

(1) The fact of agreement regarding the significance of experience supports claims to knowledge only if certain criteria are met. The kinds of agreement that count relate to events in the material world which can be tested. Take the examples of the microscopist and the drinker. The medical researcher using his microscope claims to see something nobody else has seen before. He does not keep his purported discovery to himself. By sharing it with his colleagues he hopes to have it and its importance confirmed. He hopes that they will be able to refer to experiences similar to his own. The drinker who sees fantastic animals is in no such position. He seems to see hitherto unseen and unknown creatures. Even if he wanted to share his experiences and on that basis make claims about the validity of what he claims he has seen, he will not be taken seriously.

Of course, some people can perceive what others do not. Those who do not so perceive may reasonably be persuaded that the others are making true claims about their perceptions. But the significance of those experiences is matter for examination.

8   Experience and Interpretation

Question: How shall we decide between interpretations of something that happened, whether unique public experiences e.g. a thunderstorm, or private ones e.g. visions, inner voices?

You and your friends are given a sheet of paper on which a lot of lines have been drawn. You are each asked what it is you see in the jumble. Replies will be different. One will see a horse drinking. Another will see cloud formation. Yet another will see the lines as a jumble of graffiti. We see things differently.

There has been murder in the town. Those people who are aware of it will have very different experiences. The relative, the detective, the editor of the sensational newspaper, each has his different view point of the event based on his unique experience of the event. Since they each experience the same event in different ways, let us call the phenomenon 'experiencing as'. One experiences it as a personal loss, another as a case for investigation, another as the prospect of sensational front page headline and report.

Now think of different ways of experiencing the same events. As the Chaldeans approached Jerusalem and threatened its destruction, the Jews in the city experienced it as intense fear of coming catastrophe. The prophet experienced the events as the prospective judgment of God on the city. The Chaldean soldier experienced it as prospect for slaughter and booty. The experiences are different because each brings their own immediate background into the process of interpreting the meaning of the event.

So there is an analogy between 'seeing-as' and 'experiencing-as'. Believers see the world as a world where God is present. Non-believers see the world as a series of purely natural events. We must consider that (a) there can be alternative characterisations of the event of 'seeing', 'experiencing'. (b) Something more than the fact that I experience X as Y is required to establish the validity of my interpretation. For when I try to establish my belief in its significance I must explain both what the experience was and in addition contend that it has the significance I give it. This means that I must make explanations, use arguments, give reasons. When others have similar experiences to mine and do not interpret them as I do, it appears that it is the argument I produce to support my interpretation that is the important thing. So the notion of the existence of God can collapse into something that looks like the notion of being convinced by an argument. But the argument is to be seen as the instrument leading to an interpretation. That interpretation makes possible the belief in and so the assertion of the reality of God. It also, when articulated, enables the believer to give some account of his belief.

9 Testing Experiences

The theist at some point appeals to the fact that God has revealed himself, to the fact of *revelation*. Such a one has the added conviction that experience is consonant with knowledge of God derived from revelation. For example, feeling, i.e. experiencing, guilt when one steals. This is the conviction that any God one would believe in is moral. If the purported revelation of God is incompatible with such a moral experience, one will say, 'I can't believe in that sort of God.' So experience has disconfirmed the religious claim. Conclusion: God may be more than moral but cannot be less, because of the assurance which moral experience produces. The reasonable assumption is that there must be consonance between claims on the basis of experience and claims on the basis of revelation.

There is also a broader claim: There must be consistency between our interpretation of our experience, the framework within which we interpret that experience and the rest of our knowledge.

Has one had the experience one has claimed to have had? Assuming that the answer to this question is 'Yes,' we then must ask: 'Are one's interpretations of it and the framework within which one makes them open to rational justification, or — a somewhat lesser demand — capable of being shown to be reasonable, when as a religious person, a believer, one speaks of God in connection with the experience?'

So we have to decide whether the framework within which we do our thinking is reasonable. For the Christian this means that one will justify the theistic stance.

We must also decide whether the interpretation given to our experience is itself reasonable. Here are three questions which constitute tests for experience and its claims as interpreted.

Does it harmonise with what I know? The test of **Coherence**.

Do elements in the explanation and claims harmonise with other elements? The test of **Consistency**.

Can it explain many phenomena? The test of **Expansibility**.

If the explanation we give to our experience is coherent, consistent, and expansible, it is reasonable, and there is a good chance of it being true.

However, there can be no compulsiveness about accepting the framework. There is always the possibility of doubt. The believer believes. The sceptic does not. So the belief needs justification. The believer wishes to convince the sceptic that his claim is reasonable. That entails that he is claiming more than that the experience is true for him and that that is all that matters.

10 Theists and Christians, Philosophy and Theology

The concern of philosophy is to discuss the possibility of a general religious experience or a universal capacity for religious experiences while that of the Christian theologian it is to speak of a saving relation to Christ. So what of the relation between the religious experience of the theist and that of the Christian? For the philosopher looks for a universal human consciousness of God, and the Christian theologians speaks of a specifically Christian relation with Christ. Theologians recognise this. Here is a typical statement:

> There can be no relating to Christ in which there is not
> a relation to God. Within the Christian community there is
> no religious moment in which a relation to Christ is not also
> present within it.[4]

For centuries Christian writers and teachers had been bound to the dogmatic statement defining the relation between Christ and God and also defining the person of Christ in terms of the Greek ideas of **person, substance, nature**. Jesus was 'of the same substance with' was *homoousios* as God. His person consisted of two natures in one person. As the debate raged such formulas emerged as expressing a consensus and heresy was in this way hopefully marked off from orthodoxy.

For the Christian believer the experience of Jesus Christ is inextricably interwoven with the experience of God that no such formula with its logical and ontological difficulties is required. In the experience there are two non-separable elements, 'a general awareness of God and a special relation to Christ'. So the believer knows that 'God was in Christ'.

The Greek term for 'Lord' was *kurios*. While the term was in common Roman usage, meaning 'sir' or designating a social position, e.g. Lord Sarapis, Lord Dementer, for the Christian the term 'Lord' had a sense which was exclusive to Jesus.

Paul had written that while there were many gods and many lords, for the believer there is one God and one Lord, Jesus Christ, 'through whom are all things and through whom we exist' *I Corinthians* 8:5-6. There could be only one ultimate allegiance. 'Jesus is Lord'. *Iesous kurios,* stated the commitment that identified the believer as Christian. That simple confession stated the quite irreplaceable and dominant conviction expressed in other ways in the New Testament that 'God was in Christ' revealing himself.

---

4   A. Gerrish, *A Prince of the Church*, p. 63.

There could be no competition, no other rival. There could be only one, ultimate allegiance. The Christians could not and would not worship the Emperor. So they, good citizens that they were, could not give him the token of their allegiance which was demanded, even if that meant that by refusing they would be executed. Pliny, the governor of Bithynia, in his letter to Trajan the Emperor (circa A.D. 112) wrote that he let those go who 'recited a prayer to the gods at my dictation, made supplication with incense and wine to your statue' and added, 'things which those who are really Christians cannot be made to do'.[5]

As time passed and Christians encountered new and various attempts to express this understanding, their leaders became aware that some expressions of faith were preferable to others. In the early centuries of the church the conviction that some expressions were misguided led to extended discussion of what would, in course of time, be rejected as heresy. So more complex statements of belief emerged and with them the conviction that an 'orthodox' statement of the fundamental belief about the status of Jesus the Christ, the Son, the Logos, in relation to God, could be set out to represent the faith.

The church in these early centuries was passing from the time when a simple confession of faith sufficed, when Christians were happy with confessions based on Scripture, the basic one being *Iesous kurios*, 'Jesus is Lord'. Further and widespread discussion raised problems which an appeal to the words of Scripture could not resolve. So the passage takes place from simple Christian confessions of faith to a striving for orthodox definitions of Christian doctrine and the emergence of Christian theology. These 'formulae' are intended to express the accepted belief. It was the intention of their creators by means of them to express the unity of the Christian church. This was most earnestly desired by the emperor Constantine. A united church meant a united empire.

---

5   Cf. *A New Eusebius,* pp. 13-14 (see next footnote).

The terms are philosophical and had been framed and defined by the Greek philosophers.[6] As the church discussed the question of the person of Jesus Christ, the Son and as Logos in relation to God the Father, they asked questions the answers to which they could not establish or refute by quoting passages of Scripture.

What is of interest for us is that the church turned to and adopted for its own purpose philosophical terms already available. It conducted its discussions in the conviction that an adequate and orthodox set of dogmas could be developed by employing this strategy. What follows is a brief explanation of how the philosophical term *homoousios* played an important part in the stabilising of Christian teaching in the post apostolic period. In particular the issue became that of finding a way of expressing the essential Christian belief that Father and Son are equal, that the Son is in no sense subordinate to the Father. This was in opposition to Arius who denied the essential identity of Father and Son, asserting that the Son is like, but not equal to, the Father.

It proved a difficult and arduous task to express this conviction in a way that would be acceptable to the church at large. However this was accomplished when representatives of the church met at Nicaea in A.D. 325. The council of the assembled representatives of the church introduced and approved the desired concept as they sought to express the belief that to save mankind the Saviour must be one with the Creator, and so equal with the Father. The Nicene Creed emerged. The key term was a philosophical one.

The term agreed to be appropriate was *homoousios* (*of one substance*). It is a combination of two Greek words *homos* (*one and the same, common, joint*) and *ousios*, the adjective from *ousia* (*substance, essence, being*). So to say that X is *homoousios* with Y, is to say that

6 We cannot go into detail, in this writing, either in explanation or elaboration of the issues involved. For such there is a very extensive literature. A good place to start is with the original documents. A collection of these is to be found in the indispensable two volumes, each edited by J. Stephenson. *A New Eusebius* (1957), pp. 365-366 and *Creeds, Councils and Controversies* (1972), p. 337. London: S.P.C.K.

whatever X is in its essential being, so also is Y. So the Nicene formula: 'Lord Jesus Christ is of one substance (*homoousios*) with the Father' means: Whatever the essential being of the Father is, so is the essential being of the Son.

A precedent was thus set.[7] For clarity and precision of definition, appropriate terms must be found. These may be discovered in available philosophical discussions and employed for precise theological use. Such examples are readily found in Christian theology and in confessional statements. This gave rise to interesting debates as to the appropriate relation between philosophy and the expression of Christian belief, one which has continued and continues.

BIBLIOGRAPHY

Brian Davies, *An Introduction to Philosophy of Religion*. New York Oxford University Press, 1993.

Peter Donovan, *Interpreting Religious Experience*. London: Sheldon Press, 1979.

---

7 At the later council of Chalcedon (A.D. 451) something similar took place. The question was: Given Jesus Christ was *homoousios* with God the Father, and given also that he was human, how may we speak well of the relation of these two features of his person? Greek philosophical terms served to produce an acceptable formula.

These were the terms employed:

Hypostasis	subsistence
Prosopon	person
Phusis	nature
Ousios	substance
Homoousios	of one and the same substance

The following is the statement that was accepted:

We confess our Lord Jesus Christ two natures in one person and one subsistence, of one substance with us touching the manhood and of one substance with the Father with respect to the godhead.

John Smith, *Experience and God.* New York: Oxford University Press, 1968.

J. Stephenson. *A New Eusebius*, London: S.P.C.K., 1957)

Creeds, Councils and Controversies, London: S.P.C.K., 1972.

Richard Swinburne, *The Existence of* God, Oxford: Clarendon Press, 1979.

Keith E.Yandell, *Philosophy of Religion.* London: Routledge, 1999.

ADDENDUM

John Smith, *Experience and God.* New York: Oxford University Press, 1968.

This book provides a persuasive argument for putting the concept of experience at the centre of philosophical discussions concerning the meaning of 'God'. In order that claims to religious truth within the context of an understanding of man as religious will become relevant to man as a living and thinking human being, we must examine experience to see if there are 'signs' of a divine reality present within it. We must take reality as it is presented to us within human experience and by reflecting upon it, assisted in this task by the traditions available to us, come to understand its significance as medium of the reality of God.

The question concerning God is the question concerning the meaning of human life as a whole. There are certain 'occasions' when this question presses itself upon man, where life is not ordinary but where the question about and concern for the ground and goal of human existence come to be raised. That the question is raised is a universal phenomenon. This is the basis for the argument for the essential rationality of the concept of God.

The conviction of the reality of the religious object is not arrived at by a process of deductive argument. It has its basis in the concerned questioning about the meaning of human existence as a whole, about the ground and goal of human existence. It is not arrived at by a process of deductive reasoning, as with the so-called arguments for the existence of God. He proposes the Anselmian conception of reason as an alternative to such rationalism. Anselm had described his quest as 'faith seeking understanding'. What is present in experience is to be interpreted. Within human experience one finds the 'signs' of the presence of God. The task of reason is to read these signs, not by a process of inference coming to the conclusion of a reality hitherto unknown, but by reflection upon a reality present but not understood, perhaps indeed unrecognised. The logical process is one not of demonstration but of interpretation.

The arguments for the existence of God (so-called) are not to be seen as syllogistic processes wherein one makes the move from a reality other than God deducing the necessary existence of a reality not yet known. Rather they are to be seen as processes of interpretation through which certain data given in experience come to be understood. The making intelligible of experience must be given an essential role in determining commitment to the reality of the divine presence (p. 155). 'The intelligible development of experience makes an indispensable contribution, and . . . the very intelligibility itself is a factor, and indeed the most important factor, in bringing the self to accept and commit itself to the reality of the divine presence.' The appeal to experience, as sign, via appropriate processes of understanding, is thus essentially rational, and is proposed by Smith as an alternative to different forms of irrationalism (e.g. those of Kierkegaard and Barth). He speaks of this as 'living reason' (p. 113). This is the process the self employs in attempting to find a rational pattern in its experiences.

The appeal to experience has a further aspect. We have seen that the interpretative means for the understanding of the signs of the presence of God are provided by traditions known and preserved within specific communities. Since he has proposed a generic concept of religion, he must show this concept to be applicable to different particular religious traditions. So he proposes a theory of a common 'experiential structure' of the great religions in terms of the schema of 'ideal', 'need', and 'deliverer'. The basic concept is that of 'need'. The way in which the obstacle which stands in the way of fulfilment is conceived has its counterpart in the particular kind of deliverer proposed. Although the great religious communities define the problem differently, and thus the ideal and remedy in different ways, there is still a basis of comparison in the similar structure of experience involved. The different religions represent varying responses to the same problematical situation. He had earlier in the writing analysed this in terms of question and concern about the ground and goal of human existence.

We have found Smith's suggestion of an alternative between the 'absolute distinction between immediacy and mediation, or between immediate experience and inference' (p. 52), to be a most helpful one. The category of interpreted experience recognizes both elements of immediacy and rational mediation of the reality of God as essential. Experience of God is rational since mediated through structures of interpretation.

What Smith has shown is that a rigorous philosophical treatment, which cannot be required to answer all the theological questions involved, may employ the concept of God with vigour and with decision. It is refreshing when so much undisciplined and uncritical language is spoken about God, or his death, about experience and the self, that a book of such calibre as this offers an alternative way of opening up the question on fundamental lines of empirical grounding for religious commitment. The presuppositions must be re-examined, the question of the burden of proof driving us beyond explanation and attempted theoretical justification to the issue of experienced and experienceable. The book taken as a whole presses the following question.

Taking the full range of human experience into consideration, does such consideration of such experience provide meaningful symbols for the understanding of 'God' and of propositions concerning God, whether there is a dimension of our human experience which may be the legitimate occasion for 'God-talk'? Smith's book is an invitation to take a second look, to see whether empiricism cannot be rescued from narrowness, experience from subjectivity, and reason from rationalism.

Because of the empirical grounding of faith and the rationality of the media of experience, faith is capable of an explicit philosophical definition, which can be further determined within specific religious communities. The self, in the midst of the world which impinges upon it, finds itself existing in different dimensions (e.g., the moral and the aesthetic). One such is the religious dimension. Here the matter rests within the realm of assertion. Further definition of the tricky conception of the self seems called for, especially since so much of the argument rests upon it.

A most important issue which the book raises is as to where the burden of proof lies. To a restrictive, logical empiricism which would rule out 'God-talk' Smith says: 'Show me your credentials. The burden of proof lies with you.' But he knows that this is also what the opposite side has been saying. His answer is that an adequate examination of experience will give the lie to such restrictiveness. Since this is the case, the job of the philosopher is to point the way, to point to what is assumed. One cannot go beyond experience. The question concerns its definition. The way to get such a definition is to take into account all that experience' delivers and when the definition is proposed it is an 'end-of-the-line' appeal.

TUTORIAL Paul Tillich on Faith

Reading for this tutorial:
Dynamics of Faith: New York, Harper and Brothers, 1957.
Chapters 1 and 2.

I

Of many books that treat our subject, this one is very worthwhile. In this tutorial we shall survey and hopefully stimulate interest both in the questions involved and in Tillich's treatment of them.

Before reading the suggested text, work through sections I and II.

As in other tutorials, key terms are set in bold type. Mastery of these terms is essential for understanding the issues and their particular treatment in this book. As the author remarks very early, 'faith' is a much misunderstood, and even distorted word, even though it is a key word and used as frequently as it is. Because it is a key word it deserves to be clearly and carefully understood.

A distinction is important. **Faith** is to be distinguished from **belief**. We have in an earlier chapter made the important point of distinguishing the two words. The problem of definition is that they are sometimes used as synonyms. This even in view of the fact that a believer may not have faith. The term 'faith' stands for the basic and distinctive experience of the Christian. That is the subject of this tutorial. Faith is not belief where belief is (according to Tillich) defined as **knowledge**. His point is clear, namely that belief is the result of a process of cognition. If we analyse it further we can give a stricter definition of knowledge. But that is not now our concern. His point is clear enough.

Step one. A place to begin profitably would be for you to write down, after having first given it careful thought, what you understand by the term. Do so with as few words as you can. The need to be precise in defining sharpens the thinking and enables one to clear away the unnecessary expansion and proliferation to which we are often prone. Such exercise could well show us how indefinite our understanding has been. Do not quote. If one is honest, it is often the case that a quotation is an excuse for not thinking oneself. Frame your own definition as you now understand the meaning of the term 'faith'.

Step two. With no further looking up a dictionary or other book or paper, say what you think faith is not. Write what you think would be a misunderstanding of the term. Do that also in as few words as you can.

Step three. Having performed these tasks, take other words and try to relate them to 'faith'. For example start with belief, knowledge, reason, emotion. Then go over what you have written and edit out anything not essential. Employ as few words as possible and filter out anything irrelevant or unclear.

Step four. Put your answers aside. Come back to them some time later. Meanwhile keep thinking. Then edit what you have written until you are reasonably satisfied.

Read over the contents of this tutorial while also reading portions of the book, particularly chapters one and two, 'What faith is' and 'What faith is not' (pages 1-40).

II

Step five. See whether the following terms suggest ways of approaching the subject of 'faith'. Frame at least one question in relation to each of the following pairs. When you have done this, try to refine your question or questions. Then you may be ready to give or to hear an answer.

For example: Is faith solely a conscious act? If so, is it influenced by unconscious and so, hidden motivations?

conscious/unconscious
intellectual/emotional
reason/feeling
receptive/creative.

free/determined
ego/superego

III

We now consider chapter I 'What Faith Is'.

Tillich's 'formal' definition is that faith is '**ultimate concern**'. Faith is a centred act of the whole personality: It is 'the state of being ultimately concerned', 'a total and centred act of the personal self' pp. 1, 4, 8. The first chapter explains what is involved in this definition.

The formal definition can now be expressed in different ways as the content of the concern differs. For human concerns are many, and ultimate concerns may be about different objects. For the patriot it is the nation. For the Old Testament Hebrew it is the God of justice, For many a contemporary the ultimate concern is success, or social standing, or economic power.

Faith is an act of freedom. So it is not determined by the unconscious. Nor is it identical with any rational function, although faith is a rational act. It transcends both.

Faith is not to be defined simply as a cognitive act, nor as an act of will, nor solely in terms of emotion,' feeling'. It is the unity of a personal act, in which each of these elements has a place.

So what of the expression 'ultimate concern'? There are two aspects involved. The term has both a subjective and an objective meaning. It refers both to what takes place in the personality and also refers to what the personal act of concern is about. My ultimate concern is about an ultimate concern. The centred act of my personality is about something other than me. That other may or may not be genuinely ultimate. When that is so idolatry replaces faith. When my ultimate concern is about that which is not truly ultimate, when '. . . finite realities are elevated to the rank of ultimacy' (p.12), I become an idolater.

So faith is also risk. For what one considers ultimate and about which one's concern is ultimate may not actually be ultimate. Then the realisation of one's error in making it one's ultimate concern may lead to the disintegration of the personality in the wake of such disillusionment.

IV

This section of the tutorial sets out quite simply and briefly the main contention of the second chapter 'What Faith is Not'.

There is, as we have seen, an **intellectual,** a **volitional** and an **emotional** element in the act of faith, of ultimate concern. In the experience of faith, **reason, will** and **feeling** are all involved. One of these may come to be dominant, at the expense of the others. Corresponding to these there are particular distortions of faith, the intellectualistic, the voluntaristic and the emotionalistic distortions.

In this context a distortion is defined as identifying faith with one of the functions which go to make up the total personality. Take these one by one.

Faith is not an act of knowledge, by which our author means an act of belief supported by insufficient evidence (cf. p. 31). That is what Tillich calls it: belief not faith. Faith has the certitude appropriate to it. That certainty contrasts to the probability of our ordinary and empirical knowledge. This certitude is in contrast to 'any theoretical judgment' (p. 35). He calls it 'existential'.

Neither is faith simply the 'will to believe' as if lack of evidence has to be supplemented by an act of will (p. 35). Where I do not find sufficient reason, I determine nevertheless to believe. The act of will intends to produce the sought for belief. Whether an act of will can produce such result is, in any case, dubitable. This approach misunderstands that no human effort can produce ultimate concern. The question then arises, 'What then is the source of such ultimate concern?' That leads to the topic of revelation.

A third distortion of the meaning of faith is its description as 'feeling', as human emotion. Faith is not 'a matter of merely subjective emotions' (p. 39). It is not the subjectivity of mere feeling, where there is no content and no demand. He makes the

point that the great theologian of the nineteenth century, Schleiermacher, used the term 'feeling' but defined it as 'feeling of absolute
dependence'. Tillich emphasises that, so defined, the term is related
to his 'ultimate concern' (having content and having to do with
the whole person). He then points out that, so defined, it differs
from the definition given in popular psychology, and can serve as
a constructive theological term.

Each of these distortions, with its exclusive emphasis, is a denial of faith as an affair of the whole person, an experience and a
certainty having to do with all human functions.

EXPERIENCE AND GOD: WORK SHEET

1. Attempt a definition of 'experience'? Does the definition include different 'experiences'?

2. Is there one particular kind of experience that distinguishes the religious experience? Or, are we to be content with simply describing various kinds of experience claimed to be of religious significance?

3. Does religious experience provide us with a reason for believing in God? Specify an argument from religious experience to the existence and activity of God.

4. Does an interpretation of historical events, say, the overthrow of Jerusalem as the judgment of God, or the rescue of an army from Dunkirk as the benevolent intervention of God, provide a reasonable ground for belief?

7 CREATION

A fundamental belief of theism is that God created the cosmos. How has the Christian doctrine been influenced by philosophers? Different interpretations of the meaning of creation result from and influence contrasting views about the nature of God. Is he above or within the cosmos, or in some sense both? In view of the presence of evil, could we think of this as the best of all possible worlds?

7 CREATION

1 God: Above, Within: Transcendent, Immanent

The cosmos continues to exist. The theist claims that God created the world. Those two claims imply that there are two realities, God and the world. That means that there is some relation between them. Talk about creation as beginning, and we have a question about whether the relation of God to the world at the beginning and to the world as a continuing reality is the same relation. Does the creative relation to the world continue as it was in the beginning or is there some difference between that 'original' reality and the present continuing reality? Or has God's relation to the cosmos found its fulfilment at the beginning with the existence of the cosmos?

We can put the problem in different ways by reflecting that a doctrine of providence has in Christian theology always been associated with the doctrine of creation. God's relation to the cosmos is the same, expressed in the terse phrase, 'as it was in the beginning is now and evermore shall be, world without end'.

For the cosmos continues. Speak of providence and you are often offered the image of a God supremely above the world who, from his transcendence directs events within the cosmos, acting within it to fulfil his purpose. Or, put in more piecemeal fashion as it so often is put, provides for an event here and another there as he sees the need in the individual case. At the receiving end of the act is the believer within the cosmos who discerns that providential activity, either bearing it bravely or rejoicing in it.

A different understanding of providence presents God as the great spirit within the cosmos. The events that take place therein are seen as expressions of his continuous activity and concern for the creatures. Here there is no talk of intervention.

What we must take as given is that the order of nature is consistent. We understand the workings of nature to the extent that we can discern this regularity. There can be no gate crashing into nature. An abrogation of the 'laws of nature' to produce what appears to be beneficial to some party within the cosmos would produce chaos and destroy the whole. It is irrational to conceive God as external to the universe and at the same time influencing this and that event and the whole as he intervenes at his will within the universe. For that kind of providence there is no defence.

So what alternatives are there as we accept the givenness of the cosmos, and attempt to understand its operations as far as is possible.

There is no need for any reference to either a transcendent or an immanent being to account for the operations of the cosmos. This is called humanism, or **secularism**.

The bringing into being of the cosmos was an act of God and once in being the cosmos continues without any need for further divine influence. God has set within the universe the dynamic for its continuance. This is called **deism**.

The universe and God are identical. The universe was at the beginning and in its continuance is an emanation of the divine. This is called **pantheism**.

God is within but not identical with the universe. The cosmos is as it were God's 'body'. God chooses to express himself. The cosmos is the means through which that expression is made, the medium for his self-expression. This is called **panentheism**.

These respective positions emerge as different answers given to the questions raised relative to the cosmos and as different theoretical stances are taken both in the name of faith and with regard to our scientific understanding and knowledge of the cosmos.

There are many creation stories. We can ask the same basic questions of each of them: What is its meaning? Is the story to be taken as literal? Does it describe a process of coming into being? Or is it metaphorical, detailing in symbolic terms the structure of the cosmos? We then ask, given that a vastly complex universe exists with dimensions beyond our comprehension, even when expressed in billions of light years. For what questions or kinds of question about its origin can we expect rational answers? To what sort of question is a theory of origins an answer? What is the status of an account of creation? Indeed, is the story of creation, however it is expressed, intended as an account of the coming into being of a physical world? Or does it serve some other intention? The theist remembers that it is to be read and understood within the context of the believing community at worship. It is primarily about God.

As an introduction we take contrasting accounts of the origin of the cosmos: those of Plato and of *Genesis*. In doing so we shall see what philosophical issues are relevant and illuminating.

We also mention in this chapter the views of Leibnitz. These philosophers are both of intrinsic interest. They indicate how philosophical ideas were employed to elucidate basic problems, one of these being the 'problem of evil'. Considering such ideas provides us an introduction into the discussion. It can only be a beginning.

First we indicate some important terms, whose meaning we hope to clarify in what follows: such general terms as cosmos, beginning, sensible world, transcendence, immanence, deism, dualism, *ex nihilo*, pantheism, emanation, analogy. Then the Platonic terms: forms, ideas, divine intelligence, sensible world, shadows, demiurge, receptacle.

2   Plato's Craftsman and the Production Of The Cosmos

There is an important distinction between **being**, what is and does not change, and **becoming**, what moves and changes. An idea never changes. The physical universe, a sensible entity, is always changing. But it is ordered and stable in its motions. The Greeks used the terms 'change' and 'motion' as synonyms. The temporal and changing cosmos is the result of being made a copy of the real, unchanging and ideal. This is Plato's world of Forms.

The realm of Forms contrasts to the physical world, the world of sense, the sensible world. So you can list a series of contrasts between them. The world of Forms is Real, unchanging, immaterial, apprehended by the intellect. The physical world is, in contrast to the world of Forms, unreal, changeable, material, apprehended by the senses.

Plato insists that the father of all things is beyond our comprehension but that the world's order is such that it must have a cause. The father, the *demiurge*, (the Greek word for 'craftsman') brings order out of pre-existing materials. In the Platonic account, matter places limitations on the craftsmen who brings order out of chaos, out of the irrational. Any account of the universe must include the 'variable' i.e. the irrational. The irrational is tamed by having limits imposed on its motions.[1] Then orderly motion results. But the irrationality cannot be entirely overcome. The world of sense is forever inferior to the world of Forms. It is the realm of constant change. For Plato, 'change' and 'movement' were synonyms. The evils and imperfections of the physical world result from matter.

So, for Plato, there are two basic ideas: (1) Matter is given. (2) There is a pattern from which the cosmos is copied. This pattern is the Forms. The sensible, i.e. physical world, to whatever extent it is real, gets that reality from the Forms. In *Timaeus*, as he had not done before, Plato bridges the gap between the sensible world and the Forms, the world of the intellect grasped only by mind. The

---

1   *Timaeus*, 48.

demiurge uses the Forms as the blueprint, and from it he 'copies' the visible world. Plato's account of 'creation' is that the world is brought into being as a copy of the ideal world of the Forms. It is a piece of craftsmanship.

Before the demiurge fashions the world, he creates the world-soul. Plato then portrays this soul as permeating the universe. It is intelligent and living and the visible world is its body. He tells a story about its formation.

Plato introduces space, the 'receptacle', as given. Space just is. It has always been and always will be.

The heavenly bodies resemble the Forms in that they have always been and always will be. They are nevertheless changeable and in their motion they measure time. Without that movement there is no time. Space pre-exists the formation of the cosmos. Time comes into being with the production of the physical universe.[2] Only as the heavenly bodies move can there be time. Without them there is no time. So are they eternal? Does Plato mean, from his remarks about time, that there was no beginning to the universe?

Consider the possibilities. First, time existed before the universe came into being. So time pre-exists. So it is eternal. The cosmos is created in time. So the cosmos is not eternal. Second, time and the universe are co-existent. So the creative act in an eternal time is itself eternal. Creation is not at a point in time since time is eternal. The heavenly bodies change, but they always have been and always will be. So they are 'a moving image of eternity'.[3]

Third, Time begins with the creation of the cosmos. The cosmos is not eternal. God is eternal and created time with the creation of the cosmos.

Plato recognises he is speaking about difficult and obscure matters. His account is in the form of a story with references to mathematics to indicate the proportionality and rationality of the cosmos. But we should rather speak of Plato's account as of 'formation' than creation. For his account is not a *creatio ex nihilo*.

2 *Timaeus,* 37, 38.

3 *Timaeus* 37c.

He knows that his narrative is not to be taken literally. He knows he is using the language of myth as the medium of philosophical expression. That is an invitation to understand and interpret.

3 Contrast to the *Genesis* and Christian Accounts

This is in contrast to understanding of the creation in Genesis as *creatio ex nihilo*. Plato's account is a story of order being brought to pre-existing material, the material imposing limits on the demiurge. Christian writers and theologians have been aware of this contrast between Plato and the Bible from the outset.

Plato's Forms exist as an ordered whole, independent of the craftsman, who, so to speak, copies the blueprint. Creation in *Genesis* means something else, something more than copying or imitation. In this account there is nothing to be copied. Here is invention, innovation.

Christian thinkers were attracted to Plato's account of the Forms. For Plato the world of forms was independent of mind. Very early Platonists identified the Forms with the divine mind. So a different understanding of God and of God's relation to the world resulted. The Christian interpretation of the Forms, in contrast to that of Plato, was not of an independent realm. By identifying the Forms with the divine mind they thus avoided dualism, and preserved the transcendence of the Creator to the creation. They also were able to understand the beginning of the cosmos as an act of initiative and so a creative act. In Plato the Forms from which the cosmos is copied already exist. They are not brought into being by the demiurge. So the agent in the process is often called the 'craftsman', a translation of 'demiurge' (*demiourgos*).

Whether or not you employ the idea of *creation ex nihilo* to interpret the *Genesis* account of creation, it has had an important influence in the understanding of Christians. Briefly it makes two denials by ruling out dualism and pantheism. It insists that God's act of creation was not the result of a successful struggle with an ultimate and equal power opposed to his own. Such accounts of creation as the outcome of a contest between two ultimate powers feature in the ancient world and in Gnostic systems. Christian theology also insists that the world is not an emanation from the divine being himself. The world is not God.

One important question arises. The world, the cosmos, exists. Human beings exist. Human history runs its course. But human beings do not always do good. Indeed, they plan and execute evil, sometimes on a small scale as individuals, sometimes on a staggeringly colossal scale as thoroughly evil organisations. Nor is the natural world always conducive to the well-being of human beings, with earthquakes, tsunamis, fire, storms, disease. So if we consider evil as that which destroys or reduces human well-being, we have to speak of the persistent, widespread presence of evil in the world. It seems to be endemic here, universal. According to the theist, the world is God's world. But evil is frequently destructive of human well-being and of human existence. Indeed we might speak of history as a continuing trail of one vast evil after another. So we arrive at the important question: How is it that evil is evident everywhere in a world created by a good God? This has come to be known as the problem of evil.

We can in this introductory book simply raise the question, and shall illustrate by considering one response to it. It is the interesting but questionable answer given by **G. W. Leibnitz** (1646-1714) that this world is

4   The Best of All Possible Worlds

Leibnitz was a Platonist. God is pure spirit and pure act. God is reality. Leibnitz accepted and presented the arguments for the existence of God as Thomas Aquinas had done. He accepted the reality of the world, and attempted to justify God in the face of the evil in it. His **theodicy** (vindication of God) consisted in an exposition of the view that this is the best of all possible worlds, and that as God is perfect and omnipotent, before bringing the world into existence, he would have considered all possible worlds and have chosen to create the best possible one.

The 'best possible world' is the one in which variety and reality is at a maximum. Evil is lack of reality. It is negative. It is privation, deprivation of the good. Evil for Leibnitz is thus metaphysical evil.

Have in mind three definitions of evil. **Natural evil** is that caused by the processes of nature. **Moral evil** it that which has its source in the will of man. **Metaphysical evil** is lack of being, a privation of goodness. It is finitude, imperfection. For Leibnitz metaphysical evil is fundamental. All other kinds of evil spring from that. Since Leibnitz claims that this is the best possible world and that evil is present in this world, he must explain how the best possible world contains such evil and how this presence of evil relates both to the will of God and to human freedom.

He does so by imaging God contemplating the various possibilities open to him before performing the act of creating. These are in fact 'compossibilities', that is to say some are not consistent with others. So God does not have an infinite number of possible choices. He sees the whole extent of the history of the possible worlds and then makes his choice.

The result of all these comparisons and deliberations is the choice of the best from among all these possible systems, which wisdom makes in order to satisfy goodness completely; and such is precisely the plan of the universe as it is.[4]

What is possible now becomes real as God wills it into being by his act of creating. Leibnitz speaks of God as freely creating. The production of the world is an act of divine freedom. Creation is not necessary, but an act God chooses to perform. By this act of divine freedom God decrees the existence of 'the whole sequence' which shall constitute human history. This does not mean that human beings have no freedom. A predestinarian view appears to deny the possibility of human freedom, since foreknowledge of what man will do and man's freedom in doing what he does have appeared to many people to be incompatible. Leibnitz and others, notably Au-

4 G. W. Leibnitz, *Theodicy*, 225.

gustine,[5] deny that this is the case. God can foreknow and man be free. God willed the whole course of human history within which human beings make free choices. That God knows beforehand what those choices are does not make them any the less free.

What this means is that evil is willed by God as a part of the whole history which God wills. In the best of all possible worlds, evil has a contribution to make to the whole. Indeed, it would be a fault not to permit evils, since they are instrumental to the production of good. So Leibnitz finds illustrations of evils which conduce to good, and these serve as models of the function of evil in the cosmos. Taken by itself the negative is not good, but in the context of a whole greater than itself it contributes to the total good, like discord contrasts to harmony and like shadows highlight colour. Thus evil is functional in a good world.

We raise two questions; What sort of consistent other worlds can we imagine? What status do our imaginings have with regard to the understanding of the creation? Consider what conditions would have to have to be fulfilled for a leibnitzian exercise to take place. It seems one would have to put oneself in the position of transcendence of any earthly conditions, physical and historical. One would have to stand (so to speak) in equality with the deity before the creative act and consider as he (according to the explanation) was doing. One would have to know what he knew. However, how can we speak of a 'context' before there was any cosmos, let alone a context in which we might place ourselves as the questioners?

That is impossible, and the idea beyond comprehension. How would one even in that position be able to imagine the possibilities the divine mind was contemplating? How does a creature before the event of creation discern the distinction between an imagined but impossible to create world and an imagined and possible world. How could a limited and fallible creature conclude that there were several possible worlds, give details of each and before seeing how

---

5 That God sees beforehand what we will do does not entail that we are not free in doing it. God foresees that human beings will act freely. Augustine, *The City of God*, v. 9.

the game played out in the course of the several histories, judge which was preferable to others.

5   Theistic Denial of Dualism

See 10.3.

CREATION: WORK SHEET

1. Relate the doctrine of God's providence to the conviction of the uniformity of nature, and the consistency of natural law.

2. How do different beliefs about God lead to different interpretations of providence?

3. Why did some important Christian thinkers about creation feel indebted to Plato's account of the craftsman?

4. Is God responsible for the evil that exists as a result of the creation of the cosmos?

5. Is Leibnitz's defence convincing?

8 PROVIDENCE, CAUSE AND EFFECT

We can often find out what causes what. We are aware that there is regularity in nature and take it for granted in physical and personal relations. We are often not content until we find out causes, especially of events that are of importance to us. Believers often claim that God has acted, especially when something unexpected and good has taken place, for example, when a healing takes place in answer to prayer. Should we not ask 'how?', as we ask it of how the doctor enabled a cure? If God is cause, there must be a manipulation on a physical scale, an influencing of subsequent events by introducing something new as cause.

8 PROVIDENCE, CAUSE AND EFFECT

This is the belief we are now going to consider:

God acts in the world to direct events as he sees fit. He answers prayer by hearing and responding, by acting in the cosmos.

1   Act of God?

Here is a story and a question from a well known theologian. It expresses a problem for anyone who believes that God guides the forces in the world to produce results that would not have taken place without his intervention.

The question concerns what it means to say that an event or a course of events is an 'act of God'. For if God acts within the world he must manipulate the system of causes and effects We know no other way of explaining how an event is caused. We therefore have to give due consideration to the ideas of cause and effect.

A former next-door neighbour of mine was an avid football fan who liked to follow the 'Irish'; if I remember rightly, he was a Notre Dame alumnus. But in the Chicago suburbs it is not usually possible to pick up the away games live on television from South Bend. He solved the problem one summer when I was on vacation: I came back to find an enormous antenna towering over my two-storey home. I should think it must have been capable of picking up any Big Ten game, not only from South Bend but within several hundred miles. It was like living next door to the headquarters of the state police;

only the flashing red light that warns off friendly aircraft was missing.

Seeing I was a bit apprehensive, my neighbour pointed out all the fine features of his new antenna. It was sunk deep in concrete, and he demonstrated the sturdiness of the metal frame by climbing up it for me. This, I grant, was impressive, because he had a footballer's physique that had spread with advancing years. So, I was not particularly anxious when he moved and left the antenna standing.

But it fell. During a windstorm the antenna fell on the front of my house, buckling the gutters, and then crashed through my favourite evergreen on to the lawn. Now my lawn is not a suburban showpiece, I must admit, and one of my new neighbours pointed out that the antenna could have fallen on one of my children. 'Somebody up there,' he said, 'is watching over us.' But, not having quite regained my composure, I replied thoughtlessly, 'Then why didn't he stop it from falling on my gutters?'

The insurance agent was theologically of the same persuasion as my neighbour: What had happened, he explained, was an act of God, and therefore his company could not accept financial responsibility. But when a repairman came, he attributed the fall to metal deterioration plus the force of the wind; he did not mention God. Presumably, neither my neighbours nor the insurance agent would have cared to deny the repairman's diagnosis. They would not have said he was a wicked sceptic who disbelieved in God. and I found myself asking, What exactly did God do? What does he ever do? What do we mean by 'acts of God?'[1]

(1) The Christian Theme

Providence means that God is at work in the universe, sustaining it. God is the cause of events that take place within our world.

---

1 B. A. Gerrish, *A Prince of the Church*, pp. 43-44.

(2) Relevance of Philosophical Discussion to the Christian Theme

In the normal run of life, we often know quite well how to go about giving an explanation of something that happens. We also have procedures of explaining more complex phenomena, provided we can categorise them in relation to the world of our experience, where things happen regularly and predictably. What shall we do when as believers we attempt to explain events that we say God brought about, perhaps in answer to prayer? What does it mean to bring about an event that otherwise would not have taken place?

What does it mean to say that the Creator causes events that take place within the cosmos, as believers in providence say? What does it mean to claim that God sustains and provides for the cosmos? Some Christians say that God predestines events within it, even events within a person's life, while he himself is transcendent to the cosmos. Believers also say that God causes events outside of the cosmos. There is a whole transcendent world over which God exercises control. How shall we understand and explain that claim? What status can we give to such claims if the believer chooses not to attempt to explain them but simply accept them as given?

(3) Exposition: Questions we address

What kinds of explanation are there of what takes place in the world? How can we think of God as cause of what takes place in the world? What do we mean by 'cause.' What is a cause? How shall we conceive the cause-effect relation?

To understand you have to know the language, know how the terms are used. You can't adequately state or intelligently discuss a problem unless you know how the words are being used. In philosophy, terms are used precisely and do not always have the same meanings as when they are used in our ordinary parlance.

So there are two preliminary stages:

(1). Learn the meaning of the terms,
(2). Try to state the problem using those terms.

(3). Then comes the job of trying to answer the questions, solve the problems.

Now we are going to list some relevant terms and state their meaning.

Event: something that happens, anything that takes place.

Type of event: a classification of multiple events according to a particular concept e.g. frightening, exciting, profitable, miraculous.

Phenomenon: another term for event or object.

Temporal succession: one thing happening after another.

Regularity: constancy of events happening, giving rise to expectation and so a basis for prediction of like events. The basis for laws of nature.

Contingency, contingent: (1) common understanding: sometimes unexpected or chance, non-regular happening of an event or of one event after another or of contemporaneous events. A synonym for the term is **accidental**. (2) philosophical: the simultaneous happening of two or more events.

Perception: sensing something, sometimes called experience or sense-experience.

Sense: seeing, hearing, tasting, touching, smelling.

Kinds: classes or divisions we put things into when in some respects some things are like other things, e.g. dogs, neutrons, truces, eclipses, misunderstandings

Condition: if event *b* does not happen unless event *a* happens then event *a* is a condition for event *b*. If an event does not occur without another event also occurring, that prior event is a condition for the later one: e.g. switching on the gas, getting a flame. If you don't switch on the gas, you won't get a flame.

Contiguity: togetherness in space. Bat hits ball. Bat and ball at the moment of impact are contiguous.

Constant conjunction: the relation of events that are always experienced together: blowing of whistle, hearing of sound.

Regular succession: events that are always conjoined in that one is always followed by the other: e.g. jumping into water, getting wet.

Counterfactual: a conditional statement setting together two phenomena: e.g. If A had not happened, B would not have happened, or If A does not happen, B does not happen: e.g. If the glass had not been struck with the hammer, it would not have shattered. If the glass is not struck, it does not break. The counterfactual can be negative or affirmative as e.g. If the dog should bite Leila, she will scream.

Realism: the idea that objects we perceive exist independent of our perceiving them. e.g. I see a rose. The rose is independent of my seeing it. I hear the sound of a log falling. The log is independent of my hearing it. The ball is spherical independent of my seeing it as such.

Now think:

We are aware of events following one another in temporal succession. To do so we must be able to identify objects: antenna, house. Take for example our story at the beginning of the chapter. The antenna falls on the house. We perceive a series of sensations. Our perceptions take place one after the other, i.e. in temporal succession. First I see the antenna falling. Then I see it crashing on to the house. I then hear it crashing.

Some kinds of events we always associate with other kinds of events. For example, we associate the insertion of pins in human bodies with the occurrence of pain. There is usually some order in our apprehending/experiencing of things or events. The question is. Do events which we apprehend in this order happen in this order?

Having distinguished events happening in an order from our experiencing of those events in an order, we can ask, Is the relation between the events which regularly happen and which we apprehend that of cause and effect? Is regularity of temporal succession equivalent to cause and effect?

What we usually do when we ask, 'What caused phenomenon A?' is to select only one among several causes. We never list all the possible conditions that lead to an event. When someone asks 'What caused the fire?' we do not give a list of all the physical conditions. We are not answering a question in an exam in physics. A comprehensive account could be almost endless, a whole history of the universe. We usually are satisfied with such an answer as 'The cause was a spark.' So we select the immediate condition necessary for this particular event (phenomenon), and give that as the cause of the fire. We pick out the relevant condition that suits our explanation, that under the particular circumstance counts as and is accepted as an explanation.

One last point follows from the comment about relevant conditions. Some conditions must occur if an event is to happen, but of themselves are not sufficient to produce it. For example, there must be petrol in the tank for the car to start. But that is not sufficient for the car to start. Other conditions must be present. When all the conditions that make it possible for the car to start are present, we speak of the lot as a set of **necessary conditions** and call that lot a **sufficient condition**. There usually are quite a few necessary conditions for the occurrence of an event. They must all be included in the sufficient condition. Given the sufficient condition the event will occur.

See if you have got the idea by trying the following exercise:

List some of the conditions necessary for a pie to cook. Put them all together and see whether your list constitutes a sufficient condition. Then try the same exercise for the following:

The statue topples
The ball breaks the window
The baby cries.

2   Cause as Necessary and Sufficient Condition

Take the case of **troubleshooting.** Essentially this is a search for the cause of the trouble. We have identified the trouble. The search then begins for what is responsible for it. But there are several causes, not just one. So the aim is to locate the relevant causes, and usually one or two in particular. This is done by connecting one (or more) states of affairs with others. We simply say, if this, x, had not happened, that, y, would not have. But it is sometimes extremely hard to locate the x. Often, as just remarked, there is more than one contributing state of affairs to make up the causal x : x1, x2, x3.... We do not need to be too technical to understand this.

I have a cook book open in front of me. I shall quote from it.

What went wrong?
CAKES
Fruit sinking to the bottom of the cake?

This may be caused by

Damp fruit
Sticky glace cherries.
Too soft a mixture
Opening or banging the oven door while the cake is rising
Using self raising flour where the recipe requires plain or
Using too much baking powder.[2]

This is our starting point. We shall need to add a few conditions without which nothing to do with cake, neither right nor wrong, would result, for example:

Obtain the ingredients
Mix the ingredients
Put the dough in a pan
Put the pan in the oven
Switch the oven on
Adjust to the proper temperature
Set the timer

Further possible conditions might have obtained at the inopportune moment:

---

2 *Good Housekeeping Home Baking.* London: Ebury Press, 1977, p. 121.

The ringing of the telephone
A persistent knocking at the door
A sudden attack of some illness
A lapse of memory
A power failure

It is quite clear that a simple result is the product of multiple conditions, whether what results is a well baked cake or one with some fault or other. (There are many more examples in the cook book quoted.)

We can now generalise from such an illustration and attempt to state the principle it illustrates. What results is the following definition. Cause is an **INUS condition**. That needs explaining. An effect results from a combination of different causes. There may not be just one single set of conditions that produces the same effect. No single condition in the combination is *sufficient* to produce the effect, as in the example of the cake. Cause is thus defined as **an insufficient but necessary part of an unnecessary but sufficient condition.**

What we normally do when asked for the cause is to select a single condition, and propose that as *the* cause. Different people often produce a different condition as *the* cause. They cite what they believe is the most immediate and relevant condition. If asked they would reveal that they know quite well that to cite one single cause as *the* cause is unsatisfactory as an adequate and complete explanation.

There has been a robbery and we need an explanation. So we ask 'What caused the robbery, R?' Any one of the following might be selected as *the* cause.

A The door was left unlocked.
B The lock was faulty and so easy to break.
C No-one was at home.
D The burglar found the key.
E The robber was in debt and desperate for money.

But even as we select one of these conditions and propose that as *the* cause of the burglary, we are well aware that, in addition to the one we specify there is a whole set of conditions we did not mention.

But consider the list of possible causes A to E above. Try putting them together from the symbols. That is good for you and it saves me doing it. Spell out the formulas immediately below. The same effect, R, might well have been caused by the following combinations of conditions

> A+C+E caused R
> C+D+E caused R
> B+D+E caused R

That means that no one set of these three conditions by itself is alone, i.e. exclusively, sufficient to produce the effect. There are alternatives. So if we want a formula that reflects this we will say that each of these alternatives is sufficient but is not necessary to produce the effect. Why not? It is not necessary because there are alternatives. Each of the proposed causes is an INUS condition: an insufficient but necessary condition of the effect. No one of these causes, neither A nor B nor C nor D nor E is sufficient of itself to cause R. But each one is an element in a set of conditions that jointly necessitate its effect, that is it is sufficient to produce it. The cause we single out is a necessary part of a set of conditions. When that set of conditions occurs the effect also occurs.

Conclusions:

The complex (ACE or CED or BDE) represents a condition which is both necessary and sufficient for R.

Each conjunction represents a condition which is sufficient but not necessary.

None of the single factors A, B, C, D, E is either a necessary or a sufficient condition for R.

The problem with this explanation is that we have to be quite sure that the list of causes is comprehensive before we can claim that we have discovered the necessary and sufficient condition and so the cause. Sometimes this may be possible.

3   The Concept of Event

An event is something that happens, an occurrence, a taking place. An event may be very complex, or it may be quite simple. The apparently simplest event involves relationships which can lead us into discussion of matters apparently only remotely connected with it. Every event is contained within a web of antecedent and consequent influences. Some set it in motion. Others it sets in motion. No event is isolated. Every event takes place within a totality, call it 'world.' It is possible to abstract an event in thought, to hold up one particular happening out of the catena of antecedents and consequents. Thus it may be easy, but deceptive, to think that the event is isolated, and to talk of such an event apart from the relationships in which it stands.

Let's suppose we want to inquire further back. The question then is, 'How far back?' Would we not have to take into account not only the catena of relationships we can be aware of from yesterday and from last week, but also the wide spreading relations which make our universe possible and that go back to the very beginning and include everything relevant in between? For every cause takes place within the complex system of the cosmos. Every condition demands relations with other conditions in an ordered system. A cause within the system demands the system to sustain it and to make it possible. Where the cause is a particular action of an individual person the existence of that person is taken for granted. But that person has a particular history which virtually embraces the whole of history. Why am I alive? Why do I exist so that I may, through my willing act, produce a necessary and sufficient condition for a particular state of affairs to emerge? Well there is my father and his father and his father, my mother her mother and her mother and so on, and so on.

4   God and Conditions

Without the continuing existence of a natural, ordered system, a system with *logos*, there could be no investigation, even on the simplest scale. So in considering the necessity of this complex of necessary conditions, what does it mean to say that God's action is a cause of a phenomenon or an event? What does it mean to say that God brings it about that a sufficient condition prevails and so an effect results? When the theist says that God sustains the whole system, does he say as an additional claim that he causes particular events within the system? If the theist says that the system runs independently, he may still wish to say that God is the cause of individual events and existences within that 'self-sustaining' system. That would imply that God arranges the particular set of conditions sufficient to bring the effect about. For any particular effect is, as we have seen, the product of a set of necessary and sufficient conditions. These conditions must be in place for the effect to occur. If they are not in place, they must be put in place. If God causes the effect he must arrange their co-incidence. And that is the problem. How do we know that, given the necessary and sufficient conditions for the effect, that set of conditions has been arranged by a power outside and transcendent to the system?

The problem is acute when the claim is made that a miracle has occurred. But it is also a problem when there is a quite rational, scientific explanation of the occurrence of natural events. A person extremely ill makes a remarkable recovery and the doctors can explain it in the terms of their trade. The believer may still wish to claim that God answered prayer and produced the healing. But sometimes no such medical explanation of the healing is forthcoming. The believer may then claim that God was active in the inexplicable recovery. The doctors however will not permit us to say that the incident of recovery is in principle inexplicable. They will simply confess that at present they do not know what the cause was and remain agnostic regarding the claim of divine intervention. That is in harmony with the scientific attitude in general. We may in the future find adequate explanation for what is now inexplicable. In the meantime we hold that an adequate and rational explanation is in principle possible. We must wait, work and be patient. There may be such developments in our understanding that what we cannot now explain we may be able to at some future time.

5   The Idea of a Class or Type of Event

To manage our understanding we put events and objects into classes. The class is determined by concept we create: e.g. vintage car, flu virus. So we say whenever event buying vintage car (V) occurs someone spends a lot of money (M). Which formally becomes: Whenever an event of type x occurs (in this case V) an event of type y occurs in this case (M). Or, Whenever an event of type y occurs an event of type x occurs. These examples are cases of necessary and sufficient conditions respectively.

6   The Repeatable and the Non-Repeatable

We often define the possible in terms of the repeatable. So we try to see if we are able to investigate the causes of unexpected events. We sometimes explain them by successfully probing for their causes. What puzzles us is the occurrence of the non-repeatable counter instance. What baffles us is that we sometimes do not find an explanation of it by being able to state the cause of the phenomenon in question. The fact is that we know much less about the causes of some phenomena than we do of others.

Distinguish the realm of nature from the realm of history. For history does not repeat itself. Historical events are unique. In the realm of nature we investigate by observing repeatable natural events. We are able then to classify such repeatable events and produce 'laws' to identify what we can expect to take place on the basis of observed repetition of types of events. There are no such framing of laws in historical investigation. In speaking of law governed events we are in the realm of the natural world. The historian may have to deal with reports of unusual, unrepeatable events. He does so by evaluating the plausibility of reports and witnesses as evidence. The question of the possibility of non-repeatable events from the point of view of the scientist demands a different approach. It is this we discuss here and later.

A minimal description of miracle might be in terms of 'non-repeatable counter instance'. But this description would fit other phenomena beside miracles.

The important principle of repeatableness works like this. If we can find out what the conditions are for producing a particular effect we have experienced, we may then go on to produce these conditions. When we do we shall expect the same effect to result. This is based on the fact, on which we rely, of the regularity of nature. So we ask, 'What are the necessary and sufficient conditions for producing this effect?' We have observed what these conditions have repeatedly been. Then we produce these conditions. We then expect and are regularly rewarded with the same effect. It is this expectation that sustains us in coping with life, and is anticipated in scientific research. If the expected result does not occur we re-examine the proposal we are making about the set of conditions. In this way we make progress toward knowledge.

No event is causeless. To put it in other words all events are effects. There is no event that is not an effect. When we apply this principle to the task of the historical evaluation of testimony and reports, we shall find that it excludes certain kinds of claim, such as the claims to most extraordinary events. We disallow such interpretations and say that the event *as reported* was impossible. It could not have happened. We may then go on to ask why the purported testimony included such events? What did the writer have in mind, and what would his readers understand by his writing? What were their assumptions which I do not share? What am I to understand?

A bag of buns does not feed five thousand people, let alone produce twelve baskets of leftovers. What a different world we would live in if, given the right causes, bread and fish multiplied by the thousand-fold. We could imagine contests where children with bags of food would compete to see who could feed the most people and who could produce the greatest amount of surplus. Great TV fodder that! Keep an accurate tally there! How many people did Sue feed? Weigh Johnny's group's leftovers to the ounce! Not our world! Indeed never our world!

7   Angel Activity

There is a tree whose large branches are threatening to fall on my house. I get someone to come and remove the threat to property, life and limb. If you ask me how it was done I can describe the agent who did it, the methods he employed, and the instruments he used.

If I have a loose wheel on my car, and I get it fixed, I can identify the mechanic and, within the limits of my ability, describe *how* he did *what* he did to produce the result. There has to have been a series of actions to bring about the result. We can describe in detail what those measures were.

Here is a child dying of malaria. But she does not die. The physician intervenes by introducing medicines and treatments that make all the difference. He can explain what he did, the method he employed, the particular medicines etc. he used to effect the cure, the instructions he left with his assistants etc.

If something is prevented, something must be done to prevent it. If something is accomplished something must be done to accomplish it. Often an agent is needed, in characteristic cases, to produce a different physical condition. Under normal circumstances we can quite readily describe the agent and how that agent did what was necessary to bring about the outcome.

Take a few examples in Scripture of prevention and initiation by angels, supernatural beings getting extraordinary results in the natural and human world.

'I will rebuke the devourer for you, so that it will not destroy the fruits of your soil: and your vine in the field shall not fail to bear, says the Lord of hosts' *Malachi* 3:11 (RSV).

'Then Daniel said unto the king, "O king live for ever! My God sent his angel and shut the lions' mouths and they have not hurt me"' *Daniel* 6:21 (RSV).

'And that night the angel of the Lord went forth, and slew a hundred and eighty-five thousand in the camp of the Assyrians; and when men arose early in the morning, behold, these were all dead bodies' *II Kings* 19:35 (RSV).

In each case we can ask two questions: first. *What* had to be done to produce the result? Second, *how* was it done?

What is reported in the scriptural accounts is the result of the intervention: in the first passage, that it shall be done, the destruction of the devourer; in the second and third passages that it has been done, the immobilisation of the lions and the massacre of the Assyrian army.

But *what* did the angel do in each case? *How* physically did the angel bring the result about? For there must be or have been physical intervention in each case. There must have been direct introduction of causes that were not originally in place. Nothing just happens causeless! *Ex nihilo nihil fit.* The bugs don't just stop biting. Lions don't naturally keep their mouths shut. To kill one hundred thousand human beings takes enormous energy, effort and resolution.

In the normal cases the agents could produce a detailed report of how the results were achieved. In no case is there such a report in the angel cases. Supernatural agency is simply asserted.

Perhaps the reader would like to know how the angels did what they did. Or, perhaps there are different kinds of question to be asked.

8 Open Theism

Process philosophy has had influence in many directions. Within the context of evangelical circles it has given the incentive and provided the concepts for 'open theism'. Dissatisfied with the orthodox expositions of omnipotence, omniscience and omnipresence, writers have employed the ideas from the panentheism of process philosophy to address questions concerning the relation of God to the world, including the problem of explaining how God is related to the future. So the older debate about predestination, God's foreknowledge and related topics undergoes a transformation, as the classical debates between Calvinists and Armenians are reconsidered, and in being questioned, shown to be questionable. To engage in those discussions in any detail, while interesting, would take us beyond the scope of this writing. [See 12.7]

Already in 1965 John Cobb had written:[3]

> Much that occurs is profoundly contrary to that at which God aims. The guidance of God is often, if not usually, thwarted. His purposes are therefore frequently ineffective. He constantly readjusts his aim to the partial successes and partial failures of the past so that some new possibility of achievement always lies ahead. The effectiveness of God's providential concern depends upon the receptivity and responsiveness of man, yet the outcome is not simply the product of human effort.

To pursue the topic, as discussed within evangelical circles, take as an introduction: Richard Rice, *The Openness of God*. Washington D.C.: Review and Herald 1980, and follow this with Clark H. Pinnock (ed). *The Openness of God: A Biblical Challenge to the Traditional Understanding of God*. Downer's Grove, Illinois: Inter-Varsity Press, 1994. The concern in both of these writings is to show that the 'open God' is consonant with the teachings of Scripture. and illuminating of problems debated in traditional discussions of providence, particularly the omnipotence, omniscience and omnipresence of God.

---

3   John B. Cobb, Jr, *A Christian Natural Theology*, p. 251.

CAUSE AND EFFECT: WORK SHEET

1. Distinguish event from kind of event.

2. Attempt to define the following terms in relation to different events and kinds of events e.g. the wind blows, Mary loses her hat, the leaves fall from the trees, John's car does not start, Fred's tooth aches, The house lights go off.

> priority
> succession
> regular succession
> ideas (of successive events)
> association
> contiguity
> regularity
> accidental regularity
> unique sequence
> correlation (of two events and of two kinds of events)
> necessary connection
> power (Locke's definition)

3. Give examples of the following:

(1) Two kinds of events are correlated. Neither causes the other, but there is a third event causing both.

(2) Two kinds of events are correlated. Neither causes the other. They do not have a common cause. There is nothing that determines that they happen synchronously at the times they do.

(3) Two kinds of event always occur at the same time though one is the cause of the other and not the other way around.

4. Write an essay: God at work in the world.

Questions to address; What it means to say 'x causes y.' What does it mean to say that the Creator causes events that take place within the cosmos, as believers in providence believe that God sustains and provides for the cosmos? Some Christians hold that God predestines events within it, even within a person's life, while he himself is transcendent to the cosmos. Believers also say that God causes events outside of the cosmos in the heavenly sphere. What is the status of such claims if the believer chooses not to attempt to explain them?

9 AKRASIA AND SELF-DECEPTION

'The good that I would I do not. The evil that I would not that I do' (cf. Romans 7:15). Such is Paul's description of the human predicament. It finds a parallel in the philosophers' discussion of moral weakness and then of self-deception. These concepts shed light on the Pauline assessment of the human predicament.

One knows what a better course of action would be. One chooses a worse course. We do not always convert a good intention into appropriate action.

It is not only possible but sometimes frequent that we believe a lie. We are sometimes deceived by a third party. But is it possible to tell ourselves a lie and then believe the lie we tell ourselves? Is such irrationality a feature of human life?

9 ARISTOTLE'S *AKRASIA* AND SELF-DECEPTION

1 Aristotle's Exposition

Akrasia, 'incontinence', is weakness of will, weakness of character, weakness, acting against reason. We see what it is good to do. We 'believe', we 'know', we are conscious of what it is good to do. We do something else. The term *incontinence,* the usual rendering in English of *akrasia,* suggests that one does not restrain oneself from doing what one knows that it is not good to do. It is not a case of impotence, as if one were fated. It is an activity, either positive or negative, of the self, but, it seems, of a divided self.

a. Aristotle's procedure in discussion is first, to state the beliefs commonly held; then to list questions and puzzles which such common beliefs suggest and finally to consider the essential problems these raise.

b. Plato held that if a person knows what is right, that person will do what is right. He held

> knowledge is a noble and commanding thing, which cannot be overcome, and will not allow a man, if he only knows the difference of good and evil, to do anything which is contrary to knowledge . . . . no man voluntarily pursues evil, or that which he thinks to be evil.[1]

Aristotle had Plato's position in view as he discussed *akrasia*. It is an interesting philosophical question because it is not clear how it is even possible for a rational being.

---

1 *Protagoras* 352, 358.

c. Aristotle conceives the problem widely. For him good is not always moral good. If we talk of 'wickedness' we narrow the problem unduly, since this suggests a moral dimension. Some of the problems do not have moral overtones. Put in general terms, it is the failure to convert intention into action that is the problem. We intend to do something good. We intend not to do something that is not good. But we do not do what we intend. Or, if our intention is to refrain from doing something we know is not good, we go ahead and do it anyway. We do not refrain from doing what we intend not to do. We do not restrain ourselves. We might well ask 'Is *akrasia* possible for a rational being?' Is it a paradigm case of the irrational? We see what it is good to do. We are conscious of (we 'believe', we 'know') what it is good to do. We do something else. We are conscious of what we should not do. We do it in spite of this consciousness. We do not carry out our intentions.

d. Aristotle presented us with two distinct problems: (1) Can we make sense of a person's knowingly choosing a particular worse course of action when he considers an alternative course of action, both available to him and better for him? (2) How could one's soul be in a particular state — that of having understanding and knowledge — and that state not rule?

e. Aristotle's definition of *akrasia*: a person decides that a certain course of action would be best for him and then acts against his own judgment. Aristotle widens the concept to include ordinary cases of giving in to temptation, where the agent knew better. He then gives his explanation of the phenomenon by suggesting (1) that, at the appropriate moment, when the agent decides, the knowledge is not occurring, (2) that there are cases where the relevant knowledge is not present to consciousness because the agent does not realize that the relevant facts are present, and (3) also that the knowledge has been pushed aside by passion.[2]

f. A definition of *akrasia*, stricter than Aristotle's, is of a situation in which

      i. an agent performs an action intentionally,

---

2 *Nicomachean Ethics.* I. 13.

ii. the agent believes an alternative action is open to him,

iii. the agent judges that on balance, i.e. all things considered, it would be better to perform the alternative action he does not perform rather than the one he does.

g. Discussion of *akrasia* leads easily to the problem of self-deception and its logical puzzles. Can a person deceive himself, believe what he knows is false and act in accordance with the falsehood he tells himself and believes? Is self-deception possible and if so a paradigm example of *akrasia*? Further, is it a true description of the human condition? Paul called that human condition sin, indwelling evil, and saw it as universal (cf. *Romans* 7). Is that irrationality characteristic of the human condition?

h. We have already noted that philosophical discussion can illuminate beliefs held by the Christian. Paul had given a pessimistic analysis of the human condition. He wrote:

> for that which I do I allow not: for what I would that do I not; but what I hate that do I . . . . for the good that I would I do not: but the evil which I would not that I do. Now if I do that I would not, it is no more I that do it, but sin that dwelleth within me. I find then a law, that, when I would do good, evil is present with me. *Romans* 7:15-21 (A.V.)

While the apostle focussed upon the failure to practise moral or religious obligation, Aristotle's definition of *akrasia* was of a much wider application. Aristotle's 'good' referred to my health, also to what I have to do if I wish to achieve a worthy goal etc. So smoking and laziness might well feature as illustrations of his account.

2 Holding Contradictory Beliefs. Is Self-Deception Possible?

The term **self-deception** is sometimes used in a very loose way. It is easy to put 'self' in front of 'deception' when the self has been passive in accepting a falsehood. When someone believes something false, and we consider that false belief unreasonable we may say, but say wrongly, that the person is self-deceived, when we mean only that he believes what is false and could have believed what is true instead. He is simply deceived. That deception may be the result of someone deliberately telling him a falsehood, or it may be the result of his not having looked into the evidence adequately. In any case he is simply deceived. But he has not, even if it is possible, deliberately deceived himself.

If we are going to speak carefully we will distinguish believing something false from self-deception even if self-deception entails believing something false. Something more has to be said.

So we shall distinguish two kinds of false believing: a. believing falsehood, not knowing it is false and b. believing falsehood, knowing it is false. Let's take these in turn.

a. is a common enough occurrence. There are enough agents who will benefit from our believing falsehoods, or our not believing a truth. Salesmen and politicians come immediately to mind. There are other motivations than gaining profit or power for an agent to tell you a lie and hope you will believe it. Why do parents tell children lies about Father Christmas, the Easter bunny? Motivations differ but the different instances have something in common. I am led to believe a falsehood because of the initiative of another person, or of a community.

When I am unaware that the falsehood I believe is false, I may be content with believing it and doing nothing. For I may not be aware that there are alternatives. What chance does a young child stand when the adult world conspires to have it believe the fabrications about Santa Claus? In due course the once deceived person may learn that what he has believed is false and then will abandon the belief. He may or he may not find an alternative that is reasonable and true. The rational thing to do at any rate is to abandon the belief I now know to be false.

b. The second case is that I may know that what I believe is false and still retain the false belief. This differs from (1) in my being aware of the status of my belief. I know it is false, and so irrational to believe it. I believe it nevertheless. So some response, activity, failure to act on the part of the self is required for self-deception to occur. The self is here involved as it is not in the case of being deceived by a third party. Since such self-deception is irrational we can ask whether it is really possible. If we answer that it is, we must then conclude that human existence is often irrational, that there is an endemic irrationality to our human condition, and that (as Paul has said) would be wretched indeed.

This leaves us with another problem mentioned at the outset in connection with the idea of conscious beliefs: Is it possible to hold contradictory beliefs? It seems impossible that one should hold a belief and also its contradictory. That would be to affirm and to deny the same belief at the same time, to believe that it is and that it is not so. Is it the case that sometimes we want to believe both that something is so and also to believe that it is not so. Can it happen that we are aware that we should believe something we desperately do not want to believe and then by some process or other believe the opposite without abandoning the unwelcome belief. That is quite irrational. But it does seem at least possible. What seems to take place is rather the converse. We have evidence for an unpleasant fact we do not want to accept. We want to believe the opposite. So we persist with our congenial belief. Does this result in a conflict state? Is one belief repressed in the process, but still held? Can one purposely refuse to face the truth, while believing that it is the truth that one is refusing? Or is it, as a classic treatment suggests, a 'refusal' to spell out one's engagements. One just does not engage oneself in examining, as one should, the nature and implications of what one affirms and what one refuses. The case of self-deception when this takes place amounts to a deliberate refusal to believe reasonably.[3] Jones refuses to believe that his son is guilty. A man deserted by his mistress believes he is still loved. A ship owner sends an unworthy ship to sea, knowing that it is not seaworthy but deceiving himself that it is. Someone believes he is a great artist. A Christian believes that certain miracles happen,

---

3 Fingarette, p. 47.

as the Old Testament writings suggest and reports from Lourdes maintain, while also believing in their impossibility.

One may have a belief and not be aware of it. Also one may, by a deliberate effort, become conscious of holding beliefs of which one was not previously aware. Self-deception requires a presence of two beliefs. So, remembering that a person can have a belief of which she is not aware at a given moment we can ask whether the situation is one of the following in which a person has two beliefs: The self-deceived lacks awareness of one of the beliefs, or lacks awareness of both, or has an awareness of both.

The movement in thought is from the case of a two person deception to a one person case. The question then arises whether the analogy holds. Is it rational to move from the one to the other? Can the idea of two persons with differing knowledge and belief be made an analogy of a single person's duality of belief and knowledge? Someone who deceives me causes me to believe something that he knows is false but that I do not. If the analogy applies to the one person case of self-deception, the deceiver and the deceived are one person not two. Or are they so to speak two in one? At any rate the duality must be maintained in the one person case. That person must know or have sufficient reason or evidence to show that the belief is false and yet also believe that it is true. Can there be such duality?

There are interesting parallels with *akrasia*. One writer calls self-deception and *akrasia* 'those twin puzzles'. According to Aristotle *akrasia* means acting against one's better judgment. It is a defect of character. A false belief is involved. One believes that a bad act is for the best and so accepts a false belief. How can this be? Aristotle's answer is that strong passions dominate and swamp the knowledge one has.[4] Failure is due to strong motivation.

There is a further parallel between self-deception and *akrasia*. The akratic has considered all his desires and beliefs and acts irrationally. The Aristotelian case is complicated with the acceptance of the Platonic idea that to know what is right entails acting accord-

4 *Nicomachean Ethics* VII.

ingly. So, when I know what is right how can the entailment be broken? On Plato's terms it would be impossible. Hence Aristotle in accepting that account has a very real difficulty with the idea of acting in opposition to the knowledge of what is right, what is good. He realises this, for he wrote:

> We use the word 'know' in two senses (for both the man who has knowledge but is not using it and he who is using it are said to know). It will make a difference whether, when a man does what he should not, he has the knowledge but is not exercising it, or *is* exercising it; for the latter seems strange, but not the former.[5]

He here suggests two possible situations (1) the person has knowledge but is not exercising it, (2) the person has knowledge and is exercising it. The solution is the first of these alternatives. The knowledge is dormant, not active, not brought into consciousness. So it is a blameworthy situation. The subject is culpable for not exercising himself sufficiently. The outcome is that the belief is not brought to his attention.

In self-deception the agent has apparently taken all relevant knowledge into account but has chosen to ignore some. He apparently knows and does not know simultaneously. The *akratic* acts intentionally, believing an alternative is open and judging it would he better to perform that alternative. Such things, *mutatis mutandis,* can he said of the self-deceiver. Aristotle's akratic ignores what he knows. All this involves defending the possibility of a knowledge which remains latent.

3   Two Models for Self-deception

Discussing self-deception leads us to discover answers to the questions: How do I come to hold a belief? Is it possible intentionally to get myself to believe? If so how? Do my beliefs result without my intention?

---

5   *Ibid.,* VII; 3,30.

What is clear from our experience is that, at any given point in our lives, we find ourselves with a set of beliefs. Some of these we take for granted. Others we may have struggled to achieve. The following may well be the sort of account we give of how we have sometimes come to hold a belief. We recognise evidence. We interpret the evidence. In doing so we may be motivated in various ways. We have particular desires, aversions, fears. Some beliefs are congenial to us. Other beliefs are uncongenial. Some we welcome. Some we do not. What sort of choice do we have, if any?

Self-deception is defined as believing what is false. But not all occasions when we believe falsehood are examples of self-deception. Here the false belief is, in some way initiated by the believer. It is how we come to hold the false belief that determines whether we are self-deceived. The 'self' in the term 'self-deception' indicates that we are involved in the process of believing falsely, that we are somehow active in deceiving ourselves. We may even be culpable of holding two beliefs, one of which we are aware is true and also aware that the other belief contradictory to it is false. On such an account self-deception seems impossible.

Basically there are two types of model for understanding self-deception. The traditional model is based on the analogy of one person deceiving another, sometimes called the **interpersonal model**. When Betty deceives Bill, she knows that she is getting him to believe what is false. She knows it is false, but Bill does not know that what, on her initiative he is believing, is false.

Applied by analogy to the individual the interpersonal model requires that the individual is both deceiver and deceived. The individual holds contradictory beliefs. The individual holds a true belief and a false, contradictory belief. The individual thus intends to hold a false belief, knowing or believing it to be false.

Is it the case that the self-deceived is aware and not aware at the same time? The question is, 'If I intend to deceive myself how can I not be aware of what I am doing.' But if I am aware, how can I believe my falsehood? Is the **intrapersonal model (one person)** of self-deception, derived in this way from the **interpersonal model**

(two persons), even rational? For how can one consciously and simultaneously believe two contradictory propositions? Since the situation it demands appears impossible, an alternative explanation of self-deception is demanded. In applying the interpersonal model to the intrapersonal we end with an insoluble paradox. A different basic model is needed. How shall we respond?

We can start with an obvious enough question. Is the process by which self-deception takes place deliberate? Does the subject take the required steps intentionally? Either when James and Jane are self-deceived

> a. their self-deception is intentional. They intend to believe what they know or believe is false. Or,

> b. the process is not intentional. James and Jane come to believe falsely and so they end up being self-deceived without their intention. The resulting false belief is not deliberate.

Take b as a possibility. The explanation suggested is that the process is unconscious. But it is not unmotivated The resultant self-deception occurs as a consequence of being motivated in one way or another. That motivation may be by desire or by fear or by anxiety of one kind or another.

Jane's false belief fulfils her desire, and the true belief, being unwelcome, is forgotten or consigned to the background of consciousness, or simply ignored. Something of importance is relegated, not 'spelled out'. Jane's false belief is not the result of her intending to believe falsely. It is the result of her desire that the false belief be true. Strongly desiring the false belief to be true leads her to take the further step of accepting it as true.

Jane wants to believe that her daughter will become a concert pianist. But the evidence suggests that with average grades in music and without her enthusiasm, that will not be the result. So Jane believes falsely. She becomes self-deceived. Her self-deception is not intentional. Her desire is the motive that leads her to a distorted interpretation or to a neglect of the evidence. She believes in face of the available evidence. In so believing falsely Jane is motivated by desire for the truth of her false belief and perhaps by her anxiety that it may not be true. The true belief would be most unwelcome, and so must be suppressed.

The resulting false belief may be the result of different influences motivating the subject. This happens within the context of a group or of a community, where the pressure of demand for unanimity or the desire for social acceptance on the part of the individual provides strong motivation to conform. It can result from failure to understand or from misunderstanding. Does one really believe what one does not understand, even when one professes to understand? You might convince yourself that you understand when you do not — a rather ironic form of self-deception. That is a case of asserting a belief one does not really have.

Another class of some interest is the possibility of self-deception on the part of a group, a community, a congregation. But we shall not engage in that discussion within the limits of this writing.

TUTORIAL: Fingarette's Exposition of Self-Deception

Herbert Fingarette, *Self-deception*. California: University of California Press, 2000.

Everyone who writes about self-deception gives examples of the phenomenon. Some are better than others and discussion of such examples gives rise to interesting questions. It helps us to understand what the writer means by the term. We may then ask whether the example fits the definition. Let us take some examples.

A mother believes that her criminal son is a good boy in face of the evidence (which she cannot deny) that he is a criminal.

A ship owner sends his ship to sea believing that it is sea worthy when he knows that it is not.

King Lear is self-deceived about his daughter Cordelia, who refuses to flatter him and will not exaggerate her devotion to his welfare as do her sisters.

The first two raise the basic question as to whether it is even possible to take all the evidence pro and con into account and then for the person to believe what that she knows is false.

To take the case of Lear's belief about Cordelia as self-deception provides an example of misunderstanding.

Purported cases of self-deception in a religious context are not hard to find.

All of this raises the question, 'Is self-deception even possible? How can one believe a proposition to be false when one knows it is true, or to be true when one knows it to be false. One's action may contradict one's belief and when one does not see the contradiction between one's claim or profession and one's action, another might judge that the subject is self-deceived. But such cases may not be cases of self-deception at all. The term may be applied too easily and uncritically.

The Terms of the Exposition:

lie: untruth, a statement that is false. The person telling the untruth may or may not be conscious that it is an untruth.

deceiver: a subject who gets another to believe an untruth. His action may be conscious i.e. it was that subject's intention to get the other to believe the lie.

The **analogy from other deception**: subject one tells a lie to subject two, knowing it is a lie. Subject one is thus a deceiver. Subject two believes the lie being told. Subject two is thus deceived. Subject one is a deliberate deceiver because it is his intention to get the other to credit a false statement.

The **analogy to self-deception**: For the analogy to work in the case of self-deception, two elements must be present in the case of self-deception as in the case of other deception. The features present in the case of other deception must each be present in the case of self-deception. The one subject must be both deceiver and deceived. To be deceiver he must know that the statement he is telling himself is a lie. He must know that he is telling himself an untruth and then believe that lie. To be self-deceived he must believe that the lie he is, as deceiver, telling himself is true.

Engagement: an action, belief, in which one is involved, being involved in a situation either explicit or not explicit to the subject,

Spelling out: the process of making explicit to oneself e.g. one's beliefs and motives.

Not spelling out: A wilful act: We can repress the fact of our failure to make our engagements explicit, and therefore conscious, sometimes deliberately overlooking e.g. not affirming an avowal. Then we produce a story to cover ourselves. This according to Fingarette is the beginning of self-deception.

Avowal: unconstrained admission, an inner act of acknowledgement.

Disavowal: not acknowledging that one's engagement is one's own.

Mauvaise foi: Sartre's term for self-deception.

Split ego: being engaged in the world in specific ways and not acknowledging the engagements. A failure of self identity.

A Summary of Fingarette's argument

1. To build a concept of self-deception on the model of other-deception, the cognition/perception approach, leads to paradox.

2. Sartre insists that self-deception is a conscious act of the person.

3. The Freudian defence-mechanism is an unconscious process, leading to the incapacity to recall what has been repressed.

4. Fingarette proposes to abandon the cognitive/perception approach to self-deception and proceeds to develop his own technical terminology: **spelling out** (in chapter 3) and **avowal** (in chapter 4). The context to be constructed is a **volition/action** family of terms.

5. Our engagement in the world, i.e. how we are involved, acting, experiencing, may not be clear to us because we have not spelled it out to ourselves. We have not engaged in an honest process of self-examination. So we may not be aware of our beliefs and our motivations and how our desires and beliefs influence our actions. To be fully conscious of such we must exercise a certain skill, that of 'saying' or something like 'saying,' what we are experiencing and doing. This may, but does not have to be, an explicit linguistic utterance. Normally we do not so spell out our engagements, but we could do so if we so willed. But we may not so will. Indeed, we may also avoid becoming explicit that we are not spelling out our engagement(s): i.e. fail to spell out that we are not spelling out. This is the first step toward self-deception (and its cognates, defence, *mauvaise foi*. Fingarette often classifies these together (pp. 44, 72, 82, 88), virtually identifying them. There are occasions when we should spell out our engagements to ourselves, since spelling-out is an act under our control. If we do not, we may rationalise our not doing so, and produce cover stories, disguises, etc. This 'ignoring' is genuine, a paradoxical 'wilful ignorance'. The self-deceiver now

adopts a 'self-covering policy' of not spelling out, generating an elaborate cover-story. He knows the truth which is contrary to his denials. He is both sincere and not sincere.

6. Avowal is the act of defining personal identity, i.e. of identifying oneself with one's engagements. Personal identity is constituted by avowal. This is a purposive inner act as for example when I recognise and take responsibility for my anger, my emotions, my action. Disavowal is refusal to accept one's engagement as one's own. It then becomes isolated from the influence of everything that is avowed, and entails a refusal of responsibility for what is disavowed. So the self is divided. What results is the paradox of insight with blindness in a rational being, the failure to achieve the self as a synthesis. What is initially avowed must be reaffirmed if personal integrity is to be maintained. Avowal is constitutive of personal identity, since it contributes to the formation of the self as a unity. Avowal is an action, an act, an accomplishment, not a mere happening, and so the self is an achievement. As an inner act, avowal is not identical with its expression. The doctrine of the synthesis of the self requires the concept of avowal. The self acknowledges some identity and disavows other identities.

The self deceiver isolates certain engagements from the community which is the self. This involves that one has the capacity to reject the identification of oneself engaged in the world in specific ways. Fingarette supposes that one can continue to be engaged in the world in a certain way and not acknowledge it as his personal engagement. In Freudian language, the ego has become split. Fingarette claims the support of Freud's later statement that the ego could be split. That implies, contrary to traditional Freudian teaching, that defence is (to some extent) conscious, a position Fingarette has espoused, by claiming a kinship between defence and self-deception.

Further Reading

Aristotle, *Nichomachean Ethics*, I:13; III:1-5; VII:1-10.

Herbert Fingarette, *Self-deception*. Berkeley, California: University of California Press, 2000.

SELF-DECEPTION: WORK SHEET

1. What do you think the following words or concepts mean? Give an example of each.

Wishful thinking, deception, ignorance, believing one thing (p at time^1) and another (not-p at time^2), stupidity, self-delusion, vacillation, simple lying, mistaken judgment, delusion, pretence, biased belief, suspense of judgment, irrational belief?

None of these is to be identified with self-deception. Try to distinguish each from self-deception, defined as believing the lie one tells oneself.

2. Relate each of the above to the following and give examples:
  a true\false,
  b aware\ not aware
  c available evidence,
  d to blame\ not to blame,
  e active\passive,
  f intentional\unintentional,
  g motivated\unmotivated,
  h possible\impossible,
  i probable\improbable

For example: wishful thinking may lead one to be unaware of the circumstances (b), overlook the available evidence (c), become motivated to irrational action (g), set oneself impossible goals (h).

Consciously engaging in wishful thinking may be an amusing game. What fantasies can I imagine if I were very rich!

3. Relate self-deception and examples of self-deception to the above (a –i.)

For example: allowing for the process from rejecting as false to believing as true (I am aware or not aware of the process to the falsehood believed (I am to blame for the process of such incontinence (d).

In contrast to wishful thinking where I know that it is fantasy, when self-deceived she really believes that she is a musical genius when one knows that she is not.

4. Can one know what one is not aware of? Can self-deception be unconscious? How could it then be 'deception?' Is the concept of 'repression' helpful?

5. I can believe what you don't believe. Can I believe what I don't believe? I can believe you when you lie. Can I lie to myself and 'credit my own lie'? Is there such a thing as self-deception?

10 DUALISM

Christian doctrine denies a plurality of gods. This finds expression in the teaching of creation. God is the one and supreme cause of the cosmos. There is no conflict with ultimate powers.

Christian teaching also insists on the unity of the person. When it speaks of body and soul it does not set them in opposition. In speaking of the survival of death, the unity of the person is to be preserved. Is some form of dualism here acceptable?

An explanation of how to account for mental activity cannot speak only in biological terms of brain activity. We may not neglect the fact that our experiences have a particular quality of 'feeling'.

10 DUALISM

1 The Concept

First, we explain the concept of **dualism**. We then discuss dualism in relation to three topics: the human person, creation, survival.

Monism teaches that there is ultimately only one thing, or that the many things are of one basic kind. Some early Greek philosophers held that there was just one kind of stuff and defined this basic stuff in different ways. Some said it was earth, others air (Anaximines), others fire (Heraclitus), others water (Thales). The first atomic theory taught that everything that exists is composed of one thing, or atoms in empty space. This is monism: 'one-thing-ism'. Its claim is that there is only one kind of substance. The basic idea is that there is one, common, underlying reality to whatever is. That reality is explicable in terms of one basic concept. Materialistic monism held that all that exists is matter. Physicalism is that form of materialism which teaches that everything is made up of those things with which physics deals. Opposed to physicalism is the claim that all things are spiritual, however they appear to us.

Dualism by contrast teaches that there are two basic substances. Reality is bifurcated. Mind and matter are quite distinct things (**substances**). Descartes (d. 1650) argued that as a thinking being, that is, as a subject of thought and experience, he could not exist only of physical matter. His essential being was non-material, mental. So conscious beings differ from inanimate things. These two substances have opposite properties: physical/spiritual, spatial/non-spatial, destructible/non-destructible, tangible/non-tangible, mortal/immortal. The problem this sets is how radically different sorts of thing can be in causal relations with one another. How can diametrically distinct kinds of thing integrate? How can a mental thought, say a resolution, produce a physical event? How can a physical event, say a loud noise, produce a mental event, say the experience of fear, or the thought that there is danger?

A general distinction is to be made between two forms of dualism. There is **substance dualism** teaching that mind or soul is a separate entity from matter, body. So there are two separate and distinct substances. There is **property dualism**: One thing has different kinds of properties. There are mental properties and there are physical properties. Property dualism may root in substance dualism. Descartes argued that a thought is a property.[1] He went further and reasoned:

If there is a thought, there is a substance to which it belongs.
There is a thought.
So, there is a substance to which this belongs.
This is a mental substance.

In contrast to this and with distinct characteristics is physical substance.

Having made this separation there arises the problem of saying what the relation between the separate entities, between the physical and the mental is. The crucial case is that of the mind in relation to the body in a living human being. If they are diametrical opposites how can they be in any relation? Answers to that crucial question differ, and give rise to different forms of dualism, each one of interest to the believer.

There are **several varieties of dualism**. (1) There is a two-way relationship: mind influences body and body influences mind. (2) There is a one way relationship typically that body (brain) influences mind, but mind does not influence body.

Cartesians teach that there is a two way causal connection between immaterial minds and material bodies. Descartes said that

---

1   *Meditation 2.*

what happens in the material world produces experiences in the mind and what happens in the mind produces bodily movements. 'The sticking point for Descartes is the difficulty of understanding how unextended mental substances could interact with extended material substances'.[2] Descartes never satisfactorily explained how a thinking, non-spatial substance could affect or be affected by a non-thinking, extended substance.

The following is a statement of Descartes' argument in defence of dualism:

> Many, indeed most, of our beliefs are dubitable, not scep-tic-proof.
> But what I cannot doubt is my doubting, my thinking, my existence.
> I can doubt that my body exists, but I cannot doubt that I, a thinking being, exist.
> Therefore, my mind is, I myself am, distinct from my body.

Causal interaction? If you deny that there can be a causal interaction between physical and mental, body and mind, you end up with parallelism and occasionalism. These attempts at explanation hold that mental events are exactly correlated with material events (parallelism), or that God wills both mental events and their material correlates into co-ordinated existence (occasionalism).

Epiphenomenalists teach that the causal connection between bodies and minds is a one way traffic, from bodies to minds but not from minds to bodies. Physical events in the brain (neurons moving) cause mental events. Mental events have no effects on physical events. Human behaviour is fully explicable in terms of such brain activity. Mind is thus an **epiphenomenon** of physical events, of neurological events that occur in the brain. Mind is an additional phenomenon i.e. of a non-physical kind. That an object possesses mental qualities, that there are mental properties

---

2 Heil, p. 29.

'makes no non-mental difference'.[3] What happens physically can be predicted on the physical level. All that is required to explain 'mental' events is an account of the physical processes involved. So explanation in terms of mental events is secondary. The mental has a purely epiphenomenological role. Mental events are by-products off-shoots, side-effects of material events. Something quite specific happens in my brain when have an experience of a sharp pain. It is a case of the motion of neurons. That is all the physicist can say about it. The neuroscientist gives his exclusive attention to the physical processes. He wants to discover the correlation between the brain event and the experience. Only that. So he does not have to be concerned with the problem of consciousness, and the problem of the nature of conscious experiences. He thinks about brain processes and need not and does not concern himself with the quality of the experience of smelling a rose or the feeling of pain. In short he is not concerned with **what it is like** to be an experiencing subject, that the particular experience has a distinctive experienced quality, say beauty or sharp pain. He explains it in terms of the physical and chemical activity in the brain.

Parallelism teaches that there is no causal connection between minds and bodies either one way or the other. It simply sets aside the idea of causal interaction. There may appear to be such interaction. What may appear is that minds interact with the material world. But the appearance is an illusion. We can relate two such series of events without speaking of a causal relationship. The two series of events run parallel. Between mental and material events there is no causal connection.

Occasionalism is a variant of parallelism. Both deny direct causal relations between the mental and the physical. The idea is that systems exist independently, but side by side.

I remember as a youth attempting to keep up on my motor bike with the Cornish Riviera express near Aldermaston on a stretch of the Great Western Railway between Newbury and Reading where the railway track runs parallel to the road. The motorbike

---

3   Heil, p. 49.

and the train were running parallel for a short while. Here were two independent systems side by side, but without any cause-effect relation whatever. How I performed made no difference to how the train performed. Similarly how the train performed made no difference to the way the motor-bike performed, as long as we were running parallel of course!

Occasionalism talks of God bringing it about that two sequences of events are causally related systems. God sees to it that a causal relation exists between two systems or two events. The motorbike and the train never collide. The dog bites me is one event. I bleed and feel pain are others. The biting is an event parallel to the bleeding and to the feeling of pain. God is sometimes introduced to provide the (causal) connection. God sees to it that they are related. God brings about the correlation between physical events and mental events.

A problem arises when we try to explain the idea of cause-effect and its function. We have no experience of 'cause-effect'. What we do experience is events taking place one after the other. We do not have experience of the relation we call cause-effect.

The relation of events taking place both simultaneously or one after the other are often different. One may be accidental and another may be causal. Certainly we do not have an experience of cause-effect comparable to the experience of feeling pain, or seeing a tiger. We think about the relation between the two events we experience, say pricking my finger and the experience of pain that follows and then try to provide an explanation of this complex of events and of the multitude of our regular experiences of one kind of event being followed by another kind of event, in short of the correlation of events. We employ an idea which enables us to give an explanation of the **regularity** we experience in the world. We are constantly experiencing the fact that some regular connections between events occur without exception. Some kinds of specifiable things always succeed other kinds of specifiable things. So our mind constructs the idea that there is a special connection between some of the events that regularly succeed one another. We cannot observe this connection in any way. We may then postulate a **necessary connection** and call it the cause-effect relation. We say A causes B when what we observe is **a constant conjunction between As and Bs**, and may then go on to speak of the connection as necessary. We seem to need more than constant conjunction to enable us to speak in this way and so that we can distinguish an accidental from a causal connection.

Lets take an example:

The twelve o'clock whistle sounds in a Nottingham factory.
The Nottingham workers think about knocking off work
Simultaneously the twelve o'clock whistle sounds in a Manchester factor.
The Manchester workers think about knocking off work.
Each event happens exactly and regularly at the same time.
One causes the Nottingham workers to think about knocking off work.
One causes the Manchester workers to think about knocking off work
Question: What connection is there between the two events?

The twelve o'clock whistle sounds in a Nottingham factory.

The Manchester workers think about knocking off work.

First we use the two ideas of contiguity and succession in a search for an answer to our question. What connection is there between the Nottingham whistle sounding and the Manchester workers thinking about knocking off work. For workers in the factory in Manchester who hear their whistle, the whistle and the thoughts of lunch are contiguous and successive (if not simultaneous). But not in the case of relations between Nottingham whistle sounding and Manchester workers' thoughts of lunch. The events may be successive, if not simultaneous. But they are not contiguous. In this case the relation is **accidental**, even if the events are simultaneous.

We have a term that can express this relation, but it is ambiguous. The relation is **co-incidental** in both senses of that term: i.e. it happens at exactly at the same time. It is simultaneous. But it is **not causally related**. It is also accidental. Nothing would change in Manchester, if things changed, viz. the whistle did not sound in Nottingham. That the relation is accidental is obvious when we answer the question, What would happen in Manchester if the whistle did not sound in Nottingham? The answer is obvious: Manchester workers would still think of lunch.

So, shall we rest with the thought that cause is to be defined in terms of contiguity and succession?

David Hume made the claim that **regular succession** should not be interpreted as a cause-effect relation. We do not experience cause-effect as a necessary connection between objects. He wrote that we can never perceive the tie that unites them. What we perceive is that they are in the relations of contiguity and succession. All we perceive is a constant conjunction between them, no more.[4]

(1) Arguments for dualism.

a. Things appear to us from a particular point of view. They have a particular 'feel' about them. We experience a particular quality when we taste a ripe peach, when we hear beautiful birdsong, when we see a sunset, when we feel the touch of rich velvet. You explain this, you say, by examining the brain and discern what changes are taking place there. I who am having the experience may know that such neurological changes are simultaneously taking place with my particular experience. But I also know that the account in such physical terms is inadequate to account for the quality of my particular experience. They are *my* experiences with a particular quality. No physical, scientific explanation can give an account of such experiences, the subjective experiences, of how things appear from the subjective point of view. The term **qualia** has come into use to designate the subjective quality of such experiences. Firing of neurons in the brain cannot account for the

4 *Treatise of Human Nature,* I. iii. XIV.

feel of the particular experience, say of seeing a beautiful sunset or smelling the fragrant perfume of a rose. The physical account is reductive. That means that the explanation is partial. It accounts only for the physics of the various experiences. It is reductionist in that it leaves out something important. It reduces the whole experience to explain only the physical aspect.

b. Appeal to physical things alone could not support the variety and complexity which is a feature of conscious beings.

c. ESP, out-of-the-body experiences producing reflections that enable the believer at least to contemplate or imagine the survival of soul without the body, post mortem.

2   Causal Connection

The idea is quite simple. One event results in, is the cause of another event. If event *a* had not happened event *b* would not have. Event *b* is the effect of event *a*. We can illustrate the general idea in different ways. The mallet hits the tent peg and, among other things, it causes a noise. Rain and sun act on the seed and it germinates and the plant grows. A bomb falls on a house and reduces it to rubble. In each case a physical cause produces physical effects.

Fire causes pain. This is an example of a physical event causing a mental event. Panic causes the subject to run. This is an example of a mental event causing a physical event. We take such regular causal connections for granted in our ordinary lives. We assume that we can explain what happens in the cosmos by taking for granted the assumption of such causal interaction which, we have noted using the terms of dualism, is a two way connection, physical to mental and mental to physical.

3   Creation and Dualism

Theism is monotheistic. Theism makes an emphatic denial of dualism in speaking of the divine, for example in developing its teaching about Creation. We are here in a different realm from that of the mind-body problem. The common feature is that we are presented in each case with the idea of two contrasting entities. There is also a relation of opposition. A characteristic dualistic doctrine of creation has two ultimate forces in the gargantuan struggle to produce a cosmos, one of which emerges as the victor and so succeeds in the task of creating. Monotheism repudiates this story. Christian doctrine emphatically refuses any element of plurality in its account of Creation. God, the creator, is transcendent. There are no rivals.

However a kind of dualism is to be found in some Christian accounts of the continuing universe, It is found classically in John Milton's *Paradise Lost* with the assertion of multitudes of angels who have rebelled against their creator and oppose him and his purposes in the great trans-terrestrial struggle for supremacy. Lucifer becomes Satan and exports the conflict to earth when it has been created. The creatures now participate in the struggle, the great controversy between God and Satan now gets played out in the creation. But this is not an ultimate dualism. Paradise may be 'lost' for a long while. But it is ultimately restored. The Christ figure is instrumental in restoring the creation to its sinless state. The evil, which constitutes the dualistic element, is ultimately removed.

4   The Human Person: Duality or Unity?

If the human person is essentially mind, sometimes also designated as spirit or soul, then future expectation of survival after the earthly human life will be of disembodied life. For the body is inessential. That conviction becomes the ground for the doctrine of the immortality of the soul, which has often been adopted in Christian circles. The material body is at best a kind of housing for the mind and its operations. As such, it is temporary. The crucial step is to assert that the mind or soul is the essential constituent of the person, the body a kind of container for it. These two are opposites. The soul is permanent and immortal. The body is temporal, ephemeral.

The dualist reckons with two 'substances'. Body is one and mind is the other. In designating what constitutes the human person, dualism provides a different answer from the unitary view to the question about what the human person is and also about the question of survival. The unity of the person is constituted by the relationship between mind and body. It is preserved with the survival of the body. That relationship is the problem the philosopher discusses.

When we reckon with two 'substances', the problem then is how these two different entities are related in the human person. What is the mind-body relationship? Dualism holds them in opposition. But we are aware of ourselves as a unity. Since we are such a unity we must find a way of describing and explaining that unity we know ourselves to be.

So what are '**mental objects**'? The answer is that broadly they are of two kinds: **sensations** and **thoughts**. These mental particulars, events, or states, have properties which identify them as that particular sensation or thought. I have a specific pain, or a throbbing in the root of my tooth. I have a particular thought, of the green field, for example. When I have a sensation, that sensation has a particular quality. That **phenomenological quality** goes by the name of **qualia**. It feels like something to have the throbbing pain of toothache. So of the particular quality we can ask the questions 'What is it like to . . . ?' Then we fill in the sentence by adding: 'feel that pain of toothache?', or 'smell the scent of the rose?' or 'taste a ripe peach'?

Thought is of a different order. I relate psychologically to a particular propositional content. Take, for example, my thought, 'The field is green'. I do not now have any sensation, but rather I bear a specific psychological relation to the content of that proposition.

5   Survival and Dualism

The dualistic understanding of the person sets two discrete sets of characteristics in opposition to one another. It judges that one is the essential and the other is the unessential feature of the person. The non-material soul is housed in a corporeal shell, and is the real self. The bodily is material. The bodily is perishable. The soul is imperishable. The list of contrasts continues at some length.

Thus when the body becomes old and finally dies, the soul continues. It achieves its true end in being disassociated from the confining, even imprisoning, body. That disassociation is a relief, and frees the soul for its real existence.

6   Is Some Form of Dualism Acceptable?

a Physical and Non-physical Properties

The property dualist appeals to a distinction between physical objects and non-physical properties related to physical objects. From the fact that all the objects in the world are physical objects it does not follow that all the properties of these objects are physical properties.

This assertion needs some unpacking. In one sense it does follow, i.e. if all objects are physical, any and all properties are properties of physical objects. It would thus seem quite natural to speak in a causal sense of all properties as physical properties. States of the physical are associated with different kinds of property, so all different kinds of such properties are physical. The question is whether such a causal theory has left something out, and if so, whether what has been left out can be explained in materialistic terms. If it cannot, the problem still remains whether the non-physical properties demand some thing other than the material for their explanation. If so we have a form of dualism.

Some Key Terms

As we proceed it is important to become familiar with some key terms, so as to get an understanding of the issues involved in the discussion.

Behaviourism teaches that human beings are physical mecha-
nisms; 'thoughts, feelings, and intentions, mental processes do not
determine what we do'. We react to stimuli. To understand human
beings demands that we observe human behaviour, not assuming
any other than physical reality.

Gilbert Ryle attacked the dualism of mind/body taught by
Descartes. There are not two substances, mind and body. The mind
is not a non-material entity. It is not an entity at all. He describes
the Cartesian theory as 'the ghost in the machine'. It is a category
mistake to think of the term 'mind' as designating a particular
entity, and states of mind as states of this entity. Ryle then gives a
behaviouristic account of the so-called 'states of mind', by speaking
of what the agent would do, or what he would be disposed to do
in given circumstances. Such activity is available for observation.
So statements about behaviour replace statements about mental
states. He speaks of 'fear' for example by talking about running
desperately, facial distortion, shouting etc.

He makes the reductionist statement of the century: 'There is
nothing "mental" about sensations.' The ground for this claim is
that sensations are not observable, neither by the external observer
nor by the subject having them: 'sensations are not objects of observation at all'.[5]

Reductionism. What is sophisticated and complex is explained in terms that simplify the complexity, usually at some price.
When we observe the behaviour of the human animal, give an adequate description of it, and attempt to set out the rules governing
it, we are undertaking a complex task. Before we can satisfactorily
discern a pattern in the phenomena involved we must provide an
adequate **description** of them. Only then will we be able to provide
an adequate **account**. Only then will the rules governing it prove
to be adequate. For the behaviourist, ('naturalist', 'physicalist' are
different names for the same kind of explanation), these will turn
out to be physical. So they explain human behaviour in terms of
the neurological workings of the brain.

5   *The Concept of Mind,* pp. 204, 207.

Observation of and physically accounting for such behaviour become the procedure for research. Mental processes do not determine what we do. Physical processes, in the case we are considering, neurological processes, do. The important thing to watch for here, is whether the explanation given is claimed to be the total explanation, one which explains the whole range of the phenomena in question. A reductionist explanation may be recognised for the partial and non-comprehensive explanation it is. It is when, being partial, it claims to be a complete explanation that it becomes reductionist. In the case we are interested in, it may ignore and so not give an adequate description of the phenomena involved, qualia, for example.

Qualia. When I sense the distinctive smell of the rose, that is not to be explained in physical terms. It is an 'extra'. But it is a phenomenon. It is an experience. Since inexplicable by and so of no interest to the physicalist, it has the status of an **epiphenomenon**. For philosophers **a phenomenon** is an object of perception, explicable in terms of scientific understanding. Outside the range of behaviouristic explanation, qualia are thus epiphenomena. They have no influence as causes. Physical causes in the brain account for phenomena, for example, pain. Pain is to be identified by behaviour, grimaces and cries of anguish. But parallel to the observable phenomena neurology accounts for are such qualia that we all experience and believe to be significant. What is beyond the range of the neurologist are the acute feelings of pain, what it is like to feel the sensation a deep cut makes, the pain that accompanies arthritis, the feeling of delight that accompanies the receipt of good news or the scent of a rose.

Epiphenomenalism. Such mental activities as thoughts, feelings do not and so are not to be considered as influencing our actions. The mental has no influence on the physical. It is the physical that determines how we act. So we investigate the laws that express the activity of the physical. In the philosophy of mind, this means that we allow the neurological examination of the brain to give us whatever answers are available. Mind is explained in terms of brain activity, the functioning of neurons. A state of consciousness is a by-product of the operation of the brain.

b The Identity Theory

Distinguishing mental states from physical states, we then ask, What is the relation between them? The causal theory proposes that mental states are nothing but states of the central nervous system. These physical states have causal power. They produce behaviour. But, it is to be noted, the behaviour is not identical with the mental state. Gilbert Ryle reduced mental states to **dispositions to behave** in certain ways. The underlying assumption was that the human being is nothing but a physical mechanism. So mental states are in fact nothing but physical states of the central nervous system. The critical question is whether such a view is intelligible. Behaviourism was often, following Ryle, presented as a successful response to dualism. Its limitations preclude it from that success.

An argument to the effect that there is an essential difference between physical states and mental states, is the following:

> A is a physico-chemical brain state.
> B is a mental state.
> A takes time, i.e. has genuine duration.
> B does not.
> What takes time cannot be identical with what does not.
> Therefore B and A are not identical.

To explain a brain state in physical terms and also to observe and explain behaviour by such terms is not to explain a mental state.

c Physicalism and qualia

Another anti-reductionism argument appeals to qualia. You can tell me everything there is to know about what's going on involving brain and I can put it all together, but you won't have told me about the characteristic experience itself, say, the smelling of a rose. Don't you see? Or rather, in this case, Don't you smell?

This conviction is nowhere better set out than in the following quotation:

> Tell me everything physical that is going on in a living brain, the kind of states, their functional role, their relation to what goes on at other times and in other brains, and so on and so forth, and be I as clever as can be in fitting it all together, and you won't have told me about the hurtfulness of pains. the itchiness of itches, pangs of jealousy, or about the characteristic experience of tasting a lemon, smelling a rose, hearing a loud noise or seeing the sky.[6]

For those who have the intuition, that intuition suffices. But an argument is required for those who don't. Again a very simple one suffices. Frank Jackson proposed one:

> Whatever you tell me in physical terms cannot capture the smell of a rose.
> Therefore, physicalism is false.

Similarly, he argued, one could have all the physical information about colour and lack what it means to have colour experience. So it follows (as above) that science has left something out. Physicalism does not and cannot account for a phenomenon familiar to us all.

> Qualia are left out of the physicalist story,
> So, the physicalist story is false.

If physicalism were true, it would be unnecessary to imagine or to try to understand, to know all about Fred's (or anyone else's) colour experience. We would already have the information. But we don't. So physicalism is inadequate, and so false. Jackson then defends epiphenomenal qualia with two theses: 1. The possession or absence of qualia (particular mental states) makes no difference to the physical world. 2. The mental is totally inefficacious causally. This is epiphenomenalism.

---

6 Frank Jackson, *Philosophical Quarterly*. 32 (1982), pp. 127-136. The quotation in the text is from p. 127.

d Levels of explanation

Jackson concludes that physicalism is false, but I believe his argument needs to be supplemented and his conclusion qualified. With such qualification it would read: Physicalism, if interpreted to provide an explanation covering all aspects of the experience in question, e.g. colour, is false. The impression Jackson gives in saying physicalism is false is that it can give no explanation at all. That could be quite misleading. A satisfactory explanation on one level may not be a satisfactory explanation on another level. It may not provide any explanation on that other level. But a non-comprehensive explanation is still an explanation. It is when one claims that a non-comprehensive explanation or definition is comprehensive or is the only one available that it becomes a reductionism

Jackson's objection is to the effect that the physicalist argument is reductive. His charge of its being false is to be so interpreted. His conclusion, made explicit, then would read: Physicalism, as a philosophical explanation in claiming to comprehend all aspects of the experience of (say) colour vision and similar experiences, is false. We may now make an appropriate critical observation.

The information the physicalist discovers and supplies is authentic. It serves the purpose of explaining the phenomena. To the question 'Is it or is it not the case that what you provide is all the information there is to be had?' You may well get the answer 'No!', followed by a clarification. 'My aims are quite explicit, and my method is suited to those aims. My explanation is appropriate to the aims I have. No further explanation is required. I am quite aware of experiences that cannot be explained in purely physical terms, the particular 'feel' of the smell of a rose, or the specific taste of a ripe peach. I have determined specific limits to the method of explanation, namely to account in neurological terms for the activity of the brain.' The physicalist may also claim that no further explanation is needed or can be given.

Physicalism is an extremely optimistic view of human powers. In principle it claims of its explanation, 'We have it all.' The discussion about qualia points to a 'mysterious residue' not amenable to such physicalist explanation. In this way it provides an antidote to such optimism,

e Conclusion

We have here attempted to indicate where the question of a dualism may be profitably raised, namely in relation to the so-called qualia, i.e. particular features of mental states. While it may be raised here, it is not decisively answered and (at present) further debate is likely to be productive.

BIBLIOGRAPHY

Campbell, Keith. *Body and Mind.* Notre Dame, Indiana: University of Notre Dame Press, 1984.

Descartes René *Meditations* II, VI.

Heil, John. *Philosophy of Mind.* London: Routledge, 1998. Chapter 2.

Hick, John. *Death and Eternal Life.* London: Collins, 1976.

Hospers, John. *Introduction to Philosophical Analysis* (3rd. Ed.) . London: Routledge, 1992. Chapter 6.

O'Hear, Anthony. *What Philosophy Is.* Harmondsworth: Penguin, 1985. Chapter 4.

Ryle, Gilbert. *The Concept of Mind.* London: Hutchinson. 1949.

Smith, Peter and Jones, O. R. *The Philosophy of Mind.* Part I Cambridge: University Press, 1986.

DUALISM: WORK SHEET

1 Outline the different varieties of dualism.

2 Try to explain the idea of cause-effect. How does it function?

3 What does 'causal connection' mean when thinking of mind and body (brain)?

(1) How do mind and body interact? (2) How could material things causally interact with non-material? (3) What is the status of the mental-material dichotomy? Is there a gulf to be bridged?

4 What are *qualia*? How do they feature in the discussion of dualism?

5 Explain why a Christian understanding of creation denies dualism as an explanation.

6 The idea of dualism in giving rise to a separable 'soul' leads to a doctrine of innate immortality and so provides for survival as disembodied. Explain.

11 PERSONAL IDENTITY AND THE AFTERLIFE

A conviction shared by believer and non-believer is that as human beings we are rightly held responsible for what we do. That assumes that the same person or the same group which performed past actions now performs present ones. Survival of death similarly requires that I shall be the same person post-mortem as I was ante-mortem. We discuss what it means to be a person and to claim that one is the same person after a lapse of time, long or short, before death and after death. Dualistic views speak of the person as consisting of soul and body. We consider two possibilities: immortality of the soul or resurrection of the body. We need an adequate vocabulary, and philosophers have provided the tools for the task. We shall content ourselves with considering briefly Plato's *Phaedo*, Aristotle on the Soul, Descartes and Cartesian Dualism, Locke on Identity, Hume on Identity, plus a contemporary suggestion of replication as resuscitation.

11 PERSONAL IDENTITY
AND THE AFTERLIFE

1   Identity: Importance?

For the believer the idea of personal identity is important and has many aspects. At the outset, we mention two:

a. I am responsible for my decisions and actions if and only if I continue to be the same person who made the decisions and performed the actions. If it could be shown that I am not the identical person, I cannot be held responsible for the actions of the 'other'. But is it possible that one with a bodily continuity with a person in the past could not be the same person as that one, that one has become so changed that she is a different person from what she was?

b. Believers differ in what they say about life after death. If there is life after death the question of personal identity arises. There have been two traditional and persisting beliefs about this. One is that the restoration to life will be physical. There is resurrection. The body will be restored to those who once lived. The other is that the soul at death is separated from the body and lives on as the person. Whether I am resurrected body or immortal soul, my future existence after the eschaton is only of concern to me if in that future I am the same person as I now am. In both cases continuity with the once earthly being is essential to my survival. I cannot be judged or rewarded for what someone not identical with me has been and done. Indeed 'I' can only exist as the same person as I was. For me that is what 'I' means.

But can I be the same person in the hereafter if, as resurrected, no original part of the matter that made up my body at death remains? Alternatively, Can I be the same person if as an immortal soul my body, the earthly physical housing of this soul that constitutes me the person, is no more? What in the two instances would constitute being the 'same person'?

Augustine, in his defence of the resurrection of the body had claimed that God would restore the original physical particles of the original body to the original persons whatever had happened to those particles, even if they had been eaten by cannibals.

One interesting suggestion, ignoring Augustine's fantastic idea about the resurrection of the body, is that God creates me a new being, a replica of my present self. The exact replica would think and act in the same way as I would have thought and acted had death not intervened. Would such an exact replica be 'I'?

To get ideas that address some of these questions we consider the exposition of John Locke on identify and personal identity. His treatment is a good place to start further study of the topic. [See the tutorial below.]

2   Identity and Personal Identity

What makes anything the same thing? What makes A the same as B? In one sense of the word 'same' we cannot say 'the same as something else' if when we say 'identical' we are referring to one item, when perhaps there is only the one item. What we can say is that there has been a gap of time between our perceptions of that one thing — say — the basket. So we ask, 'Is this the same basket as the one we saw yesterday?' We then make various tests, refer to criteria, to which we subject our perceptions of the basket. If we are satisfied that they pass the tests we conclude that it is the 'same' basket. Here we mean by 'same' 'identical over time'. The thing may not be material. Indeed it may not exist in the interval between the times we encounter it. Ask, 'Is that the same tune I heard last week?' Here we are not talking about a physical thing, for example the same record, the same recording. There is here only one thing. To be the 'same thing' it persists over time. So we can distinguish this meaning of 'same' as self-identical. Only one thing can be self-identical.

But in another sense of 'same' we can ask, 'Is this the same as that?' meaning 'Is this one thing the same as that other thing?' when we are talking about something that has exactly the same features as another thing. Something else, 'that thing' can be 'the same thing' as 'this thing'. In this sense more than one thing can be the same thing. We sometimes ask, 'Is that the same book as this? Is the book you are reading the same book that I am reading? So, as these two questions illustrate, we often use the terms 'same', 'identical' of more than one thing. So we think that two things can be defined as the same thing. Not only two but many. It is quite rational to say that we are all reading the same book. The teacher tells his twenty students each to bring the same book to the classroom next time. Many things can be identical.

So we have two meanings for the same (!) term. So to distinguish these meanings we speak of **identification at a time** and **identity over time**. We distinguish the two meanings by speaking of **quantitative identity** and **qualitative identity**.

With identity over time we are asking, What makes for x at time t^1 to be the same thing x at time t^2? The question is whether the identifying features we have employed fit the case in question. Is this watch I see before me the same watch that I saw before me a week ago?

With identification at a time we are asking how we identify x at any one particular time, e.g. John Smith, Reginald's office staff, the West Indies' Cricket team? At different times the constituents of each of these will be different from what they were. The present entity will be constituted differently from the past entity within the same structure. But we can nevertheless identify them by identifying their members, or enough of them within an identifiable structure. We identify them now, at a point in time. The criterion for identification here is the set of the members at a particular time. I can identify John Smith, the office staff, the cricket team, by recognising the sum of its constituent members.

3   Immortality Identity Social

Personal identity emerges in society, in this one or that one. I am what I now am as a result of interaction with the people around me and available to me. Human beings are socially formed and become persons only as they participate in particular social contexts. At the start we have no choice. Children cannot choose their parents and so cannot choose the context in which their formative years will be spent. As they grow older they will move in different contexts. As contexts change and we move from one context to another, we learn in one context what we could not learn in another. So we develop and emerge as different persons from what we were formerly. I am not what I was. I have altered. Indeed the sociologist speaks of this feature of human life, of moving from being one person to being another as 'alternation'. But in saying, 'I am different from what I was' I am repeating the personal pronoun 'I'. Repeating it suggests a real continuity. But can we speak of being the same person in view of such alternation? No-one but I was born when and where I was and of two particular parents. Whoever I now am, I am alone in these, my unique, features. Are those physical features sufficient to identify me as the same person over time? For there are other quite distinctive non-physical features that are unique to me.

The process of personal development is most often a gradual one. But there may be occasions in life when the change can be recognised as taking place almost in an instant. Alternation is to the secular person what conversion is to the religious. It may be instantaneous. It may be gradual. Such change may take place several times in the course of a person's life. The child becomes an adult by casting off the cluster of misrepresentations that have been imposed on it by well meaning adults since its earliest days. In due course the adult then becomes a different person by being exposed to a university course, by reading a set of books, by meeting someone from a background quite different from their own, by facing challenges, by suffering. The outlook and attitudes become different. Our actions take on a new character. In spite of continuity, we become different persons. To put it in a paradox. We become different persons while remaining the same. This states the problem of personal identity. We think differently. What would be very interesting would be *per impossibile* for me to have been, as it were, stabilised and preserved as a real conscious person at the age of seventeen, and for me to meet that person at the age of seventy. But it would be a different encounter from one with me at thirty! We have an interesting way of speaking of ourselves as a unit in time. 'I have changed', and 'I have not changed'. Both suggest a continuity through the passage of time. Then we add, 'in these respects', 'in those respects'. So how would it be possible for me to become a different person, so that I would say I am not the same person? Who is the 'I'? Who is the 'you'?

Any thinking about the after life that believes that consciousness continues must reckon with this phenomenon of development as a characteristic feature of the human person. We are not characteristically human if we do not develop. One problem is to conceive how we shall be the 'same person' post-mortem as we were ante-mortem. Another problem is to indicate how we may be the same person in view of the possibility of opportunities for change, for 'alternation' that we will in that future achieve. If time is limitless, there will be countless occasions for personal development, unlimited opportunities for becoming a 'different person'. Suppose we are to live for millions of years. This expression 'millions of years' gives no hint of what *everlasting* life might mean if we interpret survival in temporal terms. The longest period the biblical writer can conceive, it seems, is a millennium, a thousand years. To try to think about living through that length of time is frightening enough, given how tedious even now sometimes a day can be for us! Since all develop in the after life, there will soon come a time when there will be no more children. And we shall miss the children, of course! I hesitate to imagine social life without children! For with development, childhood recedes and disappears.

4   Personal Identity and the Afterlife

I am a material being. The question arises, 'How may we conceive the after-life for such a being?' If dualism is ruled out there are two alternatives: resurrection and re-incarnation. The question of identity hardly arises with the belief in re-incarnation. Dualism speaks of the soul, or mind, as the permanent constituent of the person in contrast to the body. The soul survives. The body does not. This leads to a doctrine of the immortality of the immaterial soul. The question of identity arises in a different way here.

The question of personal identity in connection with the after-life is this, 'Would the surviving person be I? Will I survive my death?' That may be construed to mean, 'Will the surviving person be quantitatively identical with me, the very same person, one and the same numerically? Or, the question might mean. 'Will the person after my death be qualitatively identical with me?'

There could be no resurrection if a necessary condition of identity is that of bodily identity or continuity, i.e. spatio-temporal continuity, for these reasons: There is a temporal gap between death and survival. In this time the body disintegrates. So the constituent parts of the body are not available for reconstruction. Secondly, there is a break in continuity between the two forms of the living person. Death marks the break. The resurrected person is not immediately brought to life in the moment at death. So we must search for an alternative explanation.

How is it possible to conceive of identity reaching beyond a period of non-existence, when constituent particles of an object have gone out of existence and so cannot be found. We can find examples of a kind of identity by thinking of a restoration of the original. To restore does not have to mean employing original parts to reconstitute the object, the artefact, the subject.

A boat, a bike, a watch is dismantled and its parts preserved. They will be later reassembled. When disassembled the object no longer exists, but all its parts do. There is a story from the war in the Pacific. Before the Japanese took over the island, the inhabitants dismantled their boat, and hid and preserved all the individual parts. Later they gathered and reassembled them. In this way they constituted the same boat. The preservation of the parts and their reassembly in the exact order of their original structure are essential to this concept of identity. This is not the case with the human. There can be no question of the physical parts of the human person being preserved after death. Augustine thought that every part of every human being who died and was to be resurrected could be found and reassembled. That was his big mistake. Reassembling what no longer exists is not possible.

The human body is not the same body after a period of a few years. Not a single original element remains. This takes place in the natural course of things, given the appropriate conditions. The body remains, continuous with the previous one, but without any of its previous constituents. It retains the same form and so we can recognise it as belonging to the same person after a lapse of years.

The classical and fascinating expression of the problem is that of Theseus' ship as employed by the philosopher. It is an intriguing illustration.

In the one case, the original parts of the ship are dismantled and kept in storage (like the islanders' ship). They are kept intact. Then the stored parts are put together to form the original ship. After a period of interruption, of non-existence, it now continues to exist as the same ship.

In the other case, as they begin to deteriorate and decay parts of the ship are replaced. Finally, not one of the original parts remains. But since they have been replaced a ship continues to exist without interruption.

So there are now two ships, the first having been reassembled from the original parts and the second maintained in existence by supplying replacement parts as needed, identical with but not the original parts. So the question is, 'Are both of these ships now Theseus' ship? The fact is that the ship with replacement parts has all the characteristics and performs exactly the same functions as the restored ship. So if we did not have the restored ship we would not only be content with the reconstituted ship, but say that it is identical with Theseus' original ship.

Spatio-temporal continuity can be demonstrated if we are able to show that the item in question has persisted without change over a period of time. Ask, 'Under what circumstances can an arte-fact, if disassembled, survive?' The answer is by reassembly of all its parts. The reassembled product is the same as the original if all the parts are put together in the same way as the original. We would also be quite prepared to say that this is the same boat if several of the parts had been lost and others were newly produced and fitted so as to make up the complete structure. We might even say that if all the parts had been replaced over a period of time the resultant boat would be the same as the original. So we have two criteria for identity, the second being replacement of parts.

In one case, as with Theseus' ship, the replacement of parts might result in the existence of two entities, one having been made from parts identical qualitatively with the originals, having been made to specification, the other with parts quantitatively identical i.e. the originals themselves. With which of the two resulting ships would we say is the original ship identical? Since it is clear that we might not be able to choose clearly between one answer and the other, it follows that in different circumstances we use different criteria, and that we may not have a criterion to cover all possible cases.

Would such physical continuity suffice for *personal* survival? Or is a degree of psychological connectedness necessary? So a further question arises. If bodily continuity is not sufficient for personal survival, is such continuity even necessary, or is psychological connectedness, memory and personality, sufficient?

Is the criterion for the identification for persons to be given in physical terms? Bob Jones, person a at time t^1, is identical with person b at time t^2 if a and b have the same human brain? [Cf. Locke's '**man**', below].

One man, Peter Brown continues to have the same physical features now as he had a week ago. Some of these are readily determinable by observation. In the law court, the witness is asked, 'Do you recognise this person?' At the police station witnesses may be asked to identify the criminal from a line up. In such cases recognition of the person is being made on the basis of certain physical features. This suffices in many given circumstances. The case of identical twins would provide a problem. It illustrates Locke's definition of the 'same man' as contrasted to 'same person'. For him the 'same man' is 'nothing but a participation of the same continued life by constantly fleeting particles of matter, in succession vitally united to the same organized body'. Such identity of a set of bodily parts does not constitute the person. That definition could just as well refer to 'same dog'! So identical twins would be the same men but not the same persons? For each is constituted by his own unique 'parcels of matter', to use Locke's quaint term.

We also readily identify persons over time in terms of psychological connectedness, for example in terms of memory. If after some accident I lose my memory I become a different person. If later my memories return I become my 'old self' again. My encounter with such a person would illustrate this. I remember an experience we both shared, and another and another and he does not. He has become a different person.

The question then arises: 'Can I say that I survive in the future if there exists in that future a being sufficiently psychologically connected with my past self, e.g. a being with my memories?' For having the same memories would connect a person with their past. Would I speak of my surviving after death if I found myself as existing with the same psychological features as I now possess, however the existence of such a being came about, for example if it were to have been replicated after my death, given that then I can connect my memories after survival with my memories before survival. I would of course have to be aware of those memories. I alone would be able to canvass those memories. Other persons with whom I shared them while in this existence would be able to make a judgment about me only if I communicate with them in my after death life what my post-mortem memories are and then made the comparison between the two. This is to assume that they also have retainable memories. I must be able to examine and recognise the memories. Having the same memories as the pauper will identify me as a pauper. Having the same memories as the prince will identify me as the prince, even if I were the other in my life before death.

TUTORIAL JOHN LOCKE ON PERSONAL IDENTITY:

Read John Locke, 'On Identity and Diversity,' *Essay Concerning Human Understanding*, Book II. Chapter 27.

Summary of the argument

(1) The idea of identity and diversity is formed when we compare a thing at one time and place with itself at another time and place.

(2) There is a distinction between the **identity of a man** and the **identity of a person**.

(3) A thing is the thing it is, i.e. is individuated, by its existence at a particular time and place.

(4) So with vegetables, animals and man, there is a structure supporting life, an organization whose particles change, 'one organization of life.' It is here that identity is to be found.

(5) The **identity of man** consists in that fact that he 'participates in the same continued life by constantly fleeting particles of matter' (7).

(6) The **identity of the person** consists in consciousness and in this alone (9). I am the same person as a person in the past to the extent that this consciousness can be extended backwards into the past. By 'consciousness' Locke means the 'present representation of a past action'(13). From this it follows that if I do not have consciousness of a past action I am not the same person that performed the forgotten action.

(7) The same self, or person, can exist in different substances. Different persons can exist in the same substance.

(8) The case of the prince and the cobbler. One can be the same man but not the same person. The body goes to the making of the man. It is consciousness that makes the same person whether I consist of the same substance (material or immaterial) or not. Personal identity consists in the identity of consciousness not of substance. Substance without consciousness does not constitute a person. Personal identity is equally determined by consciousness whether annexed to some individual immaterial substance or not (23). But Locke admits that it is most probable that this consciousness is joined to one individual immaterial substance (25).

(9) This entails that the same individual man may be different persons.

Exposition

Consciousness constitutes personal identity, and can be extended backwards (memory). Consciousness means the present representation of a past action. If Nigel is conscious of the same actions as Socrates, he is the same person as Socrates. Consciousness makes the same person. But 'same person' is not 'same man'. Being the same person does not consist in having the same substance, material or immaterial. The same person is that with which consciousness of the present thinking conjoins itself. If the cobbler's body 'contained' the consciousness of the prince he would be the same person as the prince. If the little finger did, even if severed from the body, it would be the prince. So, if two consciousnesses were in the same body, there would be two persons. If one consciousness were contained in two bodies then there would be one person. The same consciousness united with several different substances one after the other would be the same person. But, 'it is most probable that this consciousness is joined to one immaterial substance.' Locke rejects the views that (1) personal identity consists in bodily continuity. The same man is not the same person simpliciter. (2) To be the same person is to have one persisting soul substance. There is backward-looking memory, action ascription in the present, and forward-looking consciousness.[1] Together these provide the rationale for the use of the concept of an identical person as the bearer of responsibilities and rights.

Questions about Locke.

(1) Is the person something more than a series of co-conscious items, memories, perceptions, i.e. something that has the memories and perceptions? or

(2) Is the entity in question only a collection of co-conscious items, one series of experiences one after the other but with no unifying thread that binds them into one?

If the answer is 'Yes,' as David Hume had proposed, what is it that holds the items together, the string that binds them?

(3) There were critics. who insisted that we must be asking two different questions: 'What constitutes identity?' and 'What is evidence for personal identity? We must not confuse them. The relation between two objects constituting identity is that of continued existence. The evidence of continued existence is similarity. It is a 'natural prejudice' that when we find similarity we identify an object on two occasions. Similarity of consciousness does not constitute personal identity but is evidence for it. 'Same consciousness' does not mean identity of consciousness. Yesterday's consciousness is not the same as today's consciousness. 'Same kind of consciousness' is to be distinguished from 'same consciousness.'

BIBLIOGRAPHY

John Locke, *Essay Concerning Human Understanding.* Oxford: Oxford University Press, 1924.

J. I. Mackie, *Problems from Locke*, Oxford: Clarendon Press, 1976.

---

1   J. Mackie, *Problems with Locke*, p. 177.

IDENTITY: WORK SHEET

1. Say, at least to yourself, what each of the following questions mean. Then answer them:

Is this clock (which has had one of its parts replaced) the same one as the original?

Is this clock (which has had every one of its parts replaced) the same one as the original?

Am I the same person as I was when I was six, twenty?

2. Say whether you think the following statement is correct, after noting that it is somewhat paradoxical.

If two objects are numerically identical (= are one and the same), then anything true of the one will be true of the other. (e.g. a bicycle (seen yesterday), a bicycle (seen today).

3. Distinguish identity over time and memory

(1) If something is the same thing at a later as at an earlier time, what relation between earlier and later stages of the existence of an object must prevail which would constitute 'them' or 'it' the same thing, i.e. what is the criterion for identity? Give an example.

(2) What is the criterion for identifying something in the present, i.e. for identification? Give an example.

12 MIRACLES

Biblical writings and church traditions frequently assert the occurrence of miracles both in nature and in the human context. How shall we define the concept? Further, how shall we assess the accounts of miracle? The writers told the miracle stories with a purpose in mind. Miracles had a meaning as signs. How does the occurrence of miracles relate to well established natural or scientific laws? Are we faced with a paradox, as Hume suggested?

12 MIRACLES

1 Agency and Angel Activity

Every gardener is aware of the principle that if something, usually undesirable, is to be prevented, something must be done to prevent it. If you do not want the snails to eat your strawberries then you have to initiate some means, say deploy snail pellets, to prevent the occurrence. If something is accomplished something must be done to accomplish it. If you want the machine to start you must switch on the engine. Often a human agent is needed, in characteristic cases, to produce a new physical condition. Under normal circumstances we can quite readily describe the agent and how that agent did what was necessary to bring about the outcome.

An agent is an initiator, a necessary presence for the production of a particular outcome. It is customary to think of an agent as a human person, acting so as to produce the effect. But we may also use the term 'agent', rather than the term 'instrument' for a non-personal activity. We would not be averse to speaking of a dog as the agent for the saving of a person's life, as of a St. Bernard in a rescue mission in the mountains.

We may extend the notion of agent to include whatever it is that produces an event that without that agent would not otherwise have happened, thus including in the term what we often call an 'instrument'. The principle is quite clear: that an event would not take place without a preceding event having taken place. That preceding event is then called the 'cause' of what otherwise would not have happened. The resulting event is an 'effect'. A cause is a possible action or event. We set limits, based on our experience, as to what we are ready to accept as a possible cause, as a possible agent.

The simple point is that without the intervention of an agent, the unwanted result would not be averted, nor the desired event brought into being. An agent is thus sometimes a necessary condition for the production of the effect. A philosophical explanation takes into account both impersonal, natural events and events caused by agents.

Sometimes desirable but unexpected events happen, for example, the avoidance of a serious accident, the saving of a child's life, the receiving of unexpected succour in a time of desperate need. Such events give rise for some believers to deep relief, and to surprise at the result. This the believer expresses in an attitude of gratitude. The belief strengthens the recipient's faith. The reporting of the event in terms of angel activity is a means of expressing that thankfulness. The believer may speak of the activity of an angel or angels in producing a desirable result. It is this gracious activity of the angel that the believer celebrates and there is rejoicing as in scriptural accounts. An angel frees the apostles by opening prison doors. *Acts* 5:19. Then there is the intervention story which puts the formerly persecuted persons into a favourable position vis-á-vis their former tormentors. Cf. *Daniel* 3:28, 6:22. Accounts of destructive angel activity are also found in the biblical accounts, to the great disadvantage of one but for the beneficial advantage of the other party, for example, the angel's destruction of the Assyrians and the salvation of Hezekiah. *II Chronicles* 33:20, 21.

I have just read of a person who became unconscious and knew only of his precarious situation after he had regained consciousness. An emergency call had been made on his behalf and the ambulance and team of medics had arrived in time to save his life. Not knowing who had made the emergency call (999 in England) in his surprise and gratitude, he attributed it to his 'guardian angel'.

It reminded me of the song 'Scarlet Ribbons'. 'A little girl prayed and later received scarlet ribbons that she had so much

wanted. It was a mystery where the ribbons had come from. The
song concludes:

> If I live to be a hundred
> I shall never know from where
> Came those lovely scarlet ribbons
> Scarlet ribbons for her hair.

One would think that a little investigation in both cases would
have provided the answer. It would be one rather close at home!
Why ever does one assume that one cannot give such a down to
earth answer? Why should I think that what was required in either
of these two cases was an English speaking, technically aware, med-
ically astute, perennially attendant but supernatural, being? The
last thing one ought to be doing is to let oneself be guided by the
principle: If I cannot find an immediate explanation for an unusual
or unexpected event, postulate supernatural agency. Rather let us
assume that I will find evidence for natural causes but never for the
supernatural. And, if no explanation is available, I can always wait,
and do some thinking the while!

We sometimes hear of the supernatural when the event directly
results in personal well-being or the well-being of the community.
That is to say, when the angel activity is directed against evil, or
some threat to our well-being. Such events are sometimes called
'providential deliverances', the title of a book found on my parents'
shelf when I was a child. The idea of the providential activity of
the angel is celebrated when it produces a welcome result. It may
produce penitence and repentance when it issues in destructive
judgment.

When believers experience an event as the occasion for the
presence of God in the world, they distinguish that event from
others they take as mundane. Such events stand out therefore as
occasions for the occurrence of a religious experience. Viewed in
that light they will be regarded as of primary importance. In view
of this we have a way to define miracle. An event of particular religious significance has been happening. In this light a miraculous

event is one that provides the occasion for the believer's religious experience, however he may define that experience. There is then no problem with the concepts of regularity in the cosmos and with laws of nature.

How may acts of God, i.e. providential events, be distinguished from ordinary events? Do some natural events have a transcendental character, e.g. those initiated by human freewill? Is the fundamental problem not that of miracles but transcendence? How can we have knowledge of the transcendent?

2   Regularity

Events follow one another with a predictable regularity.

We expect future kinds of events to be similar to, of the same sort as, the kinds of events we have experienced regularly and without exception in the past.

Sometimes something unexpected happens.

We find and read purported reports of such unexpected events.

Sometimes some people take the unexpected happening to be specially significant.

Some people interpret the unusual, unexpected and unpredictable event as having a supernatural cause.

They then see it, interpret it, as having religious significance,

This may also involve them in believing that the unexpected and (by some considered) impossible event is an exhibition of the divine favour or disfavour and take it as a reason for gratitude or as a warning.

Others, acknowledging the universal regularity of laws of nature, see reports of miracles (one name for such unexpected events) as misguided if taken as descriptions of actual happenings, and so deny the reports any special significance. So they ask why such 'reports' of unrepeatable counter-instances to the laws of nature were created.

In discussing miracle we have thus two sorts of considerations. the case of the most unusual event and the appropriate interpretation of the report of the most unusual event. The first of these involves the idea of the status of laws of nature. Can you 'break' a law of nature? The second is concerned with the background beliefs that make interpretation possible. The inquiry attempts to answer two kinds of question: (1) Do miracles happen? Why do some people take some particularly unusual events as acts by the supernatural and so having special meaning for the 'believer'? (2) How shall we interpret the reporting of such events in written accounts? How trace from the 'event' to the account of the event in the book?

So we find various attitudes to the questions: those of the sceptic, the believer and the undecided.

The sceptic denies that the 'report' is of an actual event, that the event has particular significance.

The believer affirms both the occurrence of the event reported or at least that the 'report' has significance for him.

The undecided have yet to make up their mind.

3 Laws of Nature

Nature is uniform. There are regularities throughout the whole universe, and these regularities can be expressed in statements put in the form of 'laws'. The following forms represent a law of nature:

All A-events are followed by B-events.

Particular kinds of A-events are followed by particular kinds of B-events.

When we specify kinds of event we may then make predictions about what we can expect in the future. We are able to do this because we have been familiar with the connections between two kinds of events in the past. But, what precisely is the connection between the preceding event and the subsequent event? Is it more than accidental? Do the events just happen? So we report that every time the earth revolves, light dawns, clouds and sun appear.

If there is a necessary connection between the two kinds of event we may say: Given A, event B must happen. For example, that when the earth revolves the sun must appear, that when I hit a piece of glass with a heavy hammer the glass must shatter. Is that the right way of talking?

David Hume considered the alternatives. [Cf. the tutorial.]

4   Violation of Natural Law?

If someone steals your car, he has committed an offence. He has violated a law. He has disobeyed a demand, violated a specified obligation recognised by society. So what now of the concept of a violation of a natural law?

First we must make a clear distinction between law as prescriptive and law as descriptive. The law prescribes that you shall not murder. The law describes a regularity experienced in nature, that bodies attract one another (expressible in mathematical terms as many such laws are). Ethical and legal laws **prescribe** what is to be done. Scientific or natural laws **describe** what is experienced within the context of the uniformity in nature.

So the term 'violation' while at home in the context of prescriptive law, becomes problematic when we are discussing laws of nature. 'Violation' of a prescriptive law may mean that something unusual and possibly non-predictable has taken place. Mary has been found guilty of murder. She has broken, violated, the law that says, 'Thou shalt not murder', for example. But it is also out of character for Mary, meek and mild, to murder anybody. But 'violation' here does not mean irregularity. Indeed the unexpected might become a regular occurrence. If the case is understood a prediction to a possible occurrence might be possible. Take serial murder, say that of Dr. Shipman, a well known case in Britain, described as 'the world's most prolific serial killer'.

'Violation' in the context of natural law means something very different, quite simply 'occurrence of an unexpected event,' 'non-occurrence of the expected conjunction of events'. The expectation is based upon our experience of the regular association we have observed to take place between types of event. So if we make a minimal definition of miracle as occurrence of a non-repeatable counter instance to a law of nature[1] and then call it a violation of a law, then such 'violations' occur. They may not lead to modification of the law, let alone to 'paradigm change', i.e. a revised overall conception of the theory of scientific activity.

We must note that not every non-repeatable counter instance to a natural law is a miracle. We distinguish unique from repeated counter-instances.

5 The Counter-Instance

Repeated counter-instances to purported laws only show those purported laws not to be genuine laws. When such occur the law is revised or abandoned. A single counter-instance does not lead to a revision or an abandonment of the natural law.

The law of nature expresses the regularity we have observed to take place.

We observed that when event A takes place it is physically close to event B (contiguity). We have also observed that the event B regularly succeeds event A (succession). This regularity provides for expectation.

Put simply:

> Given event of type A,
> Given the covering law,
> Expect the event of type B.

Simple examples:

> This water is poured on to this fire
> Water quenches fire
> This water will quench this fire

But if a non-repeatable counter-instance to a law L occurred we could either say that: (1) L can't be a law of nature, or (2) L is such a law, but an exceptional non-repeatable counter-instance to its occurrence has occurred. Questions of proof, demonstration and falsification must then be considered. Alternative (2) is pref-

---

1   Richard Swinburne, *The Concept of Miracle*, pp. 26ff.

erable because first, the law gives correct predictions in all other circumstances and second, because the alternative is to say that no law operates.

A formula is a law if it holds without exception and if in general the predictions it enables take place.

So we may say (1) that an exception to the law takes place, and (2) that the exceptional event cannot be accounted for by another law, i.e. a formula which could be taken as a law. Therefore, the definition of the event as violation of the law is coherent. So we may say that it is logically possible that a law of nature may be violated. That is not a contradiction. Violation of a law of nature is not incoherent. The scientist may not be able to bring the observations of the unusual event he has made under any present classification or law. But he will not abandon the law on that account. If a remarkable healing has taken place, apparently without the mediation of any physician or treatment, the observer will insist on the occurrence of the event and hope for an explanation in the future. No law will be abandoned in the meantime. Testimony to the occurrence of the unique event, in such a case, must be reliable.

Now if we ask a different question we get a different answer. The question is, 'What religious significance does "miracle" have?' We now focus on the response of the believer to the reports of miracle. He takes these as referring back to the actual extraordinary event. These events become for him an occasion for religious experience. He sees them, experiences them as the occasion for his special awareness of the presence of God.

Why does the believer regard an event as a miracle? Why take it as an intervention within the realm of universal regularity? We may consider miracle as 'phenomena in the realm of physical nature which are supposed not to have been caused in a natural manner.'[2]

---

2   Friedrich D. E. Schleiermacher (1768-1834) lived at a time when a revolution was taking place in historical studies. Discussion ranged over questions about the nature of history, and about how literary documents were to be assessed as historical sources. The principle that such sources were to be evaluated according to clear principles influenced Christian

Events the believer calls miracles are seen within the realm of faith: 'the state of each individual's faith determines his judgment of the alleged miracle.' This raises the interesting question why the occurrence of miracles should be seen as divinely ordered more so than the maintenance of the whole system of the cosmos.

> it is difficult to conceive . . . how omnipotence is shown to be greater in the suspension of the independence of nature than in its original immutable course which was also divinely ordered.

Take that as a starting point and you arrive at the rule:

> interpret every event with reference to the interdependence of nature and without detriment to that principle.[3]

Then consider that 'God has prepared miracles in nature in some way incomprehensible to us'.[4] Miracle is the 'redeeming efficacy of Christ'. Physical miracles assume a relative importance in the light of that efficacy.[5]

---

understanding about the appropriate methods for assessing the narratives or the purported narratives of the Bible. It also had serious consequences for assessing the sources, composition and production of the various books of Scripture. Particular interest was shown concerning the sources and composition of the Gospels. Schleiermacher lived through this time and reckoned seriously with the implications of the new approaches, both in historical studies and in philosophy where he came to terms with the influence of Immanuel Kant.

Another long-standing attempt to demonstrate the existence of God and so to show that faith was rational was the production of the so-called 'proofs' for the existence of God by arguing from features of the physical world. Such proofs, like those from miracle and prophecy were to become questionable as the revolution in historical understanding and acceptance of the method of examination of texts was universally accepted.

3 Schleiermacher, *The Christian Faith*, p. 71.

4 *Ibid.,* p. 179-180.

5 *Ibid..* pp. 183,418.

In particular Schleiermacher cites 'answers to prayer' and regeneration as examples.[6] A quite ordinary event, one readily explicable in terms of the ordinary working of nature, may be seen as an answer to prayer by the believer who will take it as an event which would not have happened apart from the prayer. So it becomes a focus and source of a religious experience. For the believer it is the occasion of an act of God, and so an occasion for thankfulness. The believer takes God to be source and content of the experience. The believer has faith, and because of that faith can see the event or series of events in a way the unbeliever does not. 'Miracle' is the name for the event which enables that response. It is the occasion for religious experience. So 'miracle' has a definable function as a religious category. The believer relates the event to his faith in God, without which faith he would not see the ordinary event as having particular significance.

It was a popular approach in his century that one could prove the divinity of Jesus from the occurrence of miracles he performed, and that such a proof could be a basis for the believer's faith in Jesus as the Christ, resting as it did upon the authority of Scripture. The argument was a simple one.

> Scripture, i.e. the Gospels contained narratives of miracles of Jesus.
> These are to be taken as authentic reports of actual events that he caused to happen.
> That he performed such things as reported demonstrated that he was divine.
> That is a sufficient basis for having faith in him.

Such appeal to miracle was then supplemented by the accompanying attempt to prove the authority of scripture by appeal to the fulfilment of the prophecies it contained.

Schleiermacher firmly denied that there can be such proofs. Christian faith can never be based on the miracles.[7] He makes the important point that our faith in the miracles of Christ depends

---

6   *Ibid.,* p. 180.
7   *Ibid.,* pp. 448, 449.

upon our interpretation of Scripture. It 'belongs not so much to our faith in Christ directly as to our faith in Scripture'.[8]

6 Hume's paradox

a. Hume's argument about miracles.

Reasonable people proportion their belief to the evidence. They weigh the pros and the cons and do so according to their experience.

With regularly repeated events, they expect similar events in the future.

With regard to human testimony, they must weigh the probability that people are telling the truth against the possibility of falsely reporting an extraordinary event.

b. A miracle is something which violates a law of nature. So it is more credible that deception has occurred than that something contrary to our experience of the world has.

c. Testimony about miracles never amounts to proof. If universal experience and testimony on behalf of miracle conflict, accept the former.

d. Hume's concept of causation. (1) The causal relation between events is that of constant conjunction not necessitation. (2) The uniformity of nature can only be established on the basis of observation. But we cannot observe the future. We assume that what has been will be. But that is the very assumption we are trying to establish. So science rests upon non-provable assumptions.

e. Hume arrives at two conclusions, as the following examples illustrate:

(1) The best possible evidence is that x will not occur.

(2) X might conceivably occur.

So,

---

8 For an older and helpful account of this approach, see H. H. Farmer, *The World and God*. London: Nisbet, 1946. pp. 107-126. Also: Robert R. Williams, *Schleiermacher the Theologian, The Construction of the Doctrine of God*. Philadelphia: Fortress Press, 1978. pp. 90-91.

(1) The sun has always arisen.
(2) The sun may not rise tomorrow.

No contradiction is involved.

So, Hume must fail to believe in a miracle but cannot rule out the theoretical possibility that such an event might occur.

f. Is there a paradox in the definition of a miracle? If we take the following form to represent a law of nature:

All A-events are followed by B-events

then, one single instance, i.e. a counter-instance, can disprove a law of nature. It follows that if this is so, a miracle can't violate a law of nature. If it is an exception, the law of nature is destroyed.

A law of nature can't be absolutely conclusively verified but it can be falsified. But the question then arises, Does it follow that a miracle can't be a violation of a law of nature, as Hume has defined it to be?

g. Miracles are particular non-repeatable events, counter-instances to laws of nature. They are not negative, repeatable events. A negative event is one which, occurring, invalidates a law of nature by falsifying it. So they are not experimental. A genuine negative instance, one capable of destroying a law of nature is an **experimentally repeatable exception**. Miracle does not fall into this category. Miracle is a single non-repeatable event.

h. Miracles are not random events, which random events have no implications for the future. The 'deadly exception' does.

7   God's Action, Miracle and Secular Understanding

What does it require to say, God acts in the world? This question comes into sharp focus when we raise the question of miracles. As different answers are given to this question, so different answers will be given to the question about miracles.

At any rate a clear understanding of the cosmos, giving rise to an understanding of what is and what is not possible within the universe will determine our definition of miracles and our judgment as to whether they take place and then some explanation of how.

How you think about God will influence how you will speak of God's action in the world.

There are various possibilities: They range from thinking of God as impersonal to thinking of God as personal. So the idea of miracle will be developed differently or not at all. We take a sampling. *Pantheism* speaks of the world and God as one. There is no place here for personal categories. *Deism* speaks of God as active in the creation of the cosmos but thereafter the universe operates independently.

The difference between our conception of the cosmos and that of the ancients, Christians included, is that they recognised the constant operation of external, trans-human, non-physical forces to produce events within the world. We recognise the independence of nature and so in explaining it we employ empirical means. That means that any reference to the supernatural is excluded on principle.

(1) Understanding God

Certain distinctions must be made. However you designate them, these are the distinctions.

a. Traditional theism: God is understood in personal categories. He brought the world into being and acts within it as he wills.

b. Deism: God created the cosmos which, now in being, has its existence independent of its creator. The image of an absentee landlord has sometimes seemed to be appropriate.

c. Pantheism God is identified with the cosmos. What happens within the cosmos is the story of God as it is the story of the universe. This shows up in Christian theology with the principle: there is a cosmic regularity in all events. So any event may be called a miracle. Whether it is will depend on its significance for the believer. In some events the mechanical and the personal are brought together. That an event is dependent upon God should never exclude that the event has been conditioned by the system of nature.

d. **Panentheism.** All that is not God has its existence within his operation and nature. It does not identify God and the world, as does pantheism. It says that while operative within the cosmos God is more than the cosmos. God is neither absent from the cosmos (as in deism) nor is identical with the world (as in pantheism). What happens in the world has an effect on the divine reality. Creativity and so the emergence of the new takes place in the world and this creativity affects God. Panentheism does not speak of God's 'intervention' in the world for God is always present there. The analogy on which this activity of God is to be expressed is in organic rather than mechanical terms. So emerges the actual out of the possible. The theology is one of process. While for pantheism the cosmos is identical to God, for panentheism the cosmos is within God. Both are in contrast to traditionalist theism where the cosmos is other than God. The analogy of a person in relation to his body leads to different interpretations of God's relation to the world: personal and impersonal.[9]

(2) Understanding the Cosmos

1. Ancient, pre-modern: God initiates events as he wills. His agents are varied, but angels feature regularly in ancient accounts of events in the cosmos. Demons and other beings, e.g. Satan, angels, can initiate events within it. Some of these events are extraordinary and may also be unrepeatable.

To say that God is active depends on accepting the analogy from personal relations, and so on upon the appropriateness of concepts of will and purpose. It is only in the realm of the personal that concepts of will, freedom and purpose feature.

The ancients did not realise the extent to which the cosmos is explicable in terms   of universal laws.

---

9   See Norman Pittenger, *Process Thought and Christian Faith,* New York: The Macmillan Company, 1968. pp. 26-53, Schubert Ogden, *The Reality of God. New York: Harper and Row, 1966.* Chapter I pp. 1-70. Philip Clayton, *God beyond Orthodoxy: Process Theology for the 21ˢᵗ Century,* 2008. The last is available on line.

They had no notion that investigation of the universe would enable us to discover and state those laws. That required a language they did not have, the language of a sophisticated mathematics. It also required either an abandonment or a bracketing of the idea that cosmos is open to influences from outside.

2 Modern: No reference is required to some force or agency external to the universe. The account given is non-theistic. The universe is regular and phenomena are subject to understanding by assuming and explaining the regularity. Extraordinary, and apparently inexplicable events occur. The assumption is that phenomena hitherto inexplicable will with due effort come to be understood.

The question for the non-sceptic is whether within this context there is a 'space' for the introduction of the idea of an active God, and for the concept of miracles, involving as it does that God initiates events within the cosmos.

(3) Understanding the act of believing an event to be a miracle

For the classical theist the enabling beliefs are that God is related both to the cosmos and initiates events that would not otherwise take place, and also that God is also related to communities and individuals within it and responds to their well-being, needs, and pleas, for example by delivering from danger, by preventing catastrophe, or by initiating catastrophe for those he does not favour, resulting in the well- being of those he does.

The modern theist relates his understanding of God to a universe explicable in secular terms. Adjustments are obviously needed as he does so. Questions that did not arise on the traditional account have to be addressed. Theses are sometimes made in a pantheistic direction. Start with the question what does it take for a subject to interpret an event as God's action? What does it take to interpret an event as a miracle, in the context of a universe understood, as we all understand it, in secular terms. Fresh approaches to the understanding of God emerge in the process.

For example, the panentheistic interpretation of process theology, with its denial of the traditional understanding of God's unlimited omnipotence, and the naturalistic suggestion which follows. Rejecting creation *ex nihilo*, it thereby abandons the idea of supernatural incursions in the regularity of nature. So the belief that God initiates physical miracles becomes a problem.

BIBLIOGRAPHY

Mary Hesse, 'Miracles and the Laws of Nature' in C. D. F. Moule (ed.), *'Miracles'*. London: Mowbray, 1965. pp. 35-42.

Friedrich Schleiermacher, *The Christian Faith*. Edinburgh: T. & T. Clark, 1960.

Ninian Smart, *Philosophers and Religious Truth*. London: S. C. M. Press, 1969. Chapter 2

Richard Swinburne, *The Concept of Miracle*. London: Macmillan, 1970.

TUTORIAL Hume's Argument about Miracles.

Here we present David Hume's argument concerning miracles and the laws of nature. This is followed step by step at various points by explanation and clarification.

Read David Hume, *Enquiries concerning Human Understanding.* section 10 'Of Miracles'. (This became known as the Essay on Miracles).

A *Treatise of Human Nature.* I. iii. XIV.
'Of the idea of necessary connection.'

1. Reasonable people proportion their belief to the evidence. They weigh the pros and the cons and do so according to their experience.

(1) With regularly repeated events, they expect similar events in the future.

(2) With regard to human testimony, they must weigh the probability that people are telling the truth against the possibility of falsely reporting an extraordinary event.

(3) Testimony about miracles never amounts to proof. If universal experience and testimony on behalf of miracle conflict, we should accept the former.

When we encounter testimony, if wise, we do not simply accept it. We make sure it is reliable by applying certain questions both about the source and then about the reasonableness of the subject matter.

2. A miracle is something which violates a law of nature. So it is more credible that deception has occurred than that something contrary to our experience of the world has.

Here Hume applies his principle about testimony. He challenges the claim to miracle by introducing the idea of the law of nature. He takes this to be inviolable. So any claim that it has been violated is to be challenged. Testimony to that effect is to be rejected.

3. Hume's concept of causation. (1) The causal relation between events is that of constant conjunction not necessitation. (2)

The uniformity of nature can only be established on the basis of observation.

He gets now to the basic problem: the definition and application of the concept of cause and effect. The basic terms are *necessary, contiguity, succession, observation, uniformity.* We observe the constant and uniform closeness in space and the constant and uniform succession of types of events. This provides the conviction of universality. What the law claims is a connection (of contiguity and succession) occurring without exception. This we observe. Events happen this way. But we never observe that the connection is a necessary one. What we observe is one event near in time and space to another event The laws of nature do not express a *necessary* connection between the events they cover. Hume then projects this principle to the future.

But we cannot observe the future. We assume that what has been will be. But that is the very assumption we are trying to establish. So science rests upon unproveable assumptions.

4. Hume arrives at two conclusions, as the following examples illustrate:

(1) The best possible evidence is that x will not occur.
(2) X might conceivably occur.

So,

(1) The sun has always arisen.
(2) The sun may not rise tomorrow.

No contradiction is involved.

So, Hume must fail to believe in a miracle but cannot rule out the theoretical possibility that such an event might occur.

What is happening here? Distinguish between a *logical possibility*, which means that there is no contradiction involved with the claim and a *real possibility* that the claim may be true. The claim that the sun will not rise tomorrow does not involve a contradiction. It is a logical possibility. But it is practically certain, i.e. there is the highest degree of probability, that the claim is false. So we reject it as a real possibility and expect the sunrise tomorrow morning. But if the sun did not rise tomorrow we would have to adjust ourselves and our thinking (if possible) to that non-event.

OBSERVATIONS

5. Is there a paradox in the definition of a miracle? If we take the following form to represent a law of nature:

All A-events are followed by B-events

then, one single instance, i.e. a counter-instance, can disprove a law of nature. It follows that if this is so, a miracle can't violate a law of nature. If it is an exception, the law of nature is destroyed. It no longer holds.

A law of nature (e.g. all atoms have a similar structure) can't be absolutely conclusively verified but it can be falsified. No-one can examine all instances of the law. But the question then arises, 'Does it follow that a miracle cannot be a violation of a law of nature?' as Hume has defined it to be?

6. Miracles are particular non-repeatable events, counter-instances to laws of nature.

They are not negative, repeatable events. A *negative event* is one which, occurring, invalidates a law of nature by falsifying it. A genuine negative instance, one capable of destroying a law of nature, is an *experimentally repeatable exception*. Miracle does not fall into this category. Miracle is a non-repeatable event.

> If it is repeatable it is observable and given many instances a new law expressing the relation between cause and effect in these cases observed may be formed. This will differ from the law of nature which expresses the relationship between events to which these are the exception. We might then speak (as does Ninian Smart) of small scale laws having reference to the repeatable negative instances and contrast these with the large scale laws to which these are an exception. Given this probability, we may have to adjust the original laws.

Now consider this quotation:

Insisting on repeatability guards against observation bias and inaccuracy, to say nothing of dishonesty, and against freak results due to chance or unusual factors interfering with a particular observation. As such it is a crucial aspect of the objectivity and openness of science, but it demands that theories are falsified not by single observations or experiments, but by what is in effect another general hypothesis to the effect that such and such an observation is repeatable. Once again, there is scope for the defender of a theory to claim that a particular result or set of results apparently refuting the theory are not examples of a genuinely repeatable effect.

Anthony O'Hear, *An Introduction to the Philosophy of Science*, p. 62.

Note several points being made in this passage.

(1). Theories are not falsified by the single exception but only by genuine observations of repeatable phenomena.

(2) The result, even if accurately observed, may be due to elements intruding into the process of observation, thus robbing it of validity as falsifying evidence.

(3) Observation of the non-repeatable event might be the result of the inaccuracy, or bias of the observer. In that case it is inadmissible to be considered as falsifying evidence.

(4) Given that the observations are worthy the repeatable events may be explained by means of a new theory.

Think of an example of some non-repeatable event. Our newspapers have special sections where certain kinds of events are reported or anticipated. There are the marriage sections, the death, the birth sections. But there is no resurrection section. Resurrections do not happen, in contrast to the events of the other kinds which regularly do. Those who pass away do not return. So there can be no announcement: 'Roger Brown has returned and would like to meet his friends. The venue will be . . . .' Christians have claimed to believe in the unrepeatable event of Jesus' resurrection from the dead. An explanation must be given.

MIRACLES: WORK SHEET

First, Find accounts of different miracles, or what have been or are being claimed as miracles. Now note the account being given. Examine the **content** of the story being told. Then specify the **context** of the event being reported.

Second, Turn to the question of the **nature** of the events being reported. What sort of unusual event is it: natural, personal, an event that produces joy and contentment; one which produces frustration, even anger?

Third, Ask whether the interpretation of the event as miracle is a justifiable one. If I experienced such an event, would I interpret it as a miracle? Do you think that the same event could be a miracle for one person and not for another.

Reports of miracles regularly occur in religions that hold quite different beliefs. Theistic believers speak of divine intervention and express gratitude. What about unwelcome results from extraordinary events? Are some destructive events also miracles? Is there a secular meaning for the idea of 'miracle'?

If the account of miracle is a written account, ask how the event got to be presented in the written form. Ask whether it is a first hand account from the writer who has interpreted it as a miracle, or is an event more distant from the one giving the account. You might trace the process from event to account. That would be case of historical research.

By now you will have come to terms with your definition of miracle. You will have asked yourself, Do I find it satisfactory? Is my concept an adequate one? What alternatives are available to me? Is a miracle always an extraordinary, non-repeatable event? Does it include a causal agent? If so how would I begin to investigate? Could an event be a miracle to one person and not to another? Take note of the fact that believers in one religion will claim miracles which believers in another one will not recognise, while claiming miracles themselves. Does each need to do some explaining why they allow the one and disallowing the other?

Deal specifically with the following questions:

1. Why does Scripture record miracle stories?
2. What is a law of nature?
3. Would a counter-instance violate a law of nature?

13 SCIENCE AND FAITH

Often the popular understanding of scientific method is quite inadequate. Sciences have their methods of investigation and know how to construct scientific theories and employ them. Recent philosophers have questioned whether science is a rational enterprise. Frequently we meet the claim that science and religion are opposed, are always on a collision course. There can be conflict between believer and scientist only if both hold something in common. If they do not there is nothing to dispute. In that case there cannot be opposition.

13 SCIENCE AND FAITH

1   Galileo

In 1632 Galileo wrote his important work, the *Dialogue Concerning the Two World Systems*. He was condemned for a second time. A century earlier Copernicus had written his book, *On the Revolution of the Celestial Spheres*. While written in 1530, it was not published until 1543, the year of his death. He taught that the accepted system was in error in claiming that the earth was static at the centre of the universe with the sun and the planets rotating around it. Galileo constructed a telescope more advanced than previously developed and directed it toward the moons of Jupiter, which he saw revolved around the planet. He accepted the viewpoint of Copernicus and realised he had proof of a heliocentric system. But it went against the universally accepted view of the church and he met with bitter opposition until his death. The reason for the hostility was because the church pontificated in the name of religion on how the solar system was constructed. It made pronouncements about the physical on the basis of what it believed to be demanded by the dogmas of faith. The furthest thing from the mind of the church was that the understanding of the physical world, in this case the solar system, should not be within the realm of ecclesiastical pronouncement, i.e. in the realm of theology. Only when that prejudice was removed did Enlightenment take place and the door to the modern world opened. It took much time and much pain, not least on the part of the most enlightened scientists of the era. What eventuated was that the area of scientific research moved from Italy to the north and west. The initial prejudice was

absent there. Scientific progress was then to culminate in the person
of Isaac Newton (1642-1727). Other revolutions were to follow.
[See section 5 of this chapter.]

So what is to be learned from the whole sorry episode of prejudice and persecution of the best minds of several centuries, is the
importance of two principles for action.

Recognise the difference between pronouncements of science
and pronouncements of faith.

Leave alone.

The decisive difference between theological thought, argument
and conclusions and scientific thought and procedures and conclusions means that each has its own sphere of operation. The church
had drawn conclusions only available to the physicist astronomer.
It had no right to usurp the position of authoritative teacher and
require its own view to be followed. The scientist remained within
his legitimate sphere of operation. The church usurped his position,
claiming authority where it had none. It failed to recognise the autonomy of the physical scientist, while believing that as custodian
of revelation its sphere of knowledge was all encompassing. So this
belief justified the right of the pontifex to pontificate.

For both physical scientist and churchman there was, and is,
a legitimate sphere of operation when it comes to drawing conclusions and determining what one is to believe. There should be
no encroachment. Indeed, rightly understood there can be none.
The prelates learned that to their shame. Hence our principle,
'Leave alone'! It is a lesson not yet learnt in certain Christian circles. Where alternative so-called scientific accounts are provided
for the beginnings of the cosmos which are taken to be unfriendly
to believers' accounts some believers will reply, 'We shall give the
scientific world the true account of 'creation'. That is the claim.
Without embarrassment the 'creationist' challenges the scientific
account full of confidence that he is appropriately engaged in the
pseudo-scientific endeavour to establish an alternative physical explanation of the cosmos.

Modern science provided the context for life in the West. But before that the Christian West had provided the context for the beginning and development of modern science. That this is not to be taken for granted the Galileo incident makes quite clear. The Christian West first precipitated a crisis before it became clear that science was going to be made at home. It is not so much the difference between Galileo and the Aristotelians on the one hand, and Galileo and the churchmen on the other that we are now interested in. Rather that there is now, and has been from the start, conflict of interests and attitudes from within the Christian communities. Allow, as seems to be borne out by the evidence, that the Galileo trial was something of a face-saving device for the churchmen, the fact is that the conflict was made public and a severe warning given by the church of a recalcitrant, continuing attitude of hostility to new theories and explanations for the future. There would always be those who would see the progress of science as a threat to Christianity and oppose it in the name of faith. The immediate historical result of the Galileo incident was that the centre of gravity of learning in the West shifted from Italy to the North, in particular to the Netherlands and to England, where a brilliant century of discovery and scientific consolidation followed, the seventeenth, the 'century of genius'.

2 Attempts at Harmonisation

Along with the success of science, in particular of physical science, went the assurance of having discovered a method which could be relied upon to produce sure results. The earlier optimism that the final method had been discovered and that it would only take a generation or so to develop and apply it and so complete the work of science appears comic in retrospect. The interesting fact is that many of these scientists were committed Christians, some of them clergymen, for whom the interest in science was accompanied by other interests. They had to find a way of bridging between their secular scientific work and their religion. The teleological

argument served them for this purpose. Since they discerned order
in the natural world, conceived as a series of regular and reliable
occurrences, they argued from such perceived design to a designer
and identified this designer with God. The process of reasoning was
widely welcomed and readily popularised. It came to be called the
argument from design.

The more sceptical still reckoned with the idea of God as Creator, but produced a version of the doctrine of Creation, known
as Deism, which left nature quite free and independent of any
divine control. This was a way of providing for the independence
of science. The divine activity was needed to bring the cosmos into
being. But once created, after the initial act of God the universe
was self-sustaining.

The principle of Ockham's razor, namely that explanatory
principles were not to be multiplied more than was necessary, led
ultimately to the dissociation of scientific method from theological
convictions.

A kind of questioning then began and has never since ceased.
Could Christian faith and its beliefs be interpreted so that there was
harmony with the new knowledge? Thus meant, Could Christian
theology become creative and accept the fact that it had to continue to become creative? Whether it *should* or not was and is, even
now, discussed. But, since theology is the reflection by the believer
about faith and its meaning, the further question about the status
of faith became of primary importance. Hence in raising the question of Science and Christianity, we must, at the least, note two
aspects. First, Christianity may be understood as believing *p, q, r,*
the pronouncements of the faith, the propositions. The question
then raised is that of the relation between these pronouncements of
faith (scriptural, creedal and theological propositions) and scientific
claims, the propositions and claims of science.

In addition, what has been called 'religious experience' has to
be considered. Since the scientist, or the philosopher on his behalf,
has his ways of saying what constitutes valid experiencing of the
world, how is the believer's claim that there is religious experience

and that his beliefs are based upon such experience to be assessed? For the believer speaks of faith as trust, and both as response to the revelation of God.

A person holding Christian beliefs as true may be said to be Christian, since the holding of these beliefs is sufficient to distinguish him from others who hold different beliefs. The theologian works out the implications of such beliefs. But belief is rooted in the meaning of religious experience, which in one of its aspects is a stance toward the world and concerned with life, the living of life in its many aspects.

Thus two levels of claim are made by the Christian and each has significance for the question about science. On one level one may ask whether religious beliefs are compatible with the findings and the beliefs of science. This comes to focus in several ways in thinking about creation. On the other hand one may ask whether experience, or a dimension of experience, as defined by the Christian (as faith, for example) constitutes a valid experience of the world. Here at the outset it seems that the scientist has the advantage by being able to coordinate what he claims about the world with what he experiences. The scientist's claim that his experience of the world is valid is borne out by the obvious fact that that claim produces results. What relationship, if any, does the experience on which Christian theists base their claims have to the experience of the scientist? So arises the question about worldviews: the validity of the worldview made popular by science and its relation to the teachings of Christian theism. Is it one of incompatibility, or conflict, is it the way of the 'two compartments'? Or is it one of incommensurability, each independent of the other, but both authentic?

3   Incompatibility?

It will be well, at this point, to mention, if not to correct, two common misconceptions about the problem. They can be expressed quite simply, but they go rather deeper than a simple expression of them might suggest. The first is that taking note that there has been conflict in the past, and because science is 'different' from religion, they are essentially and necessarily incompatible. Being incompatible means conflict, since incompatibility means opposition. If one starts off by making the assumption of the incompatibility of science and religion, one can readily find arguments and evidence in support of such a view, and give reasons why they must be incompatible. Take any level you please, in their attitudes to the world, in their procedures of reasoning, in the modes by which their truth is established, or is claimed to be established, in their understanding and acceptance of authority, in their objectivity or subjectivity. Note that we are not here necessarily talking of two communities, two kinds of person or two persons.

If there is a problem it is because one may assume the incompatibility of the two enterprises and make sure that they are kept separate. This is the schizoid 'way of the two compartments.' The problem of the two compartments arises as the thinker understands the methods and conclusions of both science and religion. In dealing honestly with both he faces two truths or two kinds of truth. If he believes that truth is always compatible with truth even if there appears to be contradiction, even when these are truths of different kinds, he may either seek to hold the two types of truths simultaneously but separately, or, of a bolder frame of mind, seek to work out some unity between them. The alternative is incommensurability. Since there is no meeting point, there can be no opposition.

4 Misconception About Authority

The other misconception is that the Christian religion is a religion of a particular kind of authority.[1] The believer holds what

---

1 In illustration of this attitude we quote from a book on philosophy of religion:

> 'There is as much room for imagination and original thinking in science as in some of the humanities . . . . But religion does not seem to offer this kind of scope for imagination

he accepts on the basis of an ancient authority — specifically, the Bible. So he repeats the teaching of the Bible. This being the case, there is no real scope for imagination and creativity in theological thought. What the theologian does is simply to repeat the statements of the written authority he accepts.

The question concerns the kind of authority the Christian believer would accept. Is it or is it not a dogmatic authority? Does it or does it not permit imaginative and creative re-interpretation? Indeed, what is it that is being interpreted?

The alternative is that the believer holds what he believes on the basis of an ecclesiastical tradition. He accepts what the church teaches. The church's doctrines are given and so fundamental. The church's attitude to and interpretation of the Scripture is taken as normative and is often unquestioned. There often is unquestioning acceptance of tradition.

Further, if what was written in the Gospels, Epistles and Apocalypse of the New Testament in some cases and in some circles came to be accepted as having unquestioned authority, how did what is

---

and originality in interpretation. It is generally accepted that a proper way of criticising a new theology is by pointing out that it diverges from the traditional way of approaching the problems with which it deals. Admittedly, a new theology can in the course of time come to constitute on its own account an accepted tradition but only by coming to be acknowledged as the best interpretation of the fundamental doctrines of Christianity which are at all times understood to be *given* — in the Bible. The subject matter of theology is a body of doctrine. This is *given*: and although there is room for conjecture about the interpretation of particular pieces of doctrine, the doctrines themselves are not held as conjectures or hypotheses. Even if they were conjectures, the theologian would not regard himself as having the responsibility of trying to refute them. Or, even if he did, empirical methods would not be likely to strike him as appropriate.' Thomas McPherson, *Philosophy and Religious Belief.* London: Hutchinson University Library, 1974. pp. 108-110.

first written come to be written? What is written is *given*, in a sense. But before it was written there was something else. The writing was about that more fundamental *given* that provided for the basis of unique Christian reflection. If this is not considered in any assessment of the writings, serious misconception will result. The Bible, and specifically the New Testament represents a response to a more fundamental given. An adequate account of this Christian given must take account of the experience of Jesus Christ as the subject, object and source of Christian faith.

5   Theories, Laws, Hypotheses

The method of science is the conjoining of the evidence with the perceived problem. This takes place by means of particular processes of logical reasoning, guided by presuppositions. In the physical sciences, instances are conjoined with generalizations. This is done by a process of inductive reasoning. A sufficiently broad and representative set of instances is examined and on the basis of such examination generalizations are formed. Such generalizations may be extremely wide. They are then known as theories. These make possible predictions where the particular hypothesis within the context of the theory may be tested. Such presupposing of theory is a condition for experimental testing. If verified the hypothesis is then believed. If not falsified, it is retained.

On the basis of such theories, by process of deductive reasoning, the scientist may move to the narrower generalizations, which are called laws. The hypothesis is a construction, to be tested by evidence that lies in the future. The construction of an hypothesis is thus a venture. The status of the hypothesis is not that it is true or false, but that in the future it may be known to be true or false, when the necessary procedures and conditions for testing it become available. In astronomy, one may have to wait. In chemistry, one can set up the situation. The hypothesis is tested by states of affairs. It is in principle falsifiable. Its meaning is in the method of its test. Since the scientific hypothesis is tested by the instance, or by a series of instances, it is empirical. Since the test can be done by anyone, with the requisite qualifications and under particular conditions of course, it can (theoretically) be repeated, and this constitutes the objectivity of the truth claims that science makes. They are amenable to **'inter-subjective testability'**.

Critical attention to the instances covered by the testing of hypotheses makes possible the framing of laws, which are statements of regularity in nature. The law is a description of what takes place in nature. It expresses an expectation for the future on the basis of regularities observed in the past. Should the expected regularity not take place and not recur, a change may have to be made in the statement about regularity, that is the 'law' may have to be revised.[2] Confusion with the prescriptive law, in ethics or in society, sometimes suggests that a scientific law is fixed and finally authoritative. Not so. It is only a statement of what has been regularly experienced. It is descriptive, not prescriptive. Scientific language, in sum, is empirically based and symbolic.

The symbols are related according to a framework supplied by a theory and allowing an interpretation as precise and economical as possible.

Theories as paradigms are sometimes replaced. It takes place rarely, but it does happen. The coordinating symbols become entrenched and have authority in the community of scientists because of what in the past they have enabled the scientist to do. A way of thinking becomes accepted and guides research and also the humdrum work of science. The model or *paradigm* having become accepted exercises a directive function, so that observations and interpretations are made to coordinate with it. Since it is not questioned, it exercises a wide authority over the scientist's work. The working scientist accepts the model and its authority without question. The scientific community develops a technical language which enables it to perform its work. Philosophers may raise questions about the status of the theory which enables the scientist to perform his work. Are the theories so many convenient fictions, so

2   But see comments in chapter 12, 'Miracles'.

many structures produced by the mind? Do they represent what the world really is? Do they summarize the data? Are they to be seen as so many tools for investigation? Provided the theory enables the scientist to work, he may not be concerned, let alone disturbed, by such questions.

6   Crises and Revolutions in Science

The reality is that there has been wide disagreement concerning the procedures of science and also how such astonishing development in physical science has taken place. For physics is the basic discipline for the explanation of the cosmos.

We mention briefly two lines of development: (1) within science beginning with Newton, and (2) within the discipline of the philosophy of science, where, for this writing, we can only take samples. In both cases we shall see intense and wide-ranging discussion, comprehensive disagreement, and fascinating experience of puzzlement, even a sense of mystery within the disciplines of physics and philosophy of science. So for the samples, illustrating what has been termed the crisis of modern science.

From time to time, crises in science occur. A crisis takes place when the simplicity and the economy the scientist is looking for in his explanations does not result. But he does not critically examine the paradigm until he is driven to, since so much is at stake. The reason for this is that its past success as an instrument of interpretation and discovery has given it a status, which is only reluctantly called into question. But it is possible to anticipate the breakdown of the paradigm and of the language connected with it, as when the explanations which result from following a given paradigm become so complicated as to be unmanageable or incomprehensible. Also, when there are recalcitrant facts which are not explicable on the basis of the paradigm, because it is not comprehensive enough, or not expansible.

The failure on both counts of the epicyclical exposition of the Ptolemaic system of astronomy is a case in point. The epicycle was a circle around the circumference of another circle. The problem was to explain the movements of the planets. The assumption was that they must be explained by the employment of the idea of uniform cyclical motion. But appearances were contrary to what they should have been, assuming also a fixed observation point at the centre of the concentric circles representing the orbits of the planets, namely the earth. So an elaborate scheme of epicycles (circles within circles) was invented to account for the observed motions. Such a scheme could be almost endlessly refined to the point where it became meaningless. Not only could it not be comprehended when elaborated beyond a certain point. It became otiose when certain facts came to light. Then a change had to take place in fundamental attitudes.

Scientific revolutions, few and resisted, take place when there is no available alternative. Such revolutions consist in a preconception of basic ways of thinking and innovative reconstruction of vocabulary. The earlier Ptolemaic conception of the earth's relation to the sun and its place in the universe came in for challenging question from Copernicus (1473-1543), Bruno (1549-1600), and Galileo (1564-1642). This questioning and theorising eventuated in the system elaborated by Newton in the seventeenth century and became the standard for centuries of scientific interpretation and the model for the discipline's reasoning.

7 Disagreement and Development in Physics

The nineteenth and twentieth centuries produced vast achievements. Earlier in this period there was widespread belief in progress. One way this manifests itself was in the hope that science could and would provide new knowledge and the belief that this would lead to the improvement of human welfare. But later developments were to show that hope to be misplaced, leading as they did to the breakdown of the Cartesian-Newtonian cosmology. Newton's system was static. It did not reckon with time. Everything was related in ways that could be expressed in laws. These could be relied upon since the relations they attempted to express were fixed. The system was deterministic.

The shattering of the belief in progress took place in the twentieth century. We note some of the scientific developments that dictated the need for a new cosmology.

Hard matter no longer constituted the fundamental substance of nature. The **uncertainty principle** undermined and replaced strict Newtonian determinism. This breakdown resulted from a series of developments in physics, e.g. Maxwell's work on electromagnetic fields, the Michelson-Morley experiment, Becquerel's discovery of radioactivity, Planck's isolation of quantum phenomena, Einstein's special and general theories of relativity, Bohr, Heidelberg and colleagues' formulation of quantum mechanics.

> There was now no coherent conception of the world that, like Newton's *Principia*, could integrate the complex variety of new data. To incoherence was added unintelligibility: a curved space, finite but unbounded; a four-dimensional space-time continuum; mutually exclusive properties possessed by the same subatomic entity; objects that were not really things at all but processes or patterns of relationship; phenomena that took no decisive shape until observed; particles that seemed to affect each other at a distance with no known causal link; the existence of fundamental fluctuations of energy in a total vacuum.[3]

Science validated Kant's scepticism about the human mind's capacity for certain knowledge of the world in itself. But Kant was certain that the categories of human cognition were absolute. But that certainty was now eroded. Kant's fundamental *a prioris* — space, time, substance, causality — were no longer applicable to all phenomena. Leading physicists did not believe that the equations of quantum theory described the actual world.

> . . . the structure of nature may eventually be such that our processes of thought do not correspond to it sufficiently to permit us to think about it at all. Thus incoherence, unin-

3   Richard Tarnas, *The Passion of the Western Mind*, p. 358.

telligibility, and an insecure relativism compounded the earlier modern predicament of human alienation in an impersonal cosmos. [4]

A series of surprising convictions emerged. It came to be realised that the truths of science are neither absolute nor unequivocally objective; that induction cannot render general laws certain; that scientific knowledge is a product of human interpretive structures that are themselves relative, variable and creatively employed; that the act of observation in some sense produces the objective reality science attempts to explicate. What results is not only that we are left without absolutes but with no solid ground.

8 Philosophers Disagree about Science

Popular views of science are sometimes misleading. It is a common view that science is the model of rationality, that science deals with objective facts, and that its method is to establish these facts by rigorous means. Other disciplines may speculate and theorise, but not science, especially not physics. Science seeks for proof and has its methods of finding it. Here, then a is a list of some popular views about science,[5] which were challenged by T. S. Kuhn (see below) but which are still held in the popular mind.

Science attempts to discover truths about the one real world. These are true whatever we think about them and there is a unique best description of any chosen aspect of the world.

There is a sharp distinction between scientific and other theories and beliefs.

Scientific knowledge is *cumulative*. It moves forward from and builds on what is already known.

Observations are to be clearly distinguished from statements of theory. Observation and experiment provide the foundations for and justification of hypotheses and theories.

---

4 *Ibid.*, p. 359.
5 cf. Ian Hacking, *Scientific Revolutions,* pp. 1,2.

Scientists test theories by deducing observation-reports from theoretical postulates.

Scientific concepts are rather precise, and the terms used in science have fixed meanings.

Physics is the basic science to which other sciences can be reduced. It will provide the ultimate explanations.

In contrast to this it is often held that religious belief is irrational. Believers hold, without warrant, positions that cannot be demonstrated, putting forth theories without due consideration for proper justification.

An interesting disagreement became evident between two leading philosophers of science. Karl Popper and Thomas Kuhn.[6] Popper held that science does not produce knowledge that is certain, or even probable. One makes imaginative guesses, bold conjectures. For every observed fact presupposes an interpretive focus. Such conjectures are continually and systematically tested, but they cannot be proved. At any time a new test could falsify the conjecture. One cannot claim to know the real essence of things. So science is rational in that it is committed to the rigorous testing of theories, and to neutrality in searching for truth.

Kuhn denied that the practice of science conformed to the model of Popper. Rather than seeking systematic falsification of existing theories, science proceeded by seeking confirmations of the prevailing paradigm. A paradigm is a widely accepted model for procedure in the pursuit of scientific knowledge. At different periods in the history of science different models for procedure were accepted and exercised influence in guiding scientists' thinking and procedures of research. Where evidence conflicted it was interpreted so as to support the paradigm. Scientific practice makes the prevailing paradigm self-validating. However when an accumulation of conflicting data produces a paradigm crisis, new synthesis takes place, for example, from Ptolemy to Copernicus/ Galileo/ Newton, from Newton to Einstein. But revolution is not at all a

---

6   Karl Popper, *The Logic of Scientific Discovery*, 1959. Thomas Kuhn, *The Structure of Scientific Revolutions*, 1962.

rational process. The rival paradigms are seldom comparable, They are not 'commensurate'. Each paradigm creates its own *Gestalt*, its own pattern.

The older explanations are no longer adequate. They become otiose to such an extent that a new method is required. This means a total restructuring of explanation is required. Such revolutions in scientific procedure take place, but not frequently and not without pain. So the history of science is not one of linear and rational development but rather of radical shifts of vision in which a multitude of non-rational and non-empirical factors play crucial roles.[7]

Thus scientific knowledge came to be regarded as a relative matter, and this in several senses. It was relative to the observer, to his physical context, to his science's prevailing paradigm, and his own theoretical assumptions, to his culture's prevailing belief system, to his social context, and psychological predispositions, to his very act of observation. The bedrock of the Newtonian-Cartesian certainty had been shattered.

We can here only allude to great variety in the treatment of the question between philosophers of science concerning what constitutes science and whether science is rational and developmental.[8]

---

7 Whereas **Popper** had attempted to temper Hume's scepticism by demonstrating the rationality of choosing the most rigorously tested conjecture, Kuhn's analysis served to restore that scepticism.' Tarnas, *op. cit.*, p. 361.

8 We have already noted Kuhn's influential position that sociological factors have a predominant place is providing the framework within which the scientific community does its work, and how such factors provide the context and impetus for radical change.

Feyerabend sees no rationality in the development of science. He became known for the slogan 'anything goes'.

Lakatos held that theories provide structures, that some laws are more basic than others and that a research programme depends on these structures. However the fundamental principles, what he called the 'hard core', must be supplemented by other assumptions. These protect the hard core from being falsified.

9   The 'Problem' of Science and Faith

First, having specified the two realms of science and Christian faith one might propose that they be kept quite separate, within certain defined boundaries.

Since what cannot meet cannot conflict, if there is no meeting point between science and religion, there can be no conflict. Each discipline, carefully defined as to its methods, may pursue its tasks and have confidence that it will not meet opposition from the other, provided that it does not trespass beyond its own boundaries and encroach upon the other. This way of solving the problem may involve one at the outset in some serious thinking about what religious statements intend to do, how they function. For it should be clear that we are not speaking of two classes of person, but of the integrity of one, the theist, who refuses to compartmentalise himself. As theist, he is concerned about the problem of relating scientific method to that faith.

Second, one could and, since misunderstanding still prevails, one should, describe how the Christian theologian actually goes about his work. This will mean to clarify what is given and how the *given*, the religious subject matter which is the material for theology, is shaped and handled by the theologian. In carrying out such a task the autonomy of theology would be established. This autonomy, like that of any critical discipline, is a relative autonomy and can be defended as such. This would be preliminary to showing that the kind of answer given by theology is reasonable within the framework in which it is made.

A different kind of solution proposes that the methods of empirical science are the only methods for producing reliable knowledge. Since the theist does not employ such methods his proposals cannot be trustworthy. We have already paid considerable attention to the problem of defining the relationship between reason and experience as it relates to faith, and need only now remark that the proposal must be denied in the name of experience. The range of human experience must not be needlessly restricted.

One cannot reasonably claim that knowledge results only from one kind of experience, or only from one method of understanding the world.

BIBLIOGRAPHY

A. F. Chalmers, *What is this Thing called Science:* Buckingham: Open University Press, 1999. An excellent presentation of the theme.

Ian Hacking, editor. *Scientific Revolutions.* Oxford: University Press, 1981. A set of creative articles.

Thomas Kuhn, *The Structure of Scientific Revolutions. Chicago:* University of Chicago Press, 1962.

Thomas McPherson, *Philosophy and Religious Belief.* London: Hutchinson University Library, 1974. pp. 108-110.

Karl Popper, *The Logic of Scientific Discovery.* London: Hutchinson, 1980.

Richard Tarnas, *The Passion of the Western Mind.* London: Pimlico, 2000, p. 358.

Edward W. H. Vick, *Quest. An Exploration of Some Problems in Science and Religion.* London: Epworth Press, 1979. A popular introduction to the subject.

SCIENCE AND FAITH: WORK SHEET

1 Write a short essay on 'Lessons from Galileo.'

2 What do you understand by the terms: scientific method, paradigm, theory, hypothesis, law of nature?

3 Does the scientist experience the world differently from the Christian believer?

4. What is a 'scientific revolution? How are such revolutions to be accounted for?

5 What happens when scientists disagree?

6 What is the 'problem' of the relation between science and faith? Is there such a thing? If so, how does it happen? If not, why not?

BIBLIOGRAPHY

Achinstein, P., *The Nature of Explanation*. Oxford, 1983.

Aristotle, *Nichomachean Ethics*, I:13; III:1-5; VII:1-10.

Audi, Robert, *Epistemology*. London and New York: Routledge, 1998.

Campbell, Keith, *Body and Mind*. Notre Dame, Indiana: University of Notre Dame Press, 1984.

Chalmers, A. F., *What is this Thing called Science*. Buckingham: Open University Press, 1999.

Cobb John B., *A Christian Natural Theology*. Philadelphia: The Westminster Press, 1965.

Collingwood, R. G., *The Idea of History*. London: Oxford University Press, 1966.

D. J. O'Connor and Brian Carr, *Introduction to the Theory of Knowledge*, Brighton: The Harvester Press, 1982.

Davies, Brian, *An Introduction to Philosophy of Religion*. New York: Oxford University Press, 1993.

Descartes, René, *Meditations* II, VI.

Donovan, Peter, *Interpreting Religious Experience*. London: Sheldon Press, 1979.

Dray, William H., *Philosophy of History*. New Jersey: Prentice-Hall, 1964.

Fingarette, Herbert, *Self-deception*. California: University of California Press, 2000.

Gardiner, Patrick, *The Nature of Historical Explanation*. London: Oxford University Press, 1961.

Gerrish B. A., *A Prince of the Church*, London: S. C. M. Press, 1984. pp. 43-44.

Griffiths, Phillips (editor), *Knowledge and Belief*, London: Oxford University Press, 1967.

Hacking, Ian,(editor), *Scientific Revolutions*. Oxford: University Press, 1981.

Heil, John, *Philosophy of Mind*. London: Routledge, 1998. Chapter 2.

Hempel, Carl G., *Aspects of Scientific Explanation and Other Essays in the Philosophy of Science*. New York, 1965.

Hesse, Mary, 'Miracles and the Laws of Nature' in C. D. F. Moule (ed.), *'Miracles'*. London: 1965. pp. 35-42.

Hick, John, *Death and Eternal Life*. London: Collins, 1976.

Hospers, John, *Introduction to Philosophical Analysis* (3rd. Ed.). London: Routledge, 1992.

Kuhn, Thomas, *The Structure of Scientific Revolutions. Chicago:* University of Chicago Press, 1962.

Lakatos, Imre and Alan Musgrave (editors), *Criticism and the Growth of Knowledge*. Cambridge: University Press, 1979.

Leibnitz, *Theodicy.*

Locke, John, *Essay Concerning Human Understanding*. Oxford: University Press, 1924.

Mackie, J. I., *Problems from Locke*, Oxford: Clarendon Press, 1976.

Maclaren, Elizabeth, *The Nature of Belief*, London: Sheldon Press, 1976.

McPherson, Thomas, *Philosophy and Religious Belief*. London: Hutchinson University Library, 1974. pp. 108-110.

Morton, Adam, *A Guide Through the Theory Of Knowledge*. 2nd ed. Oxford: Blackwells, 1997.

O'Connor D. J. and Carr, Brian, *Introduction to the Theory of Knowledge*. Brighton: Harvester Press, 1982. pp. 164-185.

O'Hear, Anthony, *What Philosophy Is*. Harmondsworth: Penguin, 1985. Chapter 4.

Philosophy of Natural Science. Englewood Cliffs: Prentice-Hall, N.J., 1966.

Pinnock Clark H. (editor), *The Openness of God: A Biblical Challenge to the Traditional Understanding of God*. Illinois: InterVarsity Press, 1994.

Popper, Karl, *The Logic of Scientific Discovery*. London: Hutchinson, 1980.

Rice, Richard, *The Openness of God*. Washington D.C.: Review and Herald 1980.

Ryle, Gilbert, *The Concept of Mind*. London: Hutchinson. 1949.

Sabatier, August. *Outlines of a Philosophy of Religion*. London: Hodder and Stoughton, 1897.

Salmon W. C., *Statistical Explanation and Statistical Relevance*. London: 1971.

Schleiermacher, Friedrich, *The Christian Faith*. Edinburgh: T. & T. Clark, 1960.

Scruton, Roger, *Modern Philosophy*. London: Sinclair-Stephenson, 1994. pp. 97-111.

Smart, Ninian, *Philosophers and Religious Truth*. London: S. C. M. Press, 1969.

Smith, John, *Experience and God*. New York: Oxford University Press, 1968.

Smith, Peter and Jones, O. R., *The Philosophy of Mind*. Part I. Cambridge: University Press, 1986.

Stephenson. J., *A New Eusebius*, London: S.P.C.K., 1957.

    Creeds, Councils and Controversies, London: S.P.C.K., 1972.

Swinburne, Richard, *The Concept of Miracle*. London: Macmillan, 1970.

    The Existence of God. Oxford: Clarendon Press, 1979.

Tarnas, Richard *The Passion of the Western Mind*. London: Pimlico, 2000, p. 358.

Toulmin, Stephen, *The Uses of Argument*. Cambridge: University Press, 1964.

Vick, Edward W. H. *Quest. An Exploration of Some Problems in Science and Religion*. London: Epworth Press, 1979.

    History and Christian Faith. Nottingham: Evening Publications, 2003.

    Creation: The Christian Doctrine. Gonzalez, Florida: Energion Publications, 2012.

    From Inspiration to Understanding. Gonzalez, Florida: Energion Publications, 2011.

Yandell, Keith E., *Philosophy of Religion*. London: Routledge, 1999.

INDEX

A

accidental 156, 169, 195, 196, 197, 229
act of God 86, 142, 153, 154, 234, 252
agent 6, 146, 154, 166, 174, 175, 176, 179, 202, 225, 226, 245
akrasia 6, 8, 146, 154, 166, 174, 175, 176, 179, 202, 225, 226, 245
alternation 214, 215
analogy 77, 119, 120-122, 143, 184, 238
angel activity 166, 225-227
argument 3
Aristotle (384-322 B.C.) 74, 75, 103, 104, 173, 174, 175, 178, 179, 187, 210, 267
Augustine (A.D. 354-430) 9, 148, 149, 212, 217
authority 24, 27, 33, 60, 113, 234, 250, 254, 255, 257
avowal 184, 185, 186

B

Bacon, Francis (1531-1626) 104
becoming 144
behaviourism 202, 204
being 76, 144
belief 69
best explanation 84, 85, 93, 94, 95, 96, 97, 99, 102, 103
best of all possible worlds 140, 147, 149
Bruno, Giordano (1549-1600) 259

C

causal connection 50, 192, 193, 194, 196, 208
cause effect 26, 93, 94, 153–161
Chalcedon (A.D. 451) 128
Churchill 71, 74, 77, 92
class or type of event 164
coherence, coherence theory 77–79
coincidental 116
consciousness 39, 40, 47, 115, 125, 174, 179, 181, 194, 204, 215, 220, 221, 222, 226

V

W

SCRIPTURE INDEX

Old Testament

New Testament

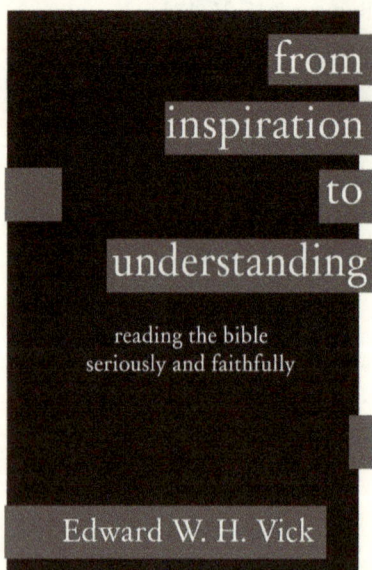

MORE FROM ENERGION PUBLICATIONS

Personal Study
Finding My Way in Christianity	Herold Weiss	$16.99
Holy Smoke! Unholy Fire	Bob McKibben	$14.99
The Jesus Paradigm	David Alan Black	$17.99
The Sacred Journey	Chris Surber	$11.99
When People Speak for God	Henry Neufeld	$17.99

Christian Living
Crossing the Street	Robert LaRochelle	$16.99
Faith in the Public Square	Robert D. Cornwall	$16.99
Grief: Finding the Candle of Light	Jody Neufeld	$8.99

Bible Study
Ephesians: A Participatory Study Guide	Robert D. Cornwall	$9.99
From Inspiration to Understanding	Edward W. H. Vick	$24.99
Learning and Living Scripture	Lentz/Neufeld	$12.99
Luke: A Participatory Study Guide	Geoffrey Lentz	$8.99
Philippians: A Participatory Study Guide	Bruce Epperly	$9.99

Theology
Creation in Scripture	Herold Weiss	$12.99
Creation: The Christian Doctrine	Edward W. H. Vick	$12.99
History and Christian Faith	Edward W. H. Vick	$9.99
The Adventists' Dilemma	Edward W. H. Vick	$14.99
The Church Under the Cross	William Powell Tuck	$11.99
The Journey to the Undiscovered Country	William Powell Tuck	$9.99
The Politics of Witness	Allan R. Bevere	$9.99
Ultimate Allegiance	Robert D. Cornwall	$9.99
Worshiping with Charles Darwin	Robert D. Cornwall	$9.99

Ministry
Clergy Table Talk	Kent Ira Groff	$9.99
Out of This World	Darren McClellan	$24.99

Generous Quantity Discounts Available
Dealer Inquiries Welcome
Energion Publications — P.O. Box 841
Gonzalez, FL_ 32560
Website: http://energionpubs.com
Phone: (850) 525-3916

www.ingramcontent.com/pod-product-compliance
Lightning Source LLC
Chambersburg PA
CBHW021136090426
42740CB00008B/807

9 781938 434549